Relationship Within

❦

INGRID FRANCES SMYER PH.D

BALBOA.
PRESS
A DIVISION OF HAY HOUSE

Balboa Press books may be ordered through booksellers or by contacting:

Balboa Press
A Division of Hay House
1663 Liberty Drive
Bloomington, IN 47403
www.balboapress.com
1-(877) 407-4847

Because of the dynamic nature of the Internet, any web addresses or links contained in this book may have changed since publication and may no longer be valid. The views expressed in this work are solely those of the author and do not necessarily reflect the views of the publisher, and the publisher hereby disclaims any responsibility for them.

The author of this book does not dispense medical advice or prescribe the use of any technique as a form of treatment for physical, emotional, or medical problems without the advice of a physician, either directly or indirectly. The intent of the author is only to offer information of a general nature to help you in your quest for emotional and spiritual well-being. In the event you use any of the information in this book for yourself, which is your constitutional right, the author and the publisher assume no responsibility for your actions.

Any people depicted in stock imagery provided by Thinkstock are models, and such images are being used for illustrative purposes only. Certain stock imagery © Thinkstock.

Printed in the United States of America.

ISBN: 978-1-4525-7829-3 (sc)
ISBN: 978-1-4525-7831-6 (hc)
ISBN: 978-1-4525-7830-9 (e)

Library of Congress Control Number: 2013913125

Balboa Press rev. date: 9/25/2013

Contents

Preface..vii

Introduction..xv

Section 1: Personal Relationships...1

Chapter 1: The Foundational Relationship 3

Chapter 2: Spiritual Resources 18

Chapter 3: Forgiveness and Healthy Relationships 28

Chapter 4: Relationship Patterns..38

Chapter 5: Your Higher Self...43

Chapter 6: Following Divine Guidance.....................................63

Chapter 7: Personal Development and Relationships...............73

Chapter 8: Positive Attitude...77

Chapter 9: Positive Thinking 88

Chapter 10: Carl G. Jung's Individuation Process 94

Chapter 11: Personality Types 100

Chapter 12: Relationship as Archetype 108

Chapter 13: The Shadow and Autonomous complexes 118

Section 2: Family Relationships...125

Chapter 1: The Family Life Cycle 127

Chapter 2: The Baby and Family 138

Chapter 3: Creating Relationships with Infants.....................146

Chapter 4: Sibling Relationship 151

Chapter 5: Autonomy and Independence 156

Chapter 6: Having a Baby..159

Chapter 7: Empty Nest...162

Chapter 8: Retirement & Senior Stage....................................166

Chapter 9: The Family as Foundation 172
Chapter 10: Benefits of Positive Family Relationships 180
Chapter 11: Strong Family Relationships 188

Section 3: Intimate Relationships 211
Chapter 1: Romantic relationships 213
Chapter 2: Fundamentals of Couples Counseling 222
Chapter 3: Attachment and Adult Relationships 227
Chapter 4: Self-Identity and Personal Boundaries 234
Chapter 5: Trust as Key to Intimacy 245
Chapter 6: Patience in a Relationship 256
Chapter 7: Curiosity in Relationships 261
Chapter 8: The Way to Solve Any Relationship Problem 266
Chapter 9: Positive Reinforcement 274
Chapter 10: Intimacy from the Neck Up 278
Chapter 11: Seven Strategies for Healthy Sexuality 282
Chapter 12: Maintaining Intimacy 295

Conclusion 303

References 309
Acknowledgements 321
About the Author 323

Preface

❦

A Relationship with Self

I am here to tell you that your relationships do not have to be on the rocks to request help. You do not have to be on the verge of catastrophe to seek a new strategy for dealing with problematic relationships. You can build affirmative relationships, but must first seek self-understanding. Maybe your relationships have been dysfunctional in the past, but this is an opportunity to reach out for guidance now. I encourage you to ask questions and inquire deeply.

This book is not a cure for negative relationship patterns, but provides you the tools to make your relationships actually work. I am not going to deny that relationships are problematic. Sometime they can be anything but easy. There are and will be challenges to face. At times relationships can be stressful, provocative, and cause angst. When significant others do not live up to our standards, or fall short of our high expectations, we become discouraged, withdrawn, angry and even vicious. Sometimes life is crammed with so many things to do we feel we are losing touch with family, friends, and intimate connections.

If you have picked up this book, chances are, you are seeking something more. Perhaps you are looking for a new way to deal with negative relationship dynamics.

Maybe a tricky relationship situation is overwhelming; you are in the dark as to what to door how to proceed. You may already feel hopeless, ready to give up, and want to run for the hills. You may want to find a mentor who has been over similar ground, or join a support group to help you bear the universal pain. Working with a therapist, counselor, or holistic life coach can help you create a relationship within. I invite you to slow down and breathe as you read along. Learn how to deal with highly charged relational situations by taking a time-honored, yet colorful and personal approach. Only your will know how you need to apply this information to your relationships.

The original force behind *Relationship Within* is my innate curiosity. I yearn for self-knowledge and am eager to understand my deeper drives and motives. They inform how I approach relationships since every creative undertaking involves dealing with other people. How we communicate to the world shines a spotlight on our particular evolution through personal, family, and intimate relationships. I offer the vision of inner healing and provide practical advice, how-to exercises, and strategies for working from the inside out. I encourage you to build lifelong self-esteem since you will need it for the journey ahead. The goal is nothing less than to be at inner peace while also asserting your destiny in the world. As Jesus said, "Be in the world, but not of it."

This book offers you a better understanding of the roles you play and how they influence your future relationships. When it comes to a relationship dynamic, what is your pet peeve? What made you this way? Were you born with innate relationship issues, or was it how your parent's raised you? What motivates you in terms of relationships? What helps your achieve your deeper objectives? What upsets your equilibrium? What makes you feel like you are losing your mind? *Relationship Within* will help you find answers to these questions.

In writing this book, I have incorporated material from countless sessions with people in counseling who candidly talked about the challenges, hardships, and setbacks in relationship building. Together we examined what was holding them back and what helped them persevere. Many people opened up about what inspires their decision-making, how they make important choices, and what they value in life. Others shared problems with self-love, secret longings, and unwarranted fears of abandonment. Nevertheless, what was most common is a deep desire to belong to the human race, to feel welcome in the universal family, and connected to the eternal.

I now invited you to come along with me on a journey to a relationship within. You need not hold back from direct experience. Test and refine my approach to see if it works for you. Develop profound gratitude for all the people in your life. This is the key for self-healing. Whether you have strong self-esteem or not, depends on how you view yourself. Self-image influences how you are in all your relationships. Inner wakefulness requires the act of bringing consciousness to how you interact, so you concentrate on the necessary changes that create positive self-esteem. Do not let anyone discourage you. Remember, it can be done!

Relationship Within offers a path to commune with elemental forces already working inside you. You had better understand the unconscious energy driving you, since it is a power to recon with. You have the awareness to examine the pros and cons, use your energy wisely, and know when divine will is at work! The real power behind a successful relationship is the relationship you have with yourself. If this relationship feels like it is turning on the hinge of fate, it might be good to work in secret until you have developed self-awareness. You gain the skill to turn any relationship into a precious gift; it becomes a crafted work of art.

The purpose of writing *Relationship Within* is to awaken you to your larger purpose. Only then can you know the full power of serving the greater good, and "paying it forward in all encounters." The art of using emotional self-control gives you the experience of self-integration and personal mastery. Open to the energy of your own heart. Inspire others to do the same. As you to dedicate your huge powers to helping others, you also create beauty in the world.

I provide a basic approach that has worked for many, and I am certain will benefit you. Follow your bliss, feel passion for life, acknowledge your innocence, allow vulnerability, and encourage openness. Something rich and juicy is already present if you rethink your approach to life. You can be optimistic since you are secure in your internal relationship. You surround yourself with the good things in life.

Whether in a peak or valley, *Relationship Within* is for you! The painting of the book represents manifestation. When you declare to the universe your true intention, it requires everything from you. If your relationships are lacking in embodied expression, and do not materialize the way you would like, you may need to focus on what holds you captive. Be willing to courageously explore what your symptoms of depression, anxiety, sadness, or anger may have to teach you. Alienation from you true spirit will stunt your growth. I know you desire to flourish, so, I challenge you to believe that you can. You can grow in wisdom and meet any relationship challenge head on by moving into what is most important. There is no need to act in undue haste. You may want to jump the gun and try to hook-up quickly with another before you go deep enough inside. I coax you on the magic carpet ride to a relationship within. Now let's get started on your alchemical process!

Knowing others is intelligence;
Knowing yourself is true wisdom.
Mastering others is strength;
Mastering yourself is true power.

If you realize that you have enough,
You are truly rich.
If you stay in the center
And embrace death with your whole heart,
You will endure forever.

Tao Te Ching (translation by Stephen Mitchell)

It has been fifteen years since I sat in a psychotherapy session, buried in a deluge of psychobabble and non-sense answers to relationship dilemmas that did not work. At that time, I was a typical Ph.D. student in clinical psychology, confident this course of study and training would help me better understand myself and other people. Like many entering a doctorate program, I was certain that psychological transformation and fulfilling relationships was achievable for most people with enough psychotherapy.

I trusted that reciprocity was possible between two people, and my relationships really could provide the motivating message of a better future. Yet I was embroiled in problems of my own that centered on trouble with my personal, family, and intimate relationships. At that time I thought, "If my aim is to assist others to connect with self-respect and dignity, I need to begin with my own inner healing." This awareness was the impetus to cultivate an extraordinary relationship, the one I have with my Higher Self. It is this path, I offer you. It is as a holistic approach, encompassing mind, body, spirit, and community.

During this phase of relational maturation, I recognized the need for personal growth and emotional healing. I was in crisis. I had recently gone through a difficult divorce. My husband and I had married because we were in love. We were hopeful of building a family together. I believed that union between two people was the one thing that would complete me. I approached my relationship with serious commitment, but was not committed to myself. I had never made the inner promise to offer up my heart and soul to myself. Years later, here I am writing to you with self-understanding based on fidelity to this inner truth. I discovered that the deck was stacked against me as long as I was not in relationship with myself.

I now know why the very thing I once thought would make me so happy, a secure marriage and family, felt like entrapment. My primary relationship (the one I had with myself) was not built on a solid foundation. I felt ensnared in a relational world of regret and disappointment. I was hurting others and myself. Even with a successful and considerate husband and two precious, loving children, I asked, how could a dream of hope and fulfillment become so heavy and painful? I felt frantically alone. Though my own self-worth was lacking, I was committed to breaking through my desperation.

I smashed the mirror of doubt, stopped second-guessing my every move, and embarked on an inner search for self-reliance. By optimizing interdependence and reconnecting with my inner self, I had to challenge my old perspectives. I began to look for inner values to guide the way I engaged others. It became clear that before I was able to reconnect with personal, family, and intimate relationships, I needed to define the real problem.

In my clinical training, I noticed how many of the individuals seeking mental health counseling asked the same shrewd questions, I had asked my therapist. Why are relationships often problematic and painful? I had to admit that the very people I love the most are the cause of a majority of my stress and suffering. Many of my coaching clients approached the problem of relationship with an air of defeat, "I want to throw in the towel and just end it all." However, in the counseling relationship, we discovered a tiny kernel of radiance underneath this personal agony.

The goddess fate shows up as "Necessity" in our life and forces us to change. Necessity is a divine energy that requires us to go deeper into our personal underworld, so to speak. When we drop a harmful relationship, we meet something fresh inside, though we may have felt it was lifeless. We encounter something intensely alive that arises from the ashes of our mistakes and disappointments. We reconnect to a forgotten internal guidance system.

The premise of this book is that we end up nowhere without an awareness of the powerful relationship we have within our self. This simple principle centers on an inner perspective: If I cherish my connection to myself, I naturally desire to grow with others. By striving to understand and give meaning to my relational experiences, I identify coping strategies, foster healing processes, and promote optimal health. I discover my happiness in the most unlikely place, within myself. Thus, relationship building is a non- linear process, based on continual growth, occasional setbacks, and learning from experience. Any relationship issues must take into account an individual's whole life, including living situation, employment, education, mental health, addiction treatment, spirituality, creativity, social networks, and community participation as determined by the person.

Empowering a person to look beyond negative perspectives that keep them stuck, supports dropping the victim attitude. A client stops assuming something is wrong with them, challenges the blame game, and allows clarity to emerge. When you can tolerate looking at how you contribute to frustrating issues in your relationships, you start to look your suffering square in the eye. Empowerment is only as good as your commitment to inner healing. It requires that you get down and dirty with what needs to change, so you form a spiritual backbone and personal character. Self-acceptance is vital in the initial stage of regaining belief in your personal resiliency since without self-respect you can never honor another.

Inner work is a direct and powerful way to approach the world of relationship. I use active imagination to help transform my dreams into a dynamic, innovative part of my life. This enables me to search my own unconscious mind where I find extraordinary strength and all the resources I need. In my own journey to relationship recovery, I begin with a mindfulness practice using a combination of Jungian dream work, cognitive behavioral therapy, meditation, and centering prayer. Introspective activity provides me a way to improve my self-management muscle, so a secure spiritual connection is established with my inner core.

During my own psychotherapy, I was searching for something deeper than symptom reduction. I wanted to get at the root of my negative attachment patterns. I witnessed how many relationships, although well intentioned, caused much harm, heartbreak, and even violence. Professional treatment was well meaning but came from a place of rescue rather than recovery. It viewed internal conflict as pathology but rarely focused on restoring people to optimal health.

I do not remember what day it was; all I know is that slowly over time after doing inner work, I spontaneously said No More. I stopped the madness and began to fall in love with me, by own radiance and wholeness. I discovered the power of true self-love. I was determined that if I continued seeking "something more" outside myself, I would just stay stuck in a downward spiral of learned helplessness. So I decided I was going to get real with me. I would be cheating myself in future relationships if I did not cultivate self-love as the foundation now.

This book is not about a quick fix to a difficult relationship, nor is it a maudlin road trip of false hopes, or an escape from tainted dreams. It is about tapping into the magic within YOU! When you courageously explode all assumptions about your relationships with others, you get real with yourself. The purpose of building a relationship within is that you strip away the artificial persona and expose your true self. Your relationships with other people become clear since you to see through the layers of your false personality that often push away true companionship and love.

Relationships Within aims to put you in touch with your core self, but many believe they need the answer to relationship problems NOW! However, relationship dynamics are multifaceted and complex. When love and intimacy collapse into violence, or sexual abuse, it is hard to deal with the emotional exploitation. Dysfunctional interactions, if we allow them to continue unchecked, cause the wheels of the relationship to come off the bus. Many cannot face inner conflict, impose artificial unity onto relationships, and repress inner voices of alarm or ambivalence. More than any form of inner work, relationship building brings our underlying inner conflicts up to the surface and out into the open. The good news is that through empowerment, you gain control over your own destiny, and influences the societal structures that support your life.

Perhaps you are reading this book because you feel confident that your relationships can be fulfilling, but you just keep making bad choices. You may find you keep ending up with manipulative friends and family members and wonder why co-dependency follows you like a shadow. You may feel that you are on a bus careening out of control, down the road to relationship ruin. Infidelity, addiction, or selfishness may have already derailed the relationship. No one consciously chooses a relationship to crash and burn. We naturally try to avoid catastrophe. As one client put it, "All I ever wanted was to belong and feel loved."

Relationship Within offers hope that it is never too late to have happy and fulfilling relationships. However, if you desire affirmative connections with others, you must have a relationship with your Higher Self. Well, there you have it: the impetus to create what you want and ought to have in your relationships. When you nurture the connection within, you recognize your relationship with yourself is a direct experience of how precious and unique you truly are. There is no one like you. This is the ultimate gift you have to offer yourself and others. Remember how you see the world is a mirror for how you actually see yourself!

Introduction

༄

Relationships are vital markers. From one stage of life to another, they point to something growing between two people over space and time.

Relationships do not arise in a vacuum, but emerge as we move into life, and reach out to others. There are no two people completely alike. Therefore no two relationships are identical. We set a realistic goal for all relationships, know they can be solid, and real. Making a conscious effort to fashion each relationship into a precious jewel brings soul to our encounters. We apply artistry because we look at each relationship as a joining of two different things, and together we create a whole greater than the sum of our parts. When two people meet in a field of interconnection this interaction produces a "third thing" that was not apparent before. We discover a shared sense of meaning as we fashion a relationship together.

Relationships are vital markers. From one stage of life to another, they point to something growing between two people over space and time. The nature of this joining is intricate and produces a deep involvement that is more than just the joining of the two separate people. The third thing that the relationship represents is something other than just you and me. My self and the other also hint at a "missing something" a subtle, invisible, yet fully embodied soul connection. We experience this comingling as something transcending the two individuals and bring sacredness to human intimacy.

I invite you to read *Relationship Within* in sequence, starting from the beginning section, but it picks up well at any part. You can read it here and there, or mull it over from time to time. I encourage you to dive into this rich, compelling material. Find some anchor point. Let it take you on an experiential journey. All human interconnection emerges from knowing that you have a relationship within. Your divine self is the spirit in you that gives your life soul. It is this divine energy that fuels self-respect while honoring the precious life of others. This sacred relationship runs toward the light. Even in the darkest and most painful places of human interaction, love rises up to meet the other as itself.

Relationship Within acknowledges that relationships change and so provides an overview of the creation of relationships as a key to making positive life transitions. Depth psychology encourages a discussion of how archetypal patterns allow us to transition into the next phase of human consciousness. The notion of psychological archetypes is one of Carl Jung's most useful and provocative contributions to human psychological development.

The Jungian archetypes provide a lens to peer inside the dynamics at work in our personal, family, and intimate relationships. I investigate how archetypal influences are alive in our object relations. Relationship archetypes such as father, mother, sister, brother, divine child, ancestor, lover, friend, teacher, healer, and stranger appear in all people, regardless of history, culture, or situation, and represent innate prototypes of human interaction. Here we enter a field that is not only individual but the healing process is always distinctive and give representations of instinctive processes in the human psyche which have a universal validity. Just as, in spite of differences, human beings all walk on two legs, have only one mouth, two eyes, and two ears, so, in spite of variation, all humans have definite and fundamental structural sameness found in the human psyche of all people. The commonality is a result of innate human archetypes.

One of the widespread archetypes the beloved seen as the hero quest or waiting on prince charming as in the search for wholeness. Thus, we conclude with a section on intimate relationships and look at erotic love as the underlying archetypal drive for completion requiring the art of soul making. Manifestations of intimacy are cross-cultural and found in legend, parable, fairy tale, and myths. In Greek mythology, Eros and Psyche are emblematic of passionate love and represent the comedy and tragedy we meet as we pursue our deepest yearning for the wholeness. Our human desire for divine union merges with the desire to find our other half or "soul mate since one mirrors the other.

You may not understand what archetypal pattern you are living out in terms of your significant relationships. Perhaps you are bewildered as to how you got into such a messy situation. I am here to tell you that you are not alone. Give yourself a break. No one actually provided you with a methodical teaching plan. Most of our parents did not formally instruct us on how to create positive relationships since they did not receive direct training from their parents. I offer a common sense way to penetrate beneath the surface of your interactions. The simple act is to create the relationship you always knew was possible. When you release emotional baggage, you have more internal space inside your relationships. By liberating stagnant energy, you discover a wellspring within.

The purpose of learning to work within is not just to resolve symptoms, deal with conflict, or to correct neurotic behavior. In considering what foster a positive relationship, I ask, "What truly makes me happy?" My happiest interactions arise when I am aware of an enduring connection to my core self. I attract the right circumstances and people into my life. I share myself with the human race because it does not matter whether those relationships fall into recognizable roles or not. I choose to relate to the world at large while also enjoying being alone. I fully explore my most significant relationship, the one I create with myself.

I invite you to consider what a significant relationship means to you. In psychodynamic terms, we call this primary human activity "object relations," as the unique way we relate to important "objects" or people in our life.

The first principle of object relations states, a relationship is comprised of a subject and an object. Simply put, the observer affects the observed; we engage others from a particular viewpoint that is based on our personal vantage.

The second principle of object relations is founded on research into how personal experience and early childhood conditioning influences all ensuing relationships. Using the framework of the object relations theory, we revision how this dynamic contributes to the success or failure of relationships over the lifespan.

The third principle is realization of projection. In relationship dynamic, it is common to think about our self and others in ways that are not accurate. This truth exposes how much our relationships arise from personal assumptions, conditioning, and personality styles.

The fourth principle states a relationship is not a static thing but a living space between two people that requires time, attention, understanding, and love.

Metaphorically, any real relationship is a shared breath between two individuals. Deep understanding connects you to something beyond the concrete world of facts. Each relationship lures us into a hidden dimension of our self that is brought to life by the other. I am not talking about some mystical state, but merely pointing to the genuine truth of engagement. Self-awareness supports clear perceptions since it helps us form effective boundaries. We distinguish between where one person ends and the other begins.

Misperception is common in relationship since it is easy to misread others intentions. We notice unconscious projections that necessitate change. We accept that each person has some level of prejudice and idiosyncratic preferences. The awareness of an interconnected field between two people brings a third area into focus; namely the relationship itself. Each person must go through various stages of personal development to form attachments and build relationships. This book explores some of the common challenges to dealing effectively with relationship inconsistency.

"Know thy Self." The ancient injunction, from the oracle at Delphi, is an early pronouncement suggesting the necessity of self-knowledge. This book is about traversing the vast territory within. To build a solid individual personality means more than just the flip of a coin. We may hope that everything will land right sides up, but at heart, this is a matter of self-knowledge. The intelligence of knowing "thy self" is at the root of all human development. It is an ancient art and yet remains remarkably contemporary since the basic core of human nature has not essentially changed in this regard.

Every one has at one time or another sought answers to relationship dilemmas. People seek psychotherapy, family therapy, couples counseling, pastoral counseling, and life coaching to help sort out personal challenges. Necessity often pushes us over the edge, a difficult relationship is spiraling out of control, and the inevitability of change invites us to seek a better way. This dynamic may come once in a lifetime or is cyclical as unresolved relationship problems continue to emerge. A growing awareness of how toxic a relationship has actually become, encourages you to recognize just how destructive it is to your physical and emotional health. You notice the ways it erodes your strength and well-being.

Let me share an example. When something is unfulfilling in my relationship (with anyone for that matter), the first thing I do is to take a step back. I notice that my tendency is to judge the other or myself. I breathe and consider how I am criticizing the situation, rather than allowing it to "Be as It Is." I ask what I may be doing to contribute to the conflict. I have learned the hard way that I must candidly evaluate my relationship situation before I react impulsively. I ask myself, what is the compensation that I am giving myself for getting angry with someone cutting me off in traffic or criticizing my work. Often the payoff is stress or more conflict.

You may be less assertive and feel sensitive about how the other makes you feel. Or else you easily become self-absorbed, depressive, and withdrawn. In such a situation ask what you may be doing to allow this person to take advantage of you. How are you an enabler or codependent? How does your emotional pattern keep the other from dealing with important personal issues? How do you begin to maximize your power from a relationship within? What can you do to make permanent changes within yourself?

I begin by looking at myself instead of the other person. By focusing on something, I can direct, I hold up a mirror to look at myself. I realize that whatever the other person is doing, I am in some way co creating the interconnected field between us. My energy field is like an attitude, it elicits, maintains, and at times even attracts negative behaviors that I do not want or respect. Other people react to my tone of voice, notice my energy, body language, and attune to subtle attitudes. By looking in the mirror, I come face to face with images of my self, I am not so proud.

You may wonder why unresolved problems from your past still trouble you. Looking at your failures; when a relationship stops working, or is no longer positive, does not have to hold you back. Perhaps what arrests you, causes you to be stuck in a relationship rut is fear of being alone.

As children, we all desire to belong. We long to feel innocent, spontaneous, and open with others. Without a caring relationship, we are lost. Many of us have been hurt, disappointed, and even heartbroken because we prematurely exposed our vulnerability to another. If this is the case, you must resolve to trust yourself. Fear, pain, suffering, and regret, can be a huge catalyst to change. Rock bottom is a good place to land. Let the desire to trust your higher self encourage self-acceptance. For many, the apprehension of separation causes fear of self-knowledge, as much if not more, than the agonizing task of getting to know the other. Being alone can be wonderful!

If everything is great and your life appears perfect on the surface, you may not be dealing honestly with emotions. Emotional dishonestly creates an environment of dissent and betrayal. If we cannot be real with our self we may need more time for introspection. A friend was angry with her husband. Sandy exclaimed, "You think I need to be less in denial? My marriage still causes me heartache. Mark thwarts my love and he does not reciprocate. I was abandoned by Mark's affaire; the relationship was unbearable since I was heartbroken."

A break-up in a relationship can be especially painful, particularly if one feels like Sandy that they have been mistreated. Sandy said, "When Mark violated the trust, by going astray, it damaged our relationship. Although it did not make me feel any better immediately, I can slowly reconnect with a relationship within." The issue that Sandy is facing around infidelity is a widespread relationship topic for others. Heartbreak and misfortune between lovers represent some of the most enduring themes in all art, music, and literature. Human relationships are ultimately one of the deepest mysteries of life. I invited you to use these affirmations as you continue reading.

I embody my personal myth in a conscious way.
I am creative, resourceful, and whole.
I forgive you, so I can love myself.

SECTION ONE:
Personal Relationships

CHAPTER ONE:
The Foundational Relationship

✢

We interact with others, in part to survive, since at core,
we are relational creatures from skin down to the bone.

Creating a positive relationship within is not easy. We all know a relationship with another presents challenges, so why would it be different with you? We have forgotten how to speak to each other in the universal language of love and respect, mainly because we do not have self-love. With all our sophisticated high-speed communication, we have lost a common idiom that makes us a relational person. The secret to being human is that we can engage in conversation with our higher self. An opportunity awaits us to develop a firm foundation. This provides a springboard to a healthy matrix of security and support. Without this basic support from parents, family, and caregivers in early life, relationships are likely to suffer.

Positive early relationships provide the capacity for us to move out into the world and form committed relationships. In the natural course of life, we build relationships from infancy into youth, as we gain maturity, age, and pass on. Some people form attachments that are so strong that the relationship continues with the loved one beyond death. There are religious practices that perform ceremony to honor the dead. Ancestor worship is a means of transmitting sacred information from the past as a way of passing vital attributes from one generation to the next. It is worthwhile to examine our relationship within and notice the role it plays in the successful navigation through life transitions, even as a passageway into death. Relationships must be responsive to the shifting tides. The truth of life is that all things change; we need to be willing to adopt flexible attitudes like wisdom and emotional intelligence to manage the inevitable changes.

Scientific research demonstrates that an inclination to connect to others is rooted in the need for survival. The human neurological system establishes connections between things, based on subjectivity. The way we take in information, process that information, and make decisions effects how we form connections. Positive and negative qualities of our relationship affect our physical and mental health in significant ways. People who have positive relationships throughout life usually live longer and have a better quality of life. Developmental psychologists work on the premise that each person must navigate the winds of change. When we build bridges to others, we all have a better change of survival. The challenge is to create a relational world where we actually consider how we form positive relationships both within the self and with others.

Symbolic Perspective of Relationship

Relationships serve different purposes and have multiplex meaning. Some of us focus on the general aspect of relationships, and others are more compelled to examine the idiosyncrasies of individual's relational stories. The exemplary meaning we ascribe to certain relationships draws us into complex intellectual, emotional, spiritual, and psychological realms. Some relationships can give us a window into dimensions we may not have considered. We all seek an authentic experience of our self and unity with our Source in the image of Higher Self, God, Allah, Atman, Yahweh, Christ Consciousness, Buddha Nature, or simply put, "All There Is."

The symbolic perspective of relationship offers a representational world of rich imagery. Relationship building is innate since it is an instinct pass on from our ancestors. By exploring these primordial rituals, artifacts, and archetypal forms from the past, modern people can use ancient representations to link us to archetypical dimensions displaying in human history today. We gain access to the mystery at the heart of relationships and try to do our part to preserve the fragile balance between the personal and collective forces at work.

Relationship building is the central activity on the life journey. Life itself is our first and primary relationship. At birth, we are miraculously born into world of relationship. We must leave the oceanic state of oneness with mother to become a separate self. From infancy through childhood, nothing stays the same. We must continue to attach, and then sever connections as we move out of childhood into the crisis of adolescent years. We mature, work, serve others, and play our part in the local community, and make our unique mark upon the world. But the most important relationship of all is the inner relationship forged in the crucible of our hearts.

Our personal, family, and intimate relationships improve when we do not expect them to provide things that we must establish. The quality of our relationships significantly influence the way we value our life, our ability to seek the higher good, and to giveback to the world. Self-esteem helps us deal effectively with life events that trigger painful relational patterns. Any worthwhile relationship must have a dual focus; to give us secure roots to grow and strong wings to soar. The relationship flies without us having to sacrifice our deeper roots. When our relationship within supports us, we fly into the unknown with courage. We know we can also rise to the challenge of the moment. Learning effective ways to deal with problematic behavior is one key to healing relationships.

Self-love forms the foundation of our most important relationship, the relationship we create with our self. The strength of all your other relationships is exactly equal to the solidity of that foundation. To love you is not just a self-esteem boosting piece of advice. It is the prerequisite to truly loving others. The Golden Rule is to do unto others, as you would like them to do unto you. You are likely to have heard it many times, expressed in different ways. Look a little closer though, and you will find that at its very center is the command to love yourself.

Self-love

First, let us dispel some myths about what it means to love your self. Self-love is not about being arrogant or egotistical. It is not about comparing yourself to others. It is not about always putting yourself first at the expense of others. It is not about always getting your way. It is not about always winning. It is not about "only looking after number one." To love myself is to be in awe of the miracle of my existence. It is to accept myself as I am. It is to know that I am the "light" parts and the "dark", the "good" and the "bad." I know the real me is above the apparent dualities of the material world. I am willing to receive as much of me as I am willing to give.

Self-love is about knowing my values, maintaining my boundaries, and honoring them. I show others how I wish them to treat me by the way I treat myself. Self-love is about being kind to me and looking after my mental and emotional states, my physical body, and the spiritual dimension of my life. It is about knowing I am worthy to receive love. Love is my inheritance and never a result of my achievements, or exterior appearance. Love is the legacy of human continued existence, and a most precious birthright.

It is an obvious statement that you cannot give something that you do not have, yet many people frantically try to love others, without having self-love. It is no surprise that in time their assets of loving kindness are exhausted. The relationship weakens, and often ends. To give love, you must first have love. This is a universal truth. To encompass love for another, you must love yourself. When I give myself the love I want to experience from others, I find all my relationships transform in miraculous ways.

Try this exercise:

Take a moment and think of those things you most need to hear from others. Consider whether you want to hear that they love you, admire you, and accept you just as you are. Take a piece of paper and write them down. Make sure to have a comprehensive inventory. This exercise demonstrates that what you most want to hear from others is often what you most need to tell yourself. You should now have a list of positive affirmations. Repeat them every day. You will soon enjoy a sense of self-love and inner peace that you never had before.

Benefits of Self-love

There is a single, intelligent consciousness that pervades the entire universe. This is an all knowing, all-powerful, all loving, all creative field of energy that is present everywhere. We call this single consciousness by many names. God, All there Is, Brahman, the Universal Mind, to name but a few. This consciousness is the source of all love. It is Love. When we recognize the truth of our oneness with the source of all love, we feel at home in the universe. Our very essence becomes love. We discover this unconditional love for our self, and tap into an unlimited reserve of abundant love for everyone, and everything. We know that to love our self is to love the one creator. This awareness puts us in a unified field of solidarity with the human community.

The benefits of self-love are astounding, and provide inner peace. It is a win-win situation for all to have self-love, and creates inner happiness, confidence, and peace of mind. When I am in alliance within, I rally to whatever circumstance may arise. I may be challenged, but not defeated, by outside events and opinions. Working from a deep connection within, enables me to make healthy relationship choices naturally. It allows me to rejoice fully in other people's good fortune, while also being more genuinely loving towards others. The more I love from within, the more I encounter the benefits of being loving.

The Buddha sought a relationship within and then once enlightened he turned back to help the world. His message is summed up in this statement. "You can search throughout the entire universe for someone who is more deserving of your love and affection than you are yourself. That person is not to be found anywhere. You yourself, as much as anybody in the entire universe deserve your love and affection." Siddhartha Gautama Buddha.

Following the wisdom of the dharma, self-love is a prerequisite to loving others. Your relationships are only as strong as the foundation of your self-love. Release any false teaching that tells you that loving yourself is selfish or egotistical. It is usually the case that people with self-loathing often are the one's that are most egotistical. So replace narcissist love with the truth; your very essence is love. Unconditional self-love is your heritage. When you know you are in alignment with the one source of all love, you are one with every thing and every one. You know that you cannot possibly experience authentic love without first loving yourself. You have discovered the truth that self-love actually is the greatest love of all.

The central purpose of a relationship with your Higher Self is to help you gain access to vital information that resides within. You are the personification and embodiment of a divine plan. In mysterious ways, your relationships help you fulfill your special purpose. The call to return to your divine self is character work. It is a human birth right that we each are given but requires taking action. You must respond to your inner vocation to deal with difficulty since it requires having access to your divine self. Answers to relationship problems are easy when you discover the real problem is separation from your Source. The underlying cause of any relationship dilemmas is the misperception of your divine nature and is the insurmountable obstacle to self-love.

The Divine Self

The Divine Self is the character that represents your fundamental nature. This star within you manifests as your inner voice, spirit guide, best friend, mother, and father. Source self is not merely a separate aspect of your ego self. This is you at the core of your being. You only need to become aware and ask this power for assistance. Source self is patient, and always waits for you to call. It is not rude or pushy but is always present. It is the secret power within. Even in your darkest hours, it will never abandon.

We can all learn to have a very real and physical communication with our Higher Self. The process is not as difficult as one would think. It just takes a little bit of practice and patience. When we develop a two-way communication with our Higher Selves, we receive guidance, and live to our fullest potential. We all experience intuition in the form of hunches. These gut feelings seem to come from out of the blue. We may have intuitions that tell us something that is irrational and illogical. We have all experienced moments when we choose to follow that guidance. Even if it does not make any normal sense, when we act on insight, we find, there was a reason why we received such guidance.

Intuitive wisdom is our Higher Self talking. The knowledge that we receive is not coming from out of nowhere. It emerges directly from the part of us that is Spirit. The perspective of this inner "knowing" brings everything into focus. Even when we cannot fully discern the fine details, we learn to trust, and tap into that extra sensory perceptive part. Do so, we bypass many difficult lessons, flow with life, and are much more alive than otherwise possible.

"What was that connection?"
I wanted it to come back and desired more of that sensation.
The feeling encompassed me. It was visceral, succulent, and nuanced.
I asked myself, "Who do I love at this moment?"

I was walking on the beach with a friend, when a feeling of deep joy overcame me. I was exhilarated, profoundly alive, and connected. It came over me for no particular reason. In this spontaneous moment of deeply connecting to everything, the crashing waves, the sea gull sounds, the feel of the sand beneath my feet, and the voice of my beloved. I was in harmony with the universe. I felt euphoric. In this instant of unfathomable belonging, I was at ease in my body, mind, and spirit. Everything tingled with aliveness. It was not I who was trembling, but the higher vibration field that encompassed me. I am not sure how long this feeling lasted, but then I noticed a shift.

The shift occurred, the moment I started to question. I began to reflect on this experience, and asked aloud, "What just happened?" "What is this unfathomable connection? What did I just experience at my core?" "What does this sense of completeness reveal about my relationship?" I felt extraordinarily alive, and noted what was happening in my body and emotions. I became aware of deep space inside; place beyond right or wrong, good or bad. It was an awareness of no self, there was no striving, and nothing to add or subtract to the now. I wanted the experience to linger. What could I do to make this feeling endure?

My conversation with my friend picked up again. I felt the residue of that moment as divine love. In the inner connection, a visceral, succulent, and nuanced place within was made known. I asked myself in silence, "Who do I love?" I asked because the experience had evoked the sensation of falling in love. I loved my friend as we walked the shoreline. Nevertheless, the feeling of epiphany was of a different nature. "What was that?" It dawned on me that I was in love with me, not my ego-identity but my divine spirit. The joyful feeling signaled a moment of homecoming; complete security within my skin.

It is one thing to feel good about our self in special moments, but quite another feeling to take the ephemeral connection and make it into a long-term relationship. Falling in love with true self is not as easy as it seems. It requires everything. I must trust myself to be my authentic self. It begins by being present to all my experiences, both the euphoric, and the distressful. The relationship I create within must be strong enough to embrace both the light at the end of the tunnel, while enduring the dark night of the soul. I encourage myself to bless all the positive aspect of my life, and to be my best advocate in the areas where I still need assistance. I examine my negative thoughts, and notice how they cause difficult emotions. I am willing to disrupt habitual patterns that cause stress. I am open to how my symptoms are survival responses. I bring loving kindness to all the unresolved aspects of my life.

If I cannot trust myself, I engage others in ways that reflect distrust. They notice this quality and there tends to be misunderstanding and relational dilemmas. As a mental health counselor, I quickly discover that the reason many come to therapy is at heart, self-hatred and lack of self-respect. If we do not like our basic self, we cannot authentically be with another person. By bringing awareness to what we are thinking, and how we judge those around us, we can see what we are up to in our relationships. We begin to see through our delusions, false fronts, and look for a deeper connection within.

Inner Child Work

One way we can jump-start this process is to nurture our "inner child." In popular psychology and Jungian therapy, the inner child represents the purest aspect of our being. It connects us to aspects of the personality that are inexperienced, innocent, and possess childlike qualities. It includes all that we learned and experienced as children before puberty. The inner child represents a partially independent entity; secondary to the waking conscious mind. The inner child is a term that has various therapeutic uses in counseling and holistic health settings. John Bradshaw, a U.S. educator and self-help movement leader, markedly used "inner child" to point to unsettled childhood experience, and the persistent dysfunctional effects of childhood abuse. In this way, inner child refers to the entire sum of mental-emotional memories stored in the sub-conscious.

Acknowledging my own problems with my inner child was most refreshing since I started getting real with the most important thing, my innocence. To be in relationship with my inner child, gives me insight about aspects of myself that I may have pushed away or ignored. Inner child work is simply giving attention to the needs of my internalized younger self. This is a direct way to learn how to break though defensive patterns from childhood and extend love, kindness, understanding, and tenderness to my inexperience or blamelessness. When I comfort, entertain, support, adore, and coach my inner child, my personal, family, intimate relationships miraculously change for the better.

I believe this is an indispensable component to building a relationship within since I spent much of my time treating my inner child roughly. I had to work on making a relationship with this immature and undeveloped part of my personality. I connect with my inner child in meditation, journal writing, and authentic dance. When I emotionally unite with my inner child, I am better able to care for others. I need to connect with my inner child since this is the direct portal into my divine innocence. Taking this simple step enhances my life in big and small ways. All of my relationships take on a new perspective. I set the captive free, and know the captive has been me.

On a practical level, my inner child helps me take care of my emotional needs. We all need to feel, and be told, we are loved. I need to feel, that I am vital and valued. You need to feel a sense of belonging. We each desire to have respect, regardless of our flaws, inadequacies, and erroneous beliefs about self and other. For example, I could work all day without getting exercise or going outside. However, I do not want my inner child stuck at the computer all day, so I try to take breaks that my inner child enjoys, like walking to work, or going to the gym during lunch.

At core, the inner child has a special intelligence. It is an inner capacity that is ingenuous and knows how to reach out to the astuteness within, often imaged as the wise old man or woman. The way that I connect to my inner wisdom or Sophia is to close my eyes and daydream. I let my thoughts float past, much like watching clouds. I engage in active imagination, a psychotherapeutic process used in inner work to help build a connection to unconscious forces within the psyche. The unconscious holds the intelligence of the imagination and gives us access to psycho-somatic states where the embodied sensation of power, confidence, and equanimity supports a connection to the divine feminine wisdom.

I call on Sophia. I align with this inner aspect of holiness since I physically experience my own sacredness. Inner child work goes hand in hand with Sophia, but for many this is an unusual topic. You may wonder if this inner work captures your attention. Only you know if you are ready to stop letting emotional issues interfere with your ability to be happy. Sophia's message is that you should concentrate on what you can realize, not on what you cannot change. You can offer your services, but inner wisdom shows that you may need to focus on the positive changes you can make within you inner child. You know what to do to improve your relationships-so do it!

Once you find the inner companions, childlike innocence and Sophia as feminine wisdom, you can ask them for guidance. Being in a relationship to your divine self requires affection and sensitivity to everything about you. The inner child encompasses the duality inherent in love and hate, good and bad, right and wrong, and sacred and profane. The key is to be acutely sensitive to the childlike emotions. Observe the sensation of being around others, and then bring attention to the residual emotions that arise in silent moments when you are alone. You notice what feels good to you and what does not. You find the middle ground, and come to a place where you feel confident that the most important relationship arises from within. Empathy with your inner child is how you know you are innocent. You did the best you could at the time.

The act of self-love is a lesson in patience. Think of any child, patience is so difficult. This is especially true when working on patience, as an adult, and coming up against selfishness driven by infantile behavior, you have not overcome from childhood. I try to check in with my inner child several times during the day. This communication helps me to create boundaries, explore what feels comfortable or not, and notice when I feel distress.

I observe how I act in various situations, and notice my habitual responses; when I am reacting to the situation rather than calmly responding. This information often comes from a negative connection to my inner child and is the source of many habitual reactions. I act in appropriate ways when I take care of my inner child since I am able to have fun times and maintain my responsibilities. I am sensitive to my emotional and physical needs, value my body, my financial obligations, and take ownership of my job. If you respect your inner child's needs, you will receive more esteem and love from others without grasping. You do not expect the other person to take care of your inner child's needs, since you have your own inner wisdom, Sophia as your divine feminine companion.

It may sound tongue and cheek to say, "I romance my self." Sometimes I treat myself to something special, or take myself on a date. I spent time doing whatever I enjoy. This may mean doing an art project, or buying a book, cuddling up next to a friend, or taking a dance class. I embrace whatever the feel-good activity is for me. I also make a list of all the things I like about myself, and refer to it in moments of self-doubt, or uncertainty. In these moments of hesitation, I have a good long talk with Sophia and realign with my innate wisdom.

This inner dialogue helps me reconnect with my inner child but it does not have to be somber or grim. I can bring childlike humor to the situation, and take myself on an adventure. Exploration comes in all shapes and sizes. From walking to the nearest park to people watch, going for a special meal, or taking a jaunt on a train to some place new. When I have a good relationship with my innocence, it is likely that my relationships with other people are positive and upbeat.

We like being around positive people who demonstrate self-love. Think about it, no one-wants to hang out with your inner saboteur or judge. My mantra is to surround myself with people who mirror a positive image back to me that reflects my capacity to be creative, resourceful, and whole.

I think we sometimes write off inner child work as egotistic, narcissistic, or just a sappy platitude. Neither could be further from the truth. Self-love that honors innocence takes an incredible amount of courage, and is an enormously worthwhile undertaking. The good news is that when you tap into self-love and become enchanted with the inner child as divine-self relationship, you know this spark is already within you now. You just have to find the ember and ignite it.

Here are a few tips for creating better relationship with your Inner Child

According to John Bradshaw, author of Home Coming: Reclaiming and Championing Your Inner Child, the process of healing your wounded inner child is one of grief, and it involves these six steps (paraphrased from Bradshaw):

1. Trust

For your wounded inner child to come out of hiding, he must be able to trust that you will be there for him. Your inner child also needs a supportive, non-shaming ally to validate his abandonment, neglect, abuse, and enmeshment. Those are the first essential elements in original pain work.

2. Validation

If you are still inclined to minimize and/or rationalize the ways in which you were shamed, ignored, or used by your parents, you need now to accept that these things truly wounded your soul. Your parents were not bad; they were just wounded children themselves.

3. Shock & Anger

If this is all shocking to you, that is great, because shock is the beginning of grief.

It is okay to be angry, even if what happened to you was unintentional. In fact, you have to be angry if you want to heal your wounded inner child. I do not mean you need to scream and holler (although you might). It is okay to be mad about a dirty deal.

I know [my parents] did the best that two wounded adult children could do. However, I am also aware that I was deeply wounded spiritually and that it has had life-damaging consequences for me. What that means is that I hold us all responsible to stop what we are doing to ourselves and to others. I will not tolerate the outright dysfunction and abuse that dominated my family.

4. Sadness
After anger comes hurt and sadness. If we were victimized, we must grieve that betrayal. We must also grieve what might have been–our dreams and aspirations. We must grieve our unfulfilled developmental needs.

5. Remorse
When we grieve for someone who has died, remorse is sometimes more relevant. For instance, perhaps we wish we had spent more time with the deceased person. In grieving childhood abandonment, you must help your wounded inner child see that there was nothing that could have been done differently. Your pain is about what happened to you; it is about your loss but you are not responsible.

6. Loneliness
The deepest core feelings of grief are toxic shame and loneliness. We were shamed by (our parents) abandoning us. We feel we are bad, as if we are contaminated, and that shame leads to loneliness. Since our inner child feels flawed and defective, she has to cover up her true self with her adapted, false self. She then comes to identify herself by her false self. Her true self is alone and isolated.

Staying with this last layer of painful feelings is the hardest part of the grief process. "The only way out is through," we say in therapy. It is hard to stay at that level of shame and loneliness; but as we embrace these feelings, we come out the other side. We encounter the self that has been in hiding. You see, because we hid it from others, we hid it from ourselves. In embracing our shame and loneliness, we begin to touch our truest self and stop feeling so alone.

Inner Child & Personal Spirituality

Working with our inner child is a form of personal spirituality that supports life transformation. This is well known. Unconditional self-love is an extension of spirituality. It works alchemy in our lives because it transforms the heavy metal of experience into the gold of inner illumination. Positive relationship dynamics arise out of a solid spiritual practice. Daily practice allows the consistent energy of love to take hold in our every day activities. What is astounding is how consistent meditation and prayer puts us in touch with inner space. It is from this inner space within that we extend sacred space to everyone. A spiritual connection means the difference between a serene relationship and one of constant conflict. We do not place unrealistic demands and expectations onto others. The bond weakens when constant worry and disappointment become the focus of the relationship. Our link to other is less than holy.

We also sustain our relationships by having a conscious and sacred purpose. Without this aim, the relationship runs on co-dependency, and meanders along with no direction. Spirituality as an activity of inner intention and requires a practice such as meditation and prayer. Prayer is the willingness to enter into a relationship with God (whatever form this takes). Meditation also provides a portal into sacred space. We approach all life situations from a more dynamic place since we operate with unconditional love.

Some people feel they do not need a relationship with something outside their ego self and do not relate with the need for a sacred resource. This may be true for some folk but many distinguish the benefits of developing a relationship within versus bolstering the ego. If someone thinks, "I cannot find the time, nor do I have the inclination to connect within," I respond with silence and know that this is a long journey. The old adage says, "You can lead a horse to water but you can't make it drink." Many need a life changing relationship or extreme situation to feel the need to identify with a higher power or acknowledge a divine resource at work behind the scenes of life.

Meditation Practice

Scientific studies demonstrate the countless benefits of engaging in a regular meditation practice. The act of quieting the mind, focusing on the rise and fall of breath, enhances over all health and well-being. Empirical data shows that mediation leads to deep states of relaxation, fosters inner security, supports positive relationships and provides an inner ground of being. Meditation becomes a refuge where we explore the dynamics of our inner life and maintain emotional equilibrium when engaging others.

Mediation is essential if we want to process all the information that surrounds us on a daily basis. It is hard to avoid the negative impact of constant media contamination. No wonder human relationships suffer. Bad news saturates our minds with suspicion. Global strife, war, poverty, and catastrophe compete with high-status celebrity scandals for airtime. The old journalistic maxim, "If it bleeds, it reads," sums it up.

We squander precious time striving for the spoils of materialism and this definitely has a negative effect on our relationships. As consumers, we barely know how to appreciate what is right in front of us. We greedily desire more and more, while hoping to find happiness in harmful attachments. In the age of instant gratification, many doubt if the trusted methods of relationship building can actually serve our deeper needs. When the media tells you, you are worth it and can have it all, and you can get something for nothing, you stop fulfilling your true needs, since a relationship within requires something from you; Inner work!

From this perspective, spirituality is an all-inclusive term for the practice of inner work through engaging prayer and meditation. The intention is to create spirited relationships with all people we encounter. We give respect to those we love and to those we may not know, or even dislike.

CHAPTER TWO:
Spiritual Resources

☘

As your practice deepens, you flow more naturally into this way of being. Meditation and prayer are methods that easily flow together.

There are many valuable spiritual resources available. They provide direction and help tailor a spiritual practice. One excellent resource is speaking with an inner guide. Meaningful relationships enhance life in so many ways. Nevertheless, we need a personal relationship with our self as a place of inner security. When our fears are diminished, deeper hopes and dreams emerge. We take time to hear the still small voice. We activate a field of intelligence that fuels the universe.

Question: "What does it mean that God speaks in a still small voice?" There is only one place in Hebrew scripture where God is said to speak in a "still small voice," and it was to Elijah after his dramatic victory over the prophets of Baal (1 Kings 18:20-40). Seeking safety from attack, Elijah hides in a cave and grumbles that Jezebel has demanded her husband to kill all of God's prophets. He alone has survived. God instructs Elijah to stand on the mountaintop. Then the Lord sent a mighty wind that shattered the rocks, sent an earthquake and fire, but His voice was in none of them. After all that, the Lord spoke to Elijah in the still small voice, or "gentle whisper."

The explanation for why God speaks in the still small voice is to show Elijah that the works of God are not always dramatic revelations or awesome manifestations. Godly silence does not automatically mean divine inactivity. Zechariah 4:6 tells us that God's work is "not by might nor by power, but by My Spirit," meaning that overt displays of power are not necessary for our Higher Power to work miracles. This still small voice speaks to us today, as it did through the prophets. The common thread in all spiritual traditions is that we can have a relationship, not only with our divine child and inner wisdom, but also with our Higher Self. Whatever Higher Power we pray to is less important than hearing how God is speaking to us. What is most important is what we do with what we hear.

The Higher Self is our inner guide and speaks most clearly to us in word and image. The more we learn to read the symbolic signs from our Source, the more ready we will be to recognize the voice when we hear it speaking to us. We draw on this enormous reservoir of support. Integrity is born out of this silent space. In the process, we learn how to focus our energy during meditation and prayer. We are able to integrate the best of who we are into our relationships.

We spend much time, money, and effort on perfecting the outer façade of our personality. Everyone must play a social role and have an identity. We create a persona much as an actor wears a mask to create a particular character. The word *persona* originates from Latin, and refers to a theatrical mask. Upbringing acculturates us to polish this outer shell and make it shine like gold. Often what we display on the outside does not match up. Not everything that glitters is gold.

The alchemy of spirituality uncovers our true spiritual gifts. Without this activity, the human heart cannot transform. We are running on spiritual emptiness and need energy to reconnect. Having lost touch with our deeper self, we cannot imagine connecting with anyone else. Insight into this difficulty helps us connect to a solid foundation. When we find that support comes from within, we bring more vitality to our relationships. Meditation, prayer, and spiritual techniques practiced daily can truly change our life. It takes going through the refiner's fire to discover all the "good stuff" that occurs in this profound alchemy. A spiritual practice helps us rise to meet the challenges of dealing with other people since it brings a refreshing quality to each relationship and fosters enduring sacred bonds.

Your Higher Self

What should you consider before seeking advice from your inner guide? First consider this as your Higher Self? The primary question is whether you feel a connection. You must feel relaxed in the exchange, as though you are speaking with a trusted friend. Your attitude should be down-to-earth and realistic while broad enough to encompass your intuition and creativity. You are not going to find a panacea to life's challenges. You can aspire to find out what makes life worthwhile. A spiritual practice provides tools that will help in all aspects of your life. Meditation and prayer take time and devotion but the benefits are astounding. As your practice deepens, you flow more naturally into this way of being. Meditation and prayer are methods that easily flow together. See what works best for you. Spirituality is a private and revered part of each person's life.

There are no hard and fast rules for creating a meditation and prayer practice. When we imagine meditation, we envision sitting cross-legged in the center of a room, eyes closed, and mindfully watching the flow of breath. That might work for some. There are those who prefer their garden to sit and commune with nature, or God. My friend delights in her meditation by sitting on a bench where she can watch hummingbirds flock to a feeder she fills with red sugar water.

One of the most frequently asked questions is, "How do I silence my mind?" How do I calm down my restless body?" Your inner guide will help you understand the levels of relaxation and ways to clear your mind. You may want to have a discussion with a meditation teacher. This may include specifics, such as how much time each meditation exercise might take, breathing techniques, and frequency of meditation. We make this passage on our own. It is natural to want to share the peace as well as the journey with those we love. It would be ideal to share what we discover in meditation. Only divulge information and insights to those we trust. Defining how the voyage will go is not possible. We cultivate the ability to understand what is going on within. Our awareness affects everyone around us.

Find a Spiritual Practice that Works

Finding devotional time is difficult. Trust that there is always time to move into a silent space in your busy schedule. You need to provide an intentional setting and allow yourself the precious time to reconnect with your authentic nature. Human connection rises to a new height and has a sacred significance. Spirituality paves the way for compassion and gratitude that are vital ingredients in the creation of a relationship. Inner contentment is the key to discovering contented outer relationships. When we are aligned from inside, we are authentic with each other. Spiritual practice moves us to new levels of self-revelation and inner fulfillment.

Remain optimistic, yet reasonable in this process. Have hope, but no expectation. You need to be careful about what to expect from your interactions in this realm. Your observing ego provides a unique perspective. From this vantage of spirit, you can consider the other's point of view. You choose a spiritual friend or mentor to help smooth the way if you become discouraged or lose your way. You find a spiritual practice that works.

Spirituality supports you and encourages living with integrity from the inside out. You become that special someone, you respect and see reflected in the mirror. All relationships are enriching when a positive, transpersonal force infuses the individual encounter. You consciously make an intentional alliance within by practice. Like most endeavors that are worthwhile, it takes devotion to a practice to build a spiritual backbone. A spiritual practice leads us through a ceremony that translates our inner dream into a memorable physical, relational experience. Working with the power of imaginative spiritual practices, we begin to develop a relationship between the conscious or outer part of our mind, and the inner, unconscious mind resulting in what is often a critical transformative experience.

The spiritual journey provides us opportunities to practice in the realm of love. It has always been a radical act to "love neighbor as self." We are born to love, but like any valuable pursuit, it requires patience, persistence, and practice. When we actively love, we are in a radical state of consciousness. The inner activity of self-love aligns with neighborly love. It is our springboard to making intentional choices in all relationships.

Many spiritual traditions support this objective. There is the command to love God. "The Greatest Commandment" taken from, the New Testament describes the first, of two commandments cited by Jesus in Matthew 22:35–40, Mark 12:28–34 and Luke 10:25–28. Jesus takes the first commandments from the Law of Moses in the Old Testament and places two commandments at the heart of New Testament Christian ethics. In Matthew, the high priests ask Jesus, "which is the great commandment in the law?" He answers, "Thou shall love the Lord thy God with all thy heart, and with all thy soul, and with thy mind", before announcing a second commandment, "Thou shall love thy neighbor as thyself."

Jesus demonstrates the ultimate value of human relationship and notes his power to bind two commandments. Commonly "love thy God" is referred to as "the first and greatest commandment" with "love thy neighbor" being referred to as "the second great commandment." However, Jesus brings a new awareness. He ties love of God with human partnership. The dance of sacred love unifies the two greatest commandments by weaving love of God with neighbor as our self. Jesus sets the law on a new course by demonstrating this relational love to include God, self, and neighbor as the new state of divine mutuality. They must go hand and hand.

The Good Samaritan

Another quality of relationship shines through in the New Testament parable of the Good Samaritan. (Luke 10:29-37). The story demonstrates in action what Jesus meant by another person's "neighbor." Luke tells of a man who befriends a stranger. The Samaritan comes to the aid of a stranger of a lower social/economic status; robbed, beaten and left to die. After relating the story, Jesus instructs the one who asks him to define "neighbor" as "Go, and do thou likewise."

In other words, Jesus is instructing the questioner to follow the conduct of the Good Samaritan. It is an illustrative narrative telling the listener what it means to love our neighbor as our self. Brotherly love or fellowship in the biblical sense is an extension of the natural care, affection, and love we extend to our family. Jesus takes it a step further by extending it to the greater community. His command goes beyond mere duty or law. It displays unfeigned love from a pure heart. It calls us to take action towards another. This is brotherly/sisterly love since it extends unconditionally to "neighbor" regardless of the outer circumstances of that person.

The story offers the image of what it might mean to love in the complete way that the Good Samaritan's act was a manifestation of selfless love to a stranger. This is a parable for awakening unconditional love. Altruism gives without getting. Ironically, the greatest gift is to love one another!

The command to love God intertwines with the mysterious desire to love another. We begin with a pure heart that is capable of setting aside projections and bias. A strong and resilent kind of love runs toward danger to help another and not away from the fray. This act acknowledges a profound connection with God and enables our heart to reach toward our neighbor even when it might put us in jeopardy. As an inner resource, we can tap into this energy to build powerful relationships throughout life even with people we do not particularly like or identify with.

Many people have only negative experience with religion, spirituality, cults, or with their family belief's about a higher power. These views convince them that there is no need for such a connection. Others remember believing as children only to receive condemnation, judgment, and fear-based reality. Rather than love from God, they got parental punishment. Our Source becomes a resource when we consider this sacred bond as a friendship. I like to approach God as I would a best friend. True friends accept us and delight in our presence. After time together, we feel good and look forward to a reunion. Having a relationship with God is like holding onto a tiny invisible thread that shows us the way, the truth, and the life. Jesus says, "As the Father loved Me, I also have loved you; abide in My Love." (JN 15:9 NKJV)

The secret to a loving relationship with our self is to make our home in God. This may sound simplistic to some, and illogical to others. However, abiding in the power of this unconditional love supports us in the arduous task of becoming conscious of our connection to God, whether we are aware of it or not. This connection becomes the foundation of all other forms of human love.

In meditation and prayer, we practice abiding in this inner resource by turning in prayer or meditation to the Source. We occupy a place in our inner home and feel a visceral connection to everyone since we are no longer a prodigal child. From this place of abiding, we are welcomed into the human family. This favorable reception supports all other relationships since we know our true connection and stop looking for love in all the wrong places. This power gives us complete security. Aligning with God offers us an individual action plan that facilitates human relationship. We believe, hope, love, and respond to our fellow humans when we engage this shared power. A loving energy is present in all our activities, projects, ambitions, and desires. When we abide in God, we feel complete. Outside of this love, we are lost in a maze of self-deception. The Psalmist, King David expresses his love for God in this psalm, "As the deer pants for the water brooks, so my soul pants for You, O God." (Ps 42:1 NAS)

A relationship must have a solid base and will not endure without this firm foundation. Self—relationship is the cornerstone of all subsequent relationships.

An Indwelling God

Without an indwelling in God, all other relationships suffer. The attempts to construct something enduring with others will be faulty. The foundation is unstable, the center cannot hold. A relationship must have a solid base and will not endure without this firm inner grounding. The analogy to constructing a foundation is not difficult to understand. It takes labor, teamwork, and tools to design and build strong, enduring relationships. As the saying goes, "no man or woman is an island unto him or herself."

We live in a relational world. From infancy onward, our personality develops in an interactive matrix. We are continuously interacting with other people. The way we learn to relate has an enormous influence on our relationship building style and capacities. When we have the appropriate tools for the task, we can dramatically change how we design relationships. We begin to understand the impact relationships have on our spiritual lives as well. We take into account how we can begin integrating this wisdom as we interface in the world.

The craft requires following certain principles. Relationships operate under a basic set of laws. Simply put, it is the law of attraction. We attract to ourselves what we put out. "You reap what you sow." "Where mind goes energy flows." The law of attraction makes the case for the boomerang theory. We send our energy out and it comes back to us. I am not just making this up. The law of attraction is the name given to the belief that "like attracts like" and that by focusing on positive or negative thoughts, one can bring about positive or negative results.

This belief arises from the idea that people and their thoughts are both made of dynamic energy. The notion that "like energy attracts like energy" is an attribute of the discoveries from the quantum field in physics. It is a model for attraction patterns in the realm of human interactions. For example, a person opens an envelope expecting to see a rejection letter, then according to the law of attraction; the law would "confirm" those thoughts and contain "a rejection." A person who expects an acceptance letter, under the same law would find an acceptance instead of a rejection. There are cases where positive or negative attitudes can produce corresponding results (principally the placebo).

Obstacles to making spiritual connections in our culture are pervasive. Positive relationships are hard to come by in a society of ever changing values. One could argue that a loving relationship is a thing of beauty much like a precious work of art that has been mistreated and appears to have no value. The first remedy to discovering hidden worth is to create a relationship with your self. This inner journey creates the gold of our relationships but requires alchemy. It takes courage and the willingness to go through the refiner's fire. To have loved our self through thick, thin, and survived the vicissitudes of our relationships is a triumph. Inner work is a costly process, and requires each person to undergo some deep sea change. Then we experience the truth from the inside out and recognize each relationship we create with another is precious.

Building a positive relationship involves giving our attention to the many facets of the other person. At the core, we each long for a human connection that is divine. A relationship that offers unconditional acceptance is full of meaning. We each have many kinds of relationships throughout our life, from casual to intimate, from mundane to spiritual. However, if we are constantly negative in our outlook toward our relationships, something is wrong. Sometimes we need to step back, take a breather from the pursuit of relationship, and start having a relationship with our self.

The ancient sage from Ecclesiastes challenge us to notice, "There is a time and a season for everything under the sun…a time to be born and a time to die, a time to mourn and a time to laugh" (Ecc 3:1,4 NKJV). When the going gets tough, and it does in relationship development, we observe how the Psalmist connects to God. They open with joy and optimism. "If the Lord had not been on our side they would have swallowed us alive" (Ps 124:1-3 NIV), "Those who trust in the Lord are like Mount Zion, which cannot be shaken" (Ps 125:1 NIV). "Our mouths were filled with laughter; The Lord has done great things for them" (Ps 126:1-3 NIV). This ancient wisdom teaches that we can rejoice regardless of our relationship situation. When we celebrate in the midst of set backs people want to know our secret.

A positive attitude offers clarity when we are in confusion, peace when in conflict, and calm in crisis. We stay cool and maintain a sense of humor that provides optimism even in the midst of violence. We turn to our ultimate resource and cooperate in God's plan. Our relationships then can convey strength to others. We use the power for "a cheerful heart is good medicine" (Pr 17:22 NLT). Even God's most tortured servant, Job was able to say, "He will fill you mouth with laughter, and your lips with shouts of joy." (Job 8:21 NRS). God put Job to the test, but he still expressed an affirmative attitude toward his challenging situation. Job models the enduring authority of the Spirit regardless of what we may be currently facing. We like Job can embrace this inner capacity for deep connection in the midst of trauma.

To create relationships that endure we need tools that build mental agility and emotional flexibility. A positive relationship calls for a vision of what is attainable and what is not. When we strive for what is beyond our reach, we burn out. We learn to let go of our trivial pursuit of happiness and let divine being bring us joy. Simplicity in each encounter forges an appropriate connection. Our actions and words correspond. We say what we mean and mean what we say. Walking the walk brings awareness to what works and what does not work. Only in practice and real lived experiences, can we increase our ability to communicate with others.

I encourage you to stay motivated when challenges arise. Bring understanding and forgiveness to your unresolved relationship dilemmas. A firm foundation in forgiveness is a prerequisite to heal any relationship.

CHAPTER THREE:
Forgiveness and Healthy Relationships

⚜

*"To forgive is to set a prisoner free and
discover that the prisoner was you."*

Lewis B. Smedes, Christian theologian

The ability to forgive self and other is a prerequisite for healthy relationships. Psychological research demonstrates how forgiveness promotes both mental and physical health. Their conclusions confirm the important role forgiveness plays in improving how we think about others. The research attempted to answer two different questions. First, are people who are naturally inclined to forgive mentally and physically healthier than those who are not? The research entailed measuring subjects' natural proclivity to forgive, or to display characteristics of forgiveness, and compared the feature of forgiveness with other mental or physical health indicators.

The second question asked by the study inquired into the issue of whether forgiveness interventions improve the mental and physical health of those who receive forgiveness. Researchers measured mental and physical health factors, pre- and post- forgiveness intervention, and compared the results with control groups who did not receive the intervention.

This study offers strong evidence that those inclined to give and receive forgiveness are more likely to experience better mental health in a variety of ways. Overall, the research demonstrates a reliable, evocative, and intelligible portrayal of the positive role forgiveness plays in the overall quality of relationships. People who forgive not only enjoy better mental health than those who do not, but are able to extend compassion to people who have harmed or violated their trust.

In addition, evidence from professionals in human services clearly demonstrates that clients who work with forgiveness interventions provide evidence that this strategy is therapeutic since it increases the client's ability to forgive. In the clinical situation, the therapist witnesses marked improvement in the client's subjective sense of happiness and peace. The life enhancements covered a wide range of psychological factors, most notably, an improved ability to forgive results in a decrease in depression, somatic, and anxiety disorders.

Additional studies compared the mental health of people who have a natural propensity to forgive with those who do not. The data demonstrates that trait forgiveness has the following mental health benefits: lower levels of stress, anxiety, and depression. In addition, forgiveness reduces harmful affects after trauma leading to better sleep and overall well-being. Results show a greater likelihood to experience significant growth, healing, and therapeutic gains after trauma. Noted is the relationship between forgiveness on the psychological and physiological index in cardiac patients. Forgiveness, when applied in clinical studies, also reveals a greater likelihood for these positive consequences to occur after one has undergone physical or psychological trauma.

Self-forgiveness

Once we experience forgiveness toward self, we extend compassion to others. Self-forgiveness is the next likely step in emotional healing. Until we bring forgiveness to ourselves, we are separate from our inner resource. This false belief of being separate from our Creator is at the core of relationship misery. To heal this, we must first correct the conviction that we are not worthy of love. This process necessitates self-forgiveness. Happiness is always available when we are in alignment with this deeper resource. You may feel you are unforgiveable for the things you have done. You may not want to tell the truth of your situation, you may feel that forgiveness is impossible. You do not want to hurt anyone now by revealing the problematic truth of your past.

Withholding self-love contributes to a feeling of disconnection. We feel alone and without a way to return to source. We experience being cut off from love. We do things that make sure we are constantly on the brink of a catastrophe or crisis. We bring negative drama into our interactions with others and wreck havoc. Our mayhem ends up causing us to act in the very way we feel is unforgivable.

One client described his self-loathing though identifying a negative habit. He reports he engages in abusive self-dialoguing. His pattern is to repeat as a mantra, "I am a loser, I am a pervert, I am bad, I am unforgivable, I am contaminated, they are going to find out about my past, and put me back in prison." When Bobby was able to change his self-concept, he began to practice radical self-forgiveness. This resulted in Bobby attracting a different set of friends and a new lifestyle.

The power of self-forgiveness demonstrates that we mirror to others, in our thoughts, words, and actions what we think about our self. Our inner reflection becomes a self-fulfilling prophecy. Negative self-appraisal signals to others that I am not worthy of respect. Low-self esteem projects an image to others of the way we treat our self and signals how we want them to treat us. The negative feedback loop interrupts the process of self-forgiveness. It changes when we begin to question our self-image and consciously check the off-putting ways we treat our self. We can look back on any experience in our past, where we are still carrying guilt or shame, and bring forgiveness. We discover power and support in the process of building responsible relationships based on self-love.

Take a specific incident from your past. Glance without judgment at what happened. What was your true intention under that particular circumstance? Can you bring forgiveness to yourself now? If you look, you will discover your intention is always to take care of yourself. Of course, from the outside that may not seem to be true. You almost certainly did it in the best way you knew at the time. A limited awareness of options caused you to make such a poor choice. Perhaps your behavior brought you and others adverse results.

My beloved grandmother who lived to be 103 years old would often say, "If you did the best you could at the time, there is no worry." I did not always understand what she meant, and had to discover the wisdom through my own experience. We each have a forgiveness lesson. Mine was forgiving all of my past actions, both good and bad. I began to see that they both came from the same fundamental place of self preservation. To survive that particular situation, I probably did the best I could at the time. My decision to act was an indication of my human survival instinct. Understanding that my relationship within supports me unconditionally, just as I am, is the foundation for my continued existence. Since I can now forgive myself and others, I experience the benefit of being loved unconditionally. I now have permission to love myself completely and this act unites my willingness to forgive others along with myself.

From this perspective, you too can love your self unconditionally. You can see into your mind, and become aware of the reasons why you did what you did. You see the clarity of your heart in the act of forgiving. In your growth process, you can look back and observe how, given what you know now; you could have done things differently. However, it is important to see the deeper reason you did what you did, and to apply self-forgiveness. It is time to let go of the weight of the past, to stop beating yourself up. Once you do this, the power of forgiveness will transform your energy field to a higher vibration. You will create a field of attraction and be a magnet for more love. Positive circumstances will enter into your life.

Forgiveness can bring deep transformation

I encourage you to keep an open mind and stay with this line of thought. This perspective holds that any heinous act, when looked out with forgiveness, can bring deep transformation. When someone commits an act of rape or murder, many believe that there is no room for forgiveness. However, if the person can reflect back on the incident and see the intention at the time, awareness dawns. They committed the act because they really believed it would make their condition better. The past act was committed as an attempt at self-care (love). At the time, they thought the negative act was the only option available. This is true for all of us, for all of our actions. Do not just take my word for it. Check it out for yourself and see what the power of forgiveness can do in your situation.

I am not excusing atrocious acts. Closing my eyes to anything that causes me pain, or inflicts suffering on another is agonizing. The aim is to bring awareness. The truth is that anything we have done is pardonable when we truthfully look directly into center of the maelstrom. We see that at the core of all our actions is the innate desire to love ourselves as best we can. If we have not yet learned how to forgive our self, we cannot forgive another. We hold the false belief that God has not forgiven us. This withholding of love creates the feeling that we are alone in the universe. Separation is actually an illusion. The separation only occurs in our own mind. We are under a delusion since unconscious separation from our Source is the most painful experience of incarnation.

Self-forgiveness, invites you to see yourself anew. Self-respect arises when you see yourself through the loving eyes of the one who is your Creator. Nothing can keep you from accessing God's unfathomable forgiveness. In truth, the need for forgiveness is not an issue. You have done nothing wrong. We are all learning and growing. Each person has an inner Source that is like the sun. This love light shines on all of our lives indiscriminately, and touches each situation unconditionally. We need to see ourselves, and love ourselves perfectly as our Creator sees us and loves us. In learning how to forgive your self, you must work on the areas in your past that bring up feelings of shame or guilt. As you work on those areas in your own life, you notice the subtle ways you still deny yourself love. When you continue to withhold love and do not forgive yourself, you feel separate from God or your innate source.

Many of us as children received punishment when we did something wrong. Unfortunately, parents and caregivers often project their own self-judgment onto others, especially their own children. This is very widespread. This universal pattern of projection had nothing to do with who we were. We tend to form ideas about ourselves from the way that other people respond to us. As children, we were too young to question the validity of these assumptions. Eventually we began to feel that we were "bad." This translated into feeling like a loser, misfit, or rebel.

You started to believe you were "bad" as your inner reality. In fact, this is the core wound. Now that you are aware of the negative dynamic of internalizing how others perceive you, you can identify the signs of negative projections in your daily life. Become aware of times when something happens that triggers you to feel angry, lonely, sad, or depressed. This may manifest in internal self-dialogue, i.e., "I am bad," "I always make the wrong choice," "I'm not good enough," "I am a loser." Watch the things you tell yourself about yourself.

The secret is to bring awareness, love, and self-forgiveness to all of these places inside ourselves. We need to travel to the situation of the relationship trauma, the incident where the original wounding happened. We go there in our feelings, memories, and bodily symptoms. Awareness supports the forgiveness process since it allows the negative images to arise while simultaneously adopting a common sense approach about ourselves. We bring humor to the situations that most trigger us into relapsing into our negative patterns of habitual response. You know they are not true.

We replace automatic negative thinking patterns with positive affirmations such as self-forgiveness. When we operate in this manner, we are more apt to forgive others. We bring a fresh view to our circumstances, and engage from a sense of being a unique, wonderful, and entirely loveable human being. This act alone is empowering. It cleanses the lens of our negative self-perception since we come to know that love is what we truly are. A client who had struggled with food addiction leading to obesity came to a radical awareness of her inner beauty. She could finally bring self-forgiveness to her body and started losing weight. She shared, "I looked in the mirror this morning and noticed something new. "What was that?" I asked. She shed a silent tear as she uttered, "I am lovable, just as I am."

"You have only one person to forgive in your journey and that is yourself. You are the judge. You are the jury. And you are the prisoner.

Paul Ferrini, Love without Conditions, page 142

As these judgments and negative beliefs come up, check into your mind, body, and spirit. See the truth: the validity of the experience, the just so story. Your core intention is to bring love to yourself. Apply self-understanding to the past, allow self-forgiveness to release all the things you felt judgment for and still judge yourself for now. Low vibrating feelings such as anxiety, anger, and hate arise as a direct result of not only the things that happened to you, but more important, the way you interpreted those events. You are not "bad" or wrong for having them. Feelings are the normal, healthy, understandable responses to painful events. Suppressing and judging them and yourself is not.

You do not need to fit someone else's idea of how you should be. You can be exactly as you are. You are unique as a physical, mental, emotional, and spiritual creature. Self-acceptance brings understanding to all the reprimand and distress you experienced due to negative behavior you perpetrated in the past. It does not mean you made a "mistake" or that you are "bad." Making "mistakes" increases self-awareness and makes it possible for your relationships to evolve. There are no "mistakes" from the viewpoint of your Creator. There are only learning events. That is what we are here to do. Our essential purpose is to build bridges across the great gaps cause by misunderstanding. Human mistakes transform from darkness into light. Our interactions find fulfillment within the mutuality of self, other, and Creator.

The Door to Abundance

When we open the door and receive forgiveness from ourselves, set free the capacity to receive abundance. We know that our wellbeing come from a place of shared abundance. It all comes through the same "doorway." This includes not only self-love, but also loving connections. We appreciate other people. Self-forgiveness completely changes our energy field. As we begin practicing it, we align our self with an advanced, supplementary, loving source of divine energy. The Law of Attraction operates in a powerful way. As we become more loving toward our self, we attract circumstances and people who are on the path to becoming more loving. Then the outer reflects the inner.

Forgive Yourself

We cannot give what we do not have. If we withhold love from others, it is because we are withholding it from ourselves. If we are withholding it from ourselves, it is because we have not fully forgiven ourselves. This is essential before we can truly forgive and love anyone else. Self-forgiveness completely changes our "outer" reality. We project onto our "outer" life what is in our internal reality.

Whenever I have a conflict with someone, that conflict is really within me. The other may have issues that need addressing or perhaps they have triggered conflict within me. However, the other is actually playing the role of a voice in my head. I notice that I am withholding love from someone else, I step back and become aware of why. Then I gain insight into how I withhold love from myself.

Whenever I judge someone, I am only judging the part of me that the other is mirroring back to me in symbolic form. In the book, *Love without Conditions*, Paul Ferrini expresses this idea; "You are not guilty of any sin, my brother/sister. But you believe that you are. And while you believe this, you will need forgiveness. It is the only way out of your self-imposed illusion." (p.146)

Self-love and Self-Forgiveness

What I am judging is a part of myself that was ashamed when I was a child. For instance, if you showed self-expression or authority as a child and it was threatening to your parents, chances are you got shamed for it. You now have issues about self-empowerment as an adult. When you bring love and self-forgiveness to the place in you that was shamed as a child, your relationship with other people in power changes. You will feel much less threatened by authority and less inclined to judge them. Forgiving them comes naturally because of forgiving yourself. Self-love and self-forgiveness is not just a one-time thing. We have to choose it repeatedly in our lives. We have to keep doing our part. Each time we choose love, we open a portal to our Creator. We are boundless and full of vigor. You tap into an energy field of light, love, and compassion. I discover that the force of loving-kindness is always here and available to me. In truth, we are it.

I am the only one who will always be with me. It is the same for you! God creates us but we are the creator of our life. The first relationship we build is with our self. Remember, a positive relationship emerges from inside. This begins with cultivating qualities of self-understanding and self-acceptance. What supports self-development is an awareness of the other within; our true self. We all need an aperture to peer inside the other. The deeper part of our self bridges us to God. Approaching our relationships with our self via a sacred attitude inspires us to extend loving kindness toward others. When we feel good about the relationship we have built with our self, we feel more connected to the other. We are more prone to give and receive love, more willing to help, inspire, educate, and extend good feelings toward all people.

Each one of us has an assortment of relationships. As Forrest Gump is famous for saying, "Life is a box of chocolates; you're never sure what's you'll get." When we reach out for the sweetness of relationships, we know that wise choices support this aspiration even if we cannot see what is on the inside. We all have informal contacts on a daily basis with strangers and mere acquaintances. What happens when we believe that relationships are dangerous? We feel we must be conniving and manipulative to get what we need or want from others. High expectations and undeveloped inner skills cause all the good things in relationships to go unnoticed. People engage in risky behaviors to obtain some of the promised highs and intoxication of another person. This strategy leads many to fight or flight syndrome.

We all have to engage people who we know little about. In this high-speed fast food way of life, it is difficult to resist the lure of a quick fix. There are countless online sites for people who are relationship seekers. Online social networking produces an attention-grabbing and painless venue for people of all ages to have relationships. Most of us admit that we do not actually know many people who "friend" us on social or professional online sites.

The attraction to social networks is understandable. We all desire to have positive human connections. This does not give us the warm, close, and intimate contact that we desire. Strangely, the social networks leave many high and dry. It is striking how contemporary technology has changed our means of meeting, dating, courtship, and even marriage.

How we come together and build relationships would barely be recognizable to my grandparent's generation. Yet the innermost needs remain the same even if the outer state of human interaction is on the decline. Relationships are under siege. Watch any news show. We all blush and are ashamed at the way we are with each other.

The zeal to connect can take on psychopathic proportions. We project unresolved complexes onto our relationship. Decency toward each other is imperative. What people are capable of doing to each other is worse than we can imagine. Outlandish and bizarre behaviors continue to confuse and even bewilder law enforcement and mental health professionals. Many ask the question, does this predicament preclude us from cultivating positive relationships. Can we be sure that another is to be trusted? To ask again, "what's actually happening in our relationships?" How can we courageously inquire into the nature of the predicament? Can we stop denying the break down in human relationships? I say, yes! We can practice skills that bring the relationship picture into focus. We can support our society by looking anew at how we teach our children to create enduring relationships.

CHAPTER FOUR:
Relationship Patterns

✤

Even harmful behavior patterns can bring new energy into our relationships.

No one can cure us of harmful relationship patterns. Destructive impulses arise inside and negatively influence our relationships. Have confidence that your relationships can dramatically change for the better. Even harmful behavior patterns can bring new energy into your relationships. Most problems we encounter can work out if we are willing to look at the issues with compassion. Even tragedy when worked on in a positive way can bring hope. This optimism will be a natural result of approaching our relationships from within. As we begin to bring awareness to how we are actually engaging in the present moment, our human connections dramatically change. Then it is simply a matter of finding value in each relationship and accepting it for what it truly brings. We appreciate and have gratitude for the joy of relating. We stop taking human interaction for granted and begin to honor our relationships. We notice them for what they are and become aware of the exquisite quality they bring.

Relationships are messy, complex and yet love is simple! We approach outer relationships in the same way we care for our inner self. The central point of reference is inside. We can act, as if relationships are important. Counterfeit connections are just that, phony. We need to be real to embody this awareness. To integrate a new vision of what is possible and attainable, we must employ a radical understanding of the hidden dimensions of projection and displacement. We need to look for what is unseen in our interaction, what we hide. We actively listen to the nuance, undertones, and subtext. We become aware that there are subtle communications going on between the lines. We notice body language, tone of voice and silences. We become acutely aware of how our style of communication and habits of interactions affect people's comfort or ease with us.

Observer Effects the Observed

Quantum physics asks us to look more intensely into the subtle interactions at work beneath the surface of matter. The law of "the observer affects the observed" demonstrates the relationship between what we see and how we see it. In the social sciences, the witness effect refers to how people observe and perceive their actions while doing them. Individuals were more able to change their behavior when taking into consideration the consequences while actually performing an act in the presence of a witness. People often do not behave in their usual manner when they know someone else is observing them.

An announced exam is used to see how well students can do when they study and put their minds to it ahead of time. While a pop quiz is used to see how well prepared they generally are. Observer bias is error introduced into measurement when observers overemphasize behavior they expect to find and fail to notice behavior they do not expect. This is why medical trials are normally double-blind rather than single-blind. Researchers see a behavior and interpret it according to what it means to them. It may mean something else to the person showing the behavior.

In science, the observer effect refers to changes that the act of observing has on the phenomenon under observation. For example, trying to observe an electron will change the path of the electron. In quantum mechanics the outcome of an unobserved event, exists in a state of probability. It (the outcome) is in all potential states at one time. The most famous example is the thought experiment Schrödinger's cat, in which the cat is neither alive nor dead until observed. Until that time, the cat is both alive and dead.

In psychological dynamics, the phenomenon of the observer effects the observed activates the relationship dynamics for good or ill. What becomes apparent is how we internally process events. In particular, we notice the way this affects how we communicate with others. It starts from within. "Who I am to myself, how I experience being me, and self-identity influence how I relate to you." Look at some of the basic truths at the heart of human interaction. The enduring spiritual traditions, the underlying psycho/somatic template, as we have discussed, is toward human connection. At the core of all religion is the urge to reconnect to a divine source. This is a powerful model for positive human interactions. It supports us engaging in this dynamic dance with others. We use our relationship with our source as the touchstone since it serves as the blueprint we follow throughout life.

The radical notion of psychological projection offers a portal into relationship difficulty. Since what we seek is not the individual person, but the capacity for conscious connection to self. The role of religious ritual is the growth of consciousness as relates to the power to make symbolic relational experience into something physical and concrete. Whether or not we are aware of it or not, much of behavior is symbolic. In this sense, a relationship is a ritual enactment that expresses in condensed form one's relationship to the inner world.

Psychological projection is the human propensity to project unwanted or disavowed feeling onto other people, groups, or institutions. Sigmund Freud, the father of psychoanalysis understood projection as a defense mechanism and conceptualized it as the primary form of psychological displacement. He noticed how a person unconsciously rejects his or her own unacceptable attributes. Instead, Freud surmised that his patients assign them to objects or persons in the outside world. Thus, projection involves projecting positive or negative qualities onto others, and is a common psychological process that can be normative or pathological.

Theoretically, projection reduces anxiety by allowing the expression of the unwanted unconscious impulses or desires through displacement. Placing onto another person your likes and dislikes is what makes the world go round. It also keeps us captive on a Merry-go-Round of difficulties. We project onto others or situations what we cannot tolerate inside our own mind, heart, and emotions. We actually believe what is on the outside, is not a reflection of our own projection, but is real.

Psychoanalysis provides a deeper look inside this dynamic. The client becomes aware of their own human tendency to project both positive and negative aspects of self onto others. This awareness offers us awareness so we take effective action in each moment without succumbing to the tendency to project or displace unwanted or unredeemed aspect of self. Everyone must forge a relationship with his or her inner life in one form or another. Consciously or unconsciously, our inner world will claim each one of us, and have its way, so it behooves us to form a conscious connection with this powerful "inner other." Only relationships that are free from projection can truly be a place to love. We become aware of what we are actually putting onto another and what they may be projecting onto us.

However, what is more important is to make it a point to stick to the basics and to incorporate your own unique footprint in whatever you do. This is always getting to know your connection to God better and will help you get the results from others that are worthwhile. John Stott writes, "Our greatest claim to nobility is our created capacity to know God, to be in personal relationship with Him, to love Him and to worship Him. Indeed, we are most truly human when we are on our knees before our creator."

As Stott eloquently puts it, it is only when we acknowledge the power of this relationship that we can stop struggling. We see that most of our problems result from a disconnection with God. Therefore, it is in this relationship that we find the simple solution. We stop trying to find problems with our relationships, and start to look within. When this heart space is uncontaminated with our projections, we notice most of our issues are naturally resolved. We feel the significance of each relationship, since we are one with our Source. The illusory notion of a separate subject/object dichotomy is necessary for socialization and personal development, but this separation often displaces our true function, to know God.

Interconnectivity

Interconnectivity is an idea used in numerous fields, i.e., psychology, cybernetics, biology, ecology, network theory, and non-linear dynamics. The concept states that all parts of a system interact with and rely on one another simply by the fact that they occupy the same system. We live in a complex system since we are all part of a multifaceted universal family called the human race. Sometimes it is impossible to investigate the complexity of this matrix and to realize our bond to others through just perceiving the individual parts. Many link the concept of interconnection with "the observer effect" and "the butterfly effect." In chaos theory, the butterfly effect is the sensitive dependence on initial conditions, where a small change at one place in a deterministic nonlinear system can result in large differences to a later state.

The name of the effect, coined by Edward Lorenz, derives from the theoretical example of a hurricane's formation being contingent on whether or not a distant butterfly had flapped its wings several weeks before. Although the butterfly effect may appear to be an esoteric and unlikely behavior, it exhibits very simple systems: for example, a relationship at the crest of change may roll into any of several possible directions depending on, among other things, slight differences in the initial situation of each of the participants, i.e. physical position and psychological attitude.

The butterfly effect is a common trope in fictional relationships when presenting scenarios involving time travel. The hypothesis suggests that a storyline diverges since a seemingly minor event may cause two significantly different outcomes. The key difference between interconnectivity in terms of a single, instantaneous change of action within a relationship suggests that even tiny changes may influence the outcome in the distant future. The butterfly effect states that while chain reactions and events alter by tiny shifts, interconnectivity deals with relational systems in dynamic equilibrium, such as family systems, ecosystems, economies, societies, etc. Interconnectedness is a perspective that acknowledges interdependency among people and a view that refers to the moral, rather than physical or scientific ways that humans design relationships.

CHAPTER FIVE:
Your Higher Self

⚜

We find strength of character; adopt a stance that advocates for tolerance and open–mindedness.

Higher self is a new age term used to describe the God concept in universal terms. Although the idea came out of mysticism it is associated with several spiritual belief systems. The basic premise of a higher self describes an eternal, omnipotent, conscious, and intelligent being. This is the real self. Blavatsky (1889) formally defined the higher self as "Atman the inseparable ray of the Universal and One Self. It is the God above, more than within, us."

In his book, *The Higher Self,* Dr. Deepak Chopra, M. D. discusses his perspective on the classical concepts of Higher Self. He weaves various perspectives including Vedic tradition and Hindu religion, with western medicine, quantum physics, and pop culture. Chopra recognizes the role of higher self in union with a divine source. In recent years, the Self-help/New Age industry encourages the idea of the Higher Self in contemporary culture in the healing arts. The vast interpretation of the Higher Self runs through the heart of faith. Some denominations believe that the Higher Self is a part of an individual's metaphysical identity.

Others teach that the Higher Self is essentially the human's tether to the heavens. The Higher Self ultimately arises out of a desire for divine union. Some envision it as a returning home. Views of Higher Self symbols are apparent in all religions and were present as the driving force of early human rituals in animism and shamanic practice. However, in recent years, the Christian, Hindu, and New Age perspectives highlight the concept as it informs our capacity for human relationships.

In the Christian Interpretation, the Bible teaches that all beings contain a tiny spark of the Holy Spirit. This spark illuminates the life path. It joins each person to the Higher Self, which is the direct link to God. The Holy Spirit is a central topic of the Christian church. The idea of the individual higher consciousness is part of a mystical strain. In Hinduism, the higher self is the same with the *Jiva* or individual self. With this perspective, the Hindu faith teaches that the higher self or Atman is not an attribute that one can control or possess. Rather the self is the subject who perceives the Higher Self as a portal that transports and channels Divine Energy. In *The Higher Self*, Deepak Chopra (2001) incorporates the views of the Hindi value system to support his claims pertaining to the divine force. Chopra suggests we acquire it with the awareness of the self. Hinduism teaches that through the examination of self-knowledge, or "Atman Janna," one can attain salvation by comprehending the true nature of self.

Most New Age literature defines the higher self as an extension of the individual personal self. The higher self is an improved self that is developed, and further along on the spiritual path than the ego self. The higher self denotes an aspect of the energy body that is both within and yet beyond the corporeal body. This Higher Self is an extension of the worldly self that has individuated as a human being. New Age text (1999) teaches that in exercising our relationship with the Higher Self, we gain the capacity to manifest the relationships that we truly desire since it encompasses serving the greater good. With this powerful source directing our future, there is nothing to fear. The self aligns with divine will and thus naturally creates its own wonderful reality.

A Spiritual Perspective

Centering our relationships on anything other than a deep rootedness with our Higher Self is a recipe for disaster. Designing an alliance with a relationship within is the remedy for all relationship wounds.

Interpersonal conflict can lead to growth but we must actively make readjustments with our perception. Deep change always comes by realigning with our Source. We bring an awareness of indivisible and non-dual wholeness that is within each person to our conscious awareness. This has the power, whether it is in the forefront of awareness or not, to find strength of character and adopt a stance that advocates tolerance and open-mindedness toward all people. A connection to Source is not an abstract idea, but a living activity that actives our reality, and is the most vital part of human interaction.

All matter emerges and returns to Source. We return to our Source in our lives by recognizing the aspect of our self that is eternal. Only then can we feel fulfillment in another. Once we know and experience this divine union are we at peace. We live as if there is nothing or no one that can cause us to fear. We may have moments of separation but we know we are complete, secure, and whole already. We experience this freedom as the presence of oneness, unity, and wholeness. In the moment of understanding, we allow things to be as they are, regardless of the situation we see that it is "just what it is." There is a sense of oneness that reveals the underlying wholeness even in duality and conflict. We notice that there is "nobody" there to create a catastrophe out of whatever thing is the problem of the moment. We learn that we can get along with anyone if we bring our higher self into the equation.

This sense of divine union is a level of consciousness that most know little about. The majority of us have had only fleeting experiences with a direct encounter with God or a Higher Power. If it has occurred, it is only in short-lived encounters when we are under the influence of a substance, falling in love, or going through a crisis. At these moments, we may get a tiny peek at what it means to connect with our ground of being. When we do not have access to this fundamental and essential level of reality, we exist in a world of separation, duality, and division. We have no safe harbor within, so we must find someone out there to blame for our insecurity. We are irresponsible, expect something for nothing, and so stop trying to create a positive relational life. The trouble takes on many guises, but at root, the attitude forces us to engage in a multitude of unconscious projections that jeopardize our relationships.

An unbiased perception towards others helps us challenge widespread narrow-mindedness that occurs between individuals and groups.

Defense Mechanisms

Nevertheless, there is a real need for psychological and physical defense mechanisms. Self-defense arises at this level of consciousness. My self comes into being, when the other, or the "not-self," manifest as the opposite. There is always a since of otherness in relating with another. We each have a separate body and personality that become the motivating force behind our need for self-preservation. When barriers between two people arise and conflict happens, there is the survival instinct toward polarity and division. In this state of relationship, you do not acknowledge a divine connection. This underlying sense of separation from others plays out on the historical stage in world wars, genocide, and global conflict. Ironically, the human proclivity to highlight divisions and then justify fundamentalist extremes actually ends up perpetuating violence and destruction in the name of religion using counterfeit images of God.

The psychology of intolerance widens the gap between individuals and groups and makes it appear unbridgeable. We can go beyond this useless disconnection and experience love directly in our hearts. When we are willing to look at our shadow projections, the conditions that trigger us to violence, we have a better chance of knowing when or when not to engage in defensive postures. The unassimilated parts of our personality, where we feel unlovable, we project out there and identify someone else as the culprit and cause of the problem. We see this negativity in the other rather than in our self. Naturally, misunderstanding and prejudice arise from this state of affaire. When we begin the practice of withdrawing our projections, we start to notice how we are creating the separation in the first place. Love makes healing possible because we withdraw the need for division, and see our similarity rather than our differences.

Returning to Source requires a relationship within since they go hand in hand, to create a trustworthy support system. Relationship with our Higher Power helps us solve problems, make good decisions, and gives us access to intuition and insight. We are in a state of ongoing dialogue with this interconnection. There are no problems, only opportunities to reconnect. Many troubles with other people are our own creations. We stop projecting unwanted aspects of our self. We resist making negative interpretations about our situation. Our relational predicaments often simply disappear since connecting within is the best remedy.

There is a reserve of divine energy available to help you work out any issue since the origin of your personal energy springs from within. This power is the true foundation of all your relationships. This resource is your only genuine gold and goal. It is an inner cornucopia of untapped riches. You discover a true storehouse of treasures and gather up your supply of wisdom, understanding, and insight, to give back to the world.

When I trust in my Higher Power and listen deeply with an open heart and mind, I am not afraid.

It is my experience that when I turn to God as my Source, I always find a way out of my stuck place or dilemma. When I trust in my Higher Power and listen deeply with an open heart and mind, I am not afraid. It allows a non-ego power to work through me so my relationships benefit the good of all, which is always the highest and best for me. Regrettably, in our society, we are having more and more difficulty with relationships. Approximately half of marriages end in divorce. People view relationships as being easily disposable and marriage as a throwaway. If it does not work out, I will find somebody else.

Online networks have become a substitute for developing real relationships. Now, there may be some good things about online sites, but the number of Face book friends you have or the number of tweets you make, really does not inform whether you have great relationships. In fact, a recent study of college students showed them to be spending almost 20 hours a week on social networking sites. Over 50% of the students felt that excessive time with their online friends was causing them to neglect other important areas of their lives.

Relationship Muscles

Relationships are important to any endeavor we undertake. There is no simple technique to build the relationship of your dreams. Nevertheless, there are steps we can take. Let us look at the things we take for granted and skills that we have not developed. We need to build our relationship muscles. Positive relationships can lower stress, improve overall heath, and create stability in families and communities. The magic is that this optimism spreads and brings us lasting fulfillment and happiness across the board.

First, we must go back to the basics. We must start with the diamond within, which is the precious potential for connection that lies deep within us, and compels us to reach out to others. We have friends, people we communicate with regularly at work, in our neighborhoods, at our schools or in our religious gathering places. Then we have close friends, people that we share with on a deeper level. Some are closer than others are. Most people do not have many close friends, but our close friends are essential.

Relationships can bring us great joy or deep distress. We cannot control what the other person in a relationship does, but we can control what we do. We live in a field of interconnection with all things. The mind and body are not separate units, but one integrated system. Everything we do, from how we think to what we feel, to what we eat, to how we sleep, all affect our personality. Psychological research establishes that the qualities of our relationships are even more important to our overall health and well-being than ever imagined. We are encouraged to take time and attention to design relationships that reflect our true values. Do not apply the "cheap and easy" mentality of consumerism to relationships with your Higher Self or other person, for that matter.

Have you ever noticed how long it takes to make microwave popcorn? Yes, we all know that popcorn can be made in only three minutes. What about delicious popcorn!" Well, that is what it says on the bag, but standing there waiting for it to pop seems like an eternity. We live in a microwave society. We have come to expect that everything in life will take only three minutes. However, the best things, the most important undertakings in life do not happen in a microwave. The relationship we create with our Higher Self and fellowship with others are two of the greatest activities in life. Yet we have scarcely understood how these relationships grow, and on what foundation relationships are best built.

It is disconcerting to see things like One-Minute Dating. Do we really expect to have a meaningful relationship with another person; much less, God or Source if all we can give that relationship is one minute of our time? We fill our schedules with so many "good" things, that we do not have time for true fellowship with others. Just because you have friends on social media does not mean you have fulfilling relationships. Many of us feel disconnected in the midst of such social media bombardment. There is an abundance of online acquaintances, but few authentic friendships. We know trivial thing about other people, and have stopped expecting anything more.

Our hunger grows for the deeper satisfaction of a rewarding companionship. Some people find this in a Divine Source, God in childhood that they knew directly when looking up at the stars on a dark night or seeing a rainbow after a storm. Others are certain that such a power source does not exist since they have never witnessed its presence, and consider such a stance illogical or just crazy. We receive conflicting information about relationships from many different and often incompatible perspectives. People cannot agree on what signifies a positive relationship. We surround ourselves by images of what it means to be in a positive relationship and yet have no clue about the underlying symbolic meaning of our drive to connect.

You may notice you still have a nagging feeling of loneliness or anxiety when speaking of relationships. That is no wonder. Our efficient machines and technology, which promised to give us more leisure time, have only increased our distress and worry. Our expectations supersede what is actually feasible or in fact productive. We have lost an appetite for the flavor of a true relationship. The fact that we are afraid of real human connection is because it takes time. If not cooked in less than three minutes, we do not want it. Somewhere between the microwave and the microchip, our society has lost something significant. We no longer have the patience or commitment to practice the art of building relationships.

By giving time to the relationship, one begins to discover the lost art of lingering. Allowing enough time to discuss the important things in life takes time. If we really want to get to know each other, we need to carve out time for self-reflection, meditation, prayer, and reverie. Reverie allows us to tap into childlike states of daydream, wistful, and trance like states of mind where we are in touch with divine imagination. This allows us to connect intensely with our inner life.

From this fresh perspective, you take action, express your preferences, and yet you know that your desire once obtained may not always bring you bliss. You gain access to a new insight, retrieve it up from your unconscious mind, and then use your reason and logic to discern the value in a practical sense.

Giving Attention to Relationships

The relationship is in the detail. How you attend to the specifics of your relationship is at heart, relationship work. It is what keeps it alive. It is of the essence to bring a new attitude toward all interactions and to work together. When you do so, your connection grows and deepens, rather than stagnates and become trivial. If you cannot simply be in the presence of another and allow your heart to open, it is hard to feel connected. When your body, mind, heart, and soul find balance, you are connecting viscerally within and with the other. You witness how everyone has something that causes them fear or triggers emotionally charged feelings. You work with others on the universal effort to apply authentic empathy and allow compassion to encircle your life.

Negative people have poor skills at building positive relationships. In fact, they are more inclined toward harmful, manipulative, co-dependent, and abusive relationships. It is essential that we develop an inner core of self-worth and respect for others and ourselves. Assuring the well-being of every person is at the foundation of civilization. Cultivating positive relationships is a worthy endeavor, since it is of utmost importance to both the survival and happiness of a human being.

The primary relationship challenge then becomes how to create a precious jewel from an unpolished stone. It requires that you discover, embrace, and develop your own divine gift. This bond is meaningful in numerous ways since it gives you a head start so you create safety for yourself and others. The propensity to yearn for another person that will complete you is actually a deeper calling to fashion a relationship with your divine self.

Questions for Reflection

When we meet with unrelenting conflict in our relationships, it may be time to step back, and to ask some deeper questions. Where is the upset in you now? Ask yourself the question, "Why do I do this?" What makes me happy in the relationship? When do I want to sing and dance? How do I stop long enough to hear the still small voice within? What causes me to struggle with my relationships? Now ask, what do you recall from that time? As you settle into this book, consider what direction your relationships are heading. How would you like to fashion each one into a treasure of great value?

I trust that the information provided will stimulate your interest in this profound and complex subject. My aim is to prompt you to look beyond the superficial meaning of your everyday encounters. The purpose is to develop awareness so you can bring insight to the peaks and valleys of your relationships, and forge new ways of engaging others. It is my desire to inspire you to arrive at a greater understanding of the ways you already communicate. Then I hope to engage you in new relationship practices. As we continue the journey together, I firmly believe that working on your relationships is of utmost importance since it is a direct link to your Divine Source, and central to your happiness, and fulfillment.

What draws you into your own unique inquiry? Move from the surface of your interactions and examine the depth. Be drawn to a profound way of relating with yourself. Then pass this intention onto others. Relationships put us into direct contact with the heart of the lifecycle. We are brought to the heights of ecstasy and to the depth of despair. We learn how multifaceted bonding is with others. Look beyond the superficial meaning of everyday encounters because you can cultivate fulfilling relationships beyond what you dreamed possible.

Let us look into what supports us aligning with our Higher Self. The key to aligning with your Higher Self is very simple but rarely stated.

Such awareness is not encouraged at this time. You align with your Higher Self by intimately getting to know how your body feels when you are in alignment. Then, when you know that feeling, you work toward maintaining it by controlling the direction of your thoughts. All positive or negative bodily feelings are rooted in your thoughts. These are either in alignment with your Higher Self or not. When your body is at ease and balanced, your thoughts are too. In this state of equilibrium, you know how it feels to be in alliance with your Higher Self. When your body feels "unsteady" in any way, your thoughts are out of kilter. It is time to discover the key alignment in order to move forward in your life.

You have felt levels of joy, harmony, happiness, passion, peace, and exuberance in your life. The difficulty is that people rarely think in terms of alignment when things are going their way. They are too busy enjoying life, which is, after all, the purpose of living. Usually people think about of alignment when they need it most or when it seems out of reach.

Alignment with the Higher Self feels different for each individual. However, the result is the same. You know you are in alignment when your mind is clear, your heart feels open, and your body feels as good as it gets. Sometimes you may not feel your body at all. It may feel light as air or you may feel like a gently floating balloon. There may be a sense of well-being and connectedness in your body. You may have an intuition or a hunch leading to a spark of creativity. On the other hand, you may feel sudden passion or happiness. You may have the physical sensation of a gentle tingle up your spine or butterflies in your stomach. No feeling is wrong. The bottom line is that you are on top of the world when you are in alignment with your Higher Self. Your body mirrors this feeling. Everything feels in flow, on course, and you have a sense of purpose.

Conditioning along cultural, familial, and systemic lines is often difficult to assess on a mental level. Your best, truest gift is how your body feels at any given time. Your body is the most sensitive instrument at your disposal for determining whether you are in alignment with your higher Self. It will serve you in amazing ways when you get to know it. Therefore, it is important in your relationships to identify comforts and discomforts. To learn to align, you first identify the ease or distress level in the most sensitive part(s) of your body. Many people discern best in their stomach and other parts of the digestive tract. Others feel a heaviness, constriction, or pain in their heart when out of alignment. Still others experience tenseness in bodily areas like their shoulders or back. Some get headaches, chills, or other bodily symptoms such as trembling. What it ultimately comes down to is that your greatest bodily challenges are actually your greatest spiritual teachers.

Once you sense discomfort in your body, you align with your Higher Self by practicing some form of relaxation or meditation. You need to take some quiet time to learn what your higher Self is trying to teach you through your body. During times of discomfort, lay back, relax, and surrender deeply. Ask your Higher Self what your body is trying to teach you and sense the answer. You may see, feel, hear, taste, or smell the answer. Your intuition may come forth boldly and you will suddenly just know what to do. The answer may come right away or it may come later when you least expect it. It is imperative that you have faith and believe that questions are answered when you are ready. No question put forth with honesty and benevolent intent is ignored.

Who is My Higher Self?

The Higher Self is not an entity separate from you. It is very much a part of you. When people speak about the higher self, they are referring to the intelligence within. It is not the intelligence like saying, "she is really smart and intelligent" but is a knowing or awakened aspect that connects to spirit and embodies your deepest truths. When you ask for help or guidance from your Higher Self, you are taking a giant Self-Help step. The Higher Self is your connection to your unconscious mind, as the essential aspect of your psyche, which is impervious to judgments or prejudices. It does not view life through murky-colored filters, nor is it a reflection of narcissistic self-whims, wishes, or ego prospects. The Higher Self can assist you by clearing a pathway to your true self since it is YOU, the best part of you!

Let us look into what supports us aligning with our Higher Self in a way that is powerful and leads to positive relationships. Sharing knowledge about how you connect within is a powerful tool. You have inner guides and spirits all along the way to befriend you since the Higher

Self holds the treasure trove of your personal history. It contains a tiny seed of light that will help you solve any predicament, find whatever you seek, and allow you to be a radiant light to others on your path.

Here are four straightforward practices you can do on a daily basis to connect with your Higher Self. You will be amazed when your practice even one on a regular basis how much more alive you feel.

1. Meditation Practice
Meditation is the basic practice for aligning with your Higher Self. Humans have practiced meditation for eons. Meditation increases life span, improves the immune system, develops mental clarity and calms the nervous system. This is a very important daily habit. Even 3 minutes of meditation can be beneficial. Try to meditate twice a day for about 15-30mins. I usually just meditate until I feel cleared and full of light, which normally takes me 20minutes.

2. Healthy Lifestyle
Having a healthy body is vital to connecting with Higher Self. It is important if you want to establish a good mind/body/spirit connection. Your spirit is already pure but your body can become contaminated and impure. Everyday try to make healthy choices when choosing what to eat. Instead of buying a soda, pour a glass of water! Also, do not smoke cigarettes. Smoking is more harmful for overall functioning that we realize. Cigarettes block the flow of vital energy, confuse, and muddle the brain with toxic chemicals. Upon quitting smoking, a friend shared that she literally became more intuitive. Obviously, do not do drugs or drink alcohol excessively. Included in this category is exercise. I do not suggest only going to a gym, but use your entire body. Play at least once a day for 30 minutes or more. It could be running outside with your dogs, playing soccer with your kids. I usually go swimming, I just love being in water.

3. Being Present
This is easier said than done. If you live in your head most of the time, it can be hard to bring yourself back into the present moment. If you

are one of those people, meditation will help. A good way to bring yourself into the moment is to focus on your breath. If you are replaying an episode in your mind that happened yesterday, you aren't living in the moment. You must let go of your worries and anything that is not positively influencing your present state of being. Pay attention to everything. Higher dimensional beings use the subtle energies to communicate.

4. Gratitude

Without the real you, there would be no moments of joy and laughter. Make a point at least once a day to list things you are grateful. In addition, sense how good it feels to be appreciative. Sometimes you may speak to your guides and you may not hear a reply. However, later you realize that they responded perfectly to what you had asked in a way than you were not expecting.

Sharing Your True Self

People who are "genuine" are much more likely to connect with others who are similar to them.

Most of us take note when we meet people who are unabashedly genuine, sharing their "true selves" with others. They seem truly happy and at peace with themselves. In addition, they seem to make friends effortlessly. A number of studies show that they are, in fact, happier than the rest of us. They also have healthier and supportive relationships. This makes intuitive sense. People who are "genuine" are more likely to connect with others who are like them. The reason for this is that their relationships reveal a deeper connection. They can create intimate connections through sharing and self-revelation. They feel good when things go well and acknowledge problems when they arise (hopefully working them through). In contrast, those who employ denial tend to disallow problems.

As an example, a man comes home frustrated by a negative review from his boss. He is worn-out after a long day at work. Without a word, he eats the dinner his wife prepared; and then he goes to bed without even a thank you. His wife is sympathetic and does the dishes. However, this is part of a larger blueprint of the relationship. The pattern consists of him taking her for granted and her putting up with it. If she is a real people-pleaser, she will disallow her building anger. The rage can spiral into a resentment that contaminates her happiness and taints their marriage. If she were more sincere with her "true self," she would also be more honest with her genuine feelings. She would recognize that she feels neglected. She may decide not to pay attention to this on occasion, but she will eventually share her hurt or frustration. While voicing her concerns might cause strain, she and her husband will have the chance to deal with the trouble and discover a resolution.

The inability to let go of the past hurt can make a new relationship virtually impossible.

The problem with sharing honestly is that you risk a negative response. No one likes criticism. As painful, as it is to experience rejection, it is devastating to experience rejection in a long-established relationship. It is much more complicated if a spouse, someone who has pledged to stand by you, abandons you. The same injury from negative responses happens in friendships, and within the family. It is not at all shocking that people stay away from that agonizing state of affairs by playing it secure and keeping up the walls to intimacy. The person with this kind of fear is not willing to take the risk to love. Unfortunately, they may wake up one day to find that they are forlorn strangers.

It is imperative to keep in mind that being authentic does not mean having to expose every thought, feeling, and vulnerability. You can be your own best judge of boundaries. People who are aware of how much to share (based on a given relationship and particular situation) can protect them selves by establishing healthy boundaries. This supports the needs of those involved and offers space. They can each be sensitive to the other person, and still be straightforward about who they are. Like so much in life, it is a dynamic dance of finding equilibrium. If you can find that balance, you can take pleasure in the many benefits of being authentic.

Awareness

Your divine nature shows you the invisible thread that leads you to where you need to be.

The art is in the detail. Bring awareness to yourself as the essence of who you truly are. To be authentic with self and other one must connect to the real self. Upbringing and conditioning of the nuclear family and society (although necessary and valuable if handled correctly) often obscures our connection to our authentic nature. Our Higher Power is like a power station. However, we have no way to access the power. When we try to speak about our Higher Self, it tends to call up a variety of images of some untouchable figure. Many consider the Higher Power to be a mystical being in some remote time zone and in a distant land. There is some amount of truth to that image.

The Higher Self is a lot more physical and more importantly, local than most people imagine. It is true that there is an aspect of us that does exist beyond our physicality. This is the unseen part that helps guide us through life. Your divine nature shows you the invisible thread that leads you to where you need to be. The Higher Self is you. The aspect that cannot help but manifest as your true nature. Once your connection to your source is solid, your individual relationships will support you throughout life. You will experience an energy that acts as an archetypal force in the guise of guide, counselor, best friend, parent, etc.

Most people do not realize that there is also a very physical component to this higher part of us. Our physical self, which includes our life situation, relationships, and so on, is the outward reflection of what is going on at a higher level. Your Higher Self will communicate with you in a variety of ways: through intuition, hunches, sudden unexpected life changes; or what I call life necessities. We may or may not choose to heed the communication. You may not listen or act on those communications.

Nevertheless, our physical self is the "receiver" of these messages. Just like a cell phone, we can receive a call or text but if we do not respond, there is very little communication. If one chooses to receive and follow that guidance, life becomes very surprising. The divine potential that is within each person is encouraged to grow. The degree to which one chooses to accept and follow the divine guidance varies. The life lessons and information gleaned through intuition and insight from the Higher Self certainly informs the quality of your relationships. Since our Divine or Higher Self is an infinite being, our own potential is infinite when we make this conscious connection.

Every individual has a blueprint, a kind of "divine template" that holds a tremendous amount of information.

Besides being someone who acts as a guide for us, what is this Higher Self? What is the function and what does that have to do with our relationships. What role does it play in our everyday experience? In order to understand the true purpose, it is imperative to know one essential concept. Every individual has a blueprint, a kind of "divine template" that holds a tremendous amount of information. This blueprint exists in every single atom of our being. The amount of information that this blueprint carries is phenomenal, covering every aspect of who we are, what we are doing here, every lifetime we have ever experienced, as well as all "potentialities" of who we can be.

The central purpose of our Higher Self is to help us gain access to the information that resides within this blueprint. In essence, you are the personification and embodiment of that divine plan. The call to return to your divine self is the most sacred right of all people. You find the answer to any question you could ever have. The divine self answers every problem, overcomes all obstacles. This Self is our essence, our inner voice, spirit guide, best friend, mother, father, and inner healer. Source self is not only part of us; this is us at the core of our being. We only need to become aware and ask for assistance. Source self is patient and always waiting for our call. It is always on the other end as a presence and secret power within.

The knowledge that we receive is not coming from out of nowhere! It comes directly from the part of us that is Spirit.

We can all learn to have a very real and physical communication with our Higher Self. The process is not as difficult as one would think. It just takes a little bit of practice so we can live out this potential. We can learn to follow divine guidance so that we can live to our fullest potential. We have all experienced hunches, or gut feelings that seemingly come from out of the blue. This premonition tells us something that does not always appear to be logical. We have all experienced moments when we choose to follow that guidance, even if it did not make sense. There was a reason why we were guided in that direction. This is our Higher Self talking. The knowledge that we receive comes directly from the part of ourselves that is Spirit. If we could learn to tap into that knowing part, we would be able to bypass many difficult lessons. The flow of our life would be much freer, on target, and yet fluid.

After graduating from Yale divinity school and working in hospital chaplaincy, I encountered spiritual direction as a tool for connecting to deeper inspiration. I worked with others to help them tap into a deeper relationship with a Higher Self. Spiritual direction for many seekers manifests as a struggle with sickness, the need for healing, and preparation for death. In spiritual direction, the person seeks a spiritual path by sharing stories of his or her encounters with the divine. During the meetings, the spiritual director encourages the seeker to identify, examine, and explore how he or she is experiencing spiritual struggles. Creating the life that you have always imagined is not always certain, but that is the point of connecting to your Higher Self.

You open up to your doubts and fears as well as embracing your underlying hopes dreams, and prospects. As a spiritual director, I move the discussion toward what you need to look at in terms of ongoing spiritual concerns. The director listens, reflects, and asks questions to assist the seeker in a process of self-reflection and spiritual growth. Spiritual direction develops a profound relationship with the sacred aspect of being human. It is not psychotherapy, counseling, or career planning but allows the support of a professional trained as a guide and companion.

Setting Aside Sacred Time

Most of us are so busy during the day that we have a difficult time hearing that quiet, voice of higher guidance. Whether we know it or not, our higher self is speaking to us always and at all times. We just cannot hear the voice of our higher guidance because of the noise of cell phones, teleconferences, and gossip. We need to set aside some sacred time to connect directly and consciously to our source. Daily rituals are perfect for that.

Importance of Consistency

If you already have a daily ritual, you are one-step ahead. Make sure to do that ritual with as much consistency as possible. In spiritual circles, people have discovered that the consistency of doing a ritual at the same time every day increases the level and quality of the connection with our higher power. If you do not have a ritual, you can try meditation, or you can try this simple walking ritual.

Walking Meditation Ritual

Here is the way I practice a daily walking meditation ritual.

1. I decide what amount of time or what distance I want to walk each day (you can adjust this to suit your needs). I walk thirty minutes back and forth to work 5 days a week. I live in urban Boston and walk through the city and Public Gardens, Boston Commons and over Beacon Hill. The walk provides a variety of pleasant scenery that enhances the benefit of the walking ritual.

2. The first half of the walk, I get to talk. I talk to my inner wisdom. I speak from the heart and talk about what is on my mind. I inquire into what is going on in my life or what I am in conflict with or what I want.

I have an inner self-dialogue about anything that is important to me or that I need help with or just want to celebrate.

3. The second half of the walk, I get to listen. I take in everything my guides or the Universe is trying to express to me. I feel my feelings, feel the sensations in my body, hear the sounds around me, smell the smells, and take in the sights. I become an instrument of listening and absorbing. I take this walk daily at about the same time every day, (from 6:30-7:00AM) and return trip (3:00-3:30PM).

I have established a consistent connection with my deeper self and higher power. In other words, it is a scheduled appointment between God and my self. It is a time when I can truly connect, listen and feel heard. My life has already increased in richness, depth, and understanding. Enjoy connecting to the dance of life and feel the renewal of the mind, body, and spirit when you engage with this simple yet profound practice.

Example of taking action:

I will share with you a personal experience about taking action. A few years ago, I was looking for a new job after having created a successful guesthouse business. I had been self-employed as a small business entrepreneur and holistic life coach. I did not take the normal route of looking in employment guides, asking friends, or applying to on-line job sites. I had a longing to connect with something deeper. I began to take action by tuning into my Higher Self for guidance toward a more rewarding job. In my practice, I found one of the simplest ways to connect is by creating a daily ritual. Whether you meditate, do yoga, read inspirational books, or just take a walk, doing a daily ritual creates a doorway through which a higher power can enter your life.

I spent a lot of time and energy reworking my resume, making phone calls to friends and colleagues. I let go and let God in. It all flows. My prospective interview all came together. I got the job on the spot. I had made a conscious choice to find guidance from my Higher Self, and it manifested in a career in the field of mental health.

It did not just happen. It took inner preparation. I got an intuitive hit to send out my resume to a particular human resource company and then followed up on that. I applied to the first job. Ironically, within a few hours, I had an interview, and the next day I had a perfect job. The job presented me with an enormous challenge. The situation manifested at just the opportune moment and offered me a place to share my psychology experience and training as a doctor of clinical psychology. I knew from that moment, "this was the job for me." I took possession of the residential counselor position and joined a clinical treatment team.

CHAPTER SIX:
Following Divine Guidance

⚜

You discover that this is it; the miracle and the glorious being that we embody. This is the goal of every soul incarnate and nothing less.

I was working with a same sex couple who were symbolizing their relationship by deciding to buy a house together. The house hunting began to hit a wall. They came for life coaching to help with this obstacle in their relationship. Ann opened the session by saying "When we first were looking for a new home, we just did the typical things that people do when looking for a place to live, and it did not work." Betsy joined in, "We spent weeks of looking and were frustrated." I asked what happened. Ann added, "As soon as we consciously decided to follow divine guidance, we found a place in a few hours. To top it off, we not only found our new home quickly, but it was a very enjoyable experience in the process."

In the previous session, we discussed how we accomplish more in our daily life when we dialogue with our divine self. Ann shared, "I trust that it will guide us to where we need to be." The session revealed that there are amazing benefits from developing a conscious communication with our Higher Self. The relationship issues that were upsetting the relationship between Ann and Betsy began to dissipate. They brought understanding to each other's needs and were able to reach out to a higher self to guide the housing decision. Betsy added, "It takes attentiveness to use my inner wisdom. I discover that this life is it, and I want to share it with Ann. I find gratitude for the miracle we embody." Ann chimed in, "This is what I desire, to feel at home with Betsy, both of us whole in body and spirit."

Betsy had been dragging her feet and fearful about moving forward. Ann said, "But once Betsy began tapping into her deeper source, she knew we could accomplish this move together." When we can begin to live a life of fullness, as spiritual beings, we live into our fullest and grandest expressions. Betsy was able to share a new vision with Ann. "I now believe we can develop our true gifts and find fulfillment beyond our wildest dreams."

The way this couple began to achieve their dream was to get to know and accept each other from the view of a Higher Self. This takes time, staying power, and kindness. It is not getting something for nothing. We must make the choice, do the work, and heal the parts of ourselves that tell us to be limited and small. Ann echoed how she experiences this new perspective, "Trusting my source is not always an easy process for me, but it is the most rewarding one that I can have, and it is the reason I am here." Betsy had the last word, "this is how I now bring divine will into the equation since it provides more clarity and gives profound meaning to what once seemed a basic decision making process.

Mirror, Mirror on the Wall

Have you looked in the mirror lately? I mean, truly looked in the mirror. What did you see? Did the image reflected back to you, shock or surprise you? Did it look like you? Did it meet the image you hold of yourself in your mind? If it did not match, what were the differences? What was the image telling you? What do you think the image is that you are projecting out to the world? Does it match your inner view? How has it changed from a year ago, or from 5 years or even 10 years? Think about the image you have of yourself. Has it evolved over the years as you have? Do you still see yourself in your 20's even though you are in your 50's?

So often, we lock an image in our mind of who we think we are, never changing it or enhancing it as we adjust to the world. We upgrade our technology, cell phones, computers, and even our relationships.

However, we forget to upgrade our inner view of ourselves. Is your self-image outdated? Think about how much you have changed and ask yourself if your image is outdated? Is your inner image stuck in the 70's, while your outer self approaches the world in the latest fashions?

Internal imaging is not only about your body image, it is about your entire being. Body image is a powerful subject in the media. Many celebrities are coming forward to speak about their struggles with substance abuse, sex addiction, and self-image. While the pressure they are under comes so much from their high visibility and the demands of the industry. It is also self-imposed. Insecurity about their appearance exists deep within their being. As the great teacher, Jesus reminds us, our house or self-identity if built on sand will not stand against the vicissitudes of time.

Think about your inner foundation. Is it stable or rickety? If you do not feel stable and sure of yourself, what steps can you take? First, identify that the image is just that- an image. The image is not a real thing, but just a picture or idea you filed away in your memory. That snapshot has been subjected to years of media, family, and societal influences. The snapshot is no longer a clear or accurate picture of your reality. Subjected to many layers of distortion our self-image resembles a digitally enhanced, high-tech caricature. However, this image is just a picture. It is no longer the truth. After many years of distortion, it requires clarity. Sorting through the layers takes time and effort. It takes patience and commitment, along with a good deal of compassion, and self-nurturing.

As you peel away the layers, it is important to clarify the truth. Ask yourself if the image you are seeing is the truth of your being. Listen to your intuition. Feel the answer deep within your belly. Ask yourself; is the truth I have attached to that image true? Is it your belief or society's? Is it your mother's voice you hear, or maybe another's? Then ask what motivates that particular image. Is it motivated to please mother? Is it motivated to please father's image of you? Could it be motivated by attracting attention, or by not wanting to attract attention? What is the deepest motivator?

The impetus to connect with another often arises as a way to avoid feelings of loneliness. Lonesomeness and feeling alienated motivates some people to reach out and want to connect. In others, it only causes them to retreat deeper inside themselves. Do not let your relationships become motivated by the need to meet some fictional inner standard? Once you have identified your motivators, you can address the core issues. You can face the emotion that you connected to the belief and release it. Then replace the belief with a new truth.

Seek your inner path and find the light of your own truth, then radiate that light out for the world to see.

This technique has helped me to raise self-esteem by using mirroring work. This exercise is a summary from Dale Carnegie's hugely influential book, *How to Win Friends and Influence People.*

Dale Carnegie suggests that you look at yourself in the mirror. Then he coaches you to practice various styles of smiling in front of a mirror and decide which smile makes you look great. Practice smiling like that in front of mirror. Every time you smile in front of the mirror look at your eyes and tell yourself that you look good.

Select powerful messages to use as a self-esteem affirmation like "I feel good about myself." When you look at yourself in the mirror look at your eyes, smile, and say your powerful messages. During your day, every time you see a mirror, smile and say a powerful message to affirm yourself.

I find this exercise simple but effective. I have used this mirror activity for the past few years and treat it as a game, and find it very entertaining. I challenge myself to say my powerful messages every time I see a mirror. I was very surprised to experience how an ordinary mirror could change my life like a magic mirror.

I create my own reality as I define my own truths. I build my life and mold my identity as I create my own images. My self-image is a representation as is your self-image. It is up to each person. You are the creator of your world. To regain our power sometimes requires additional support from friends, family, or counseling. The best reflection can come from another, who can help to assist us in sorting out the facts from the fiction.

I am the only one who knows the truth for me. Others can try to define it for me. You can look to others who will help you ask questions and uncover your truth. We know that it is up to each person. When we seek empowerment from within, we are less likely to need other sources to help us feel that we fit in and belong. The inner path supports us finding the light of our own truth. Then we radiate that light out for the world to see. You are a unique being with your own inner beauty and shining light. If you recognize it, own it and value it. Let that be the new image you show to the world. Many people today are running blindly, haphazardly seeking their elusive higher Self. They feel so disconnected from life that they change directions repeatedly without thought.

When you are fearful and anxious about life without knowing why there is no peace. This is a root cause of the current pandemic of stress-related disorders. Challenge yourself to practice a method to help you align with your higher Self through the wisdom of your body. Recognize that you have a connection to a higher power and can turn to this resource when you need it. Once you align in this way, you are forever empowered. Your purpose becomes clear, you are on track, and your life dances and flows with grace and ease.

Very few people know what it feels like to align with the Higher Self, since embodying a complete life is rare. This means that you respect others needs, and wants since you desire the best for them. "Doing unto others as you would have them do unto you" is a way we can use our higher self to reach out to those in need. When we extend compassion to another person, we demonstrate that they are worthy and that their lives matter. We practice true love. The fact that we all share the same spiritual mystery should become a source of consolation. Do not be conditioned to believe that suffering and adversity are normal and necessary in relationship building. This is not the truth. Conditioning teaches us to turn inconsequential events into fierce dramas. Believing that hardship and drama are necessary only makes it so.

I try to experience the encounter with my Higher Self with innocence. I trust that my Higher Self wants me to enjoy life, but this power also understands the nuances of my hopes and fears. The Infinite knows all my material needs, personality preferences, and behavioral patterns. My Source is intimately aware of the lessons I have come here to learn, and gently pushes me toward my true-life purpose. The Higher Self holds all your secrets and strengths too. It faithfully waits for you to claim this power, and God is in no hurry. This power source is aware of your eternal and multidimensional nature. Tapping into this resource is the rudder that steadies your vessel and carries you with inner authority throughout life.

Spirituality and stress relief: Make the connection

When we develop a relationship and know how our personality influences the other, we have better access to the stress relief that having a connection to a higher Power offers.Taking the path less traveled by exploring your spirituality can lead to a clearer life purpose. Some stress relief tools are very tangible: exercising more, eating healthy foods and talking with friends. A less tangible but no less useful way to find stress relief is through spirituality. What is spirituality really? For many this term is rather vague.

Spirituality has many definitions, but essentially, helps to give life meaning and fulfillment. Spiritual connection is not only relying on a specific belief system or even religious devotion. Spiritual lives emerge from a deep connection that arises from within and extends out to others. The development of a personal value system and the search for meaning in life is spirituality.

For many, spirituality takes the form of religious observance, prayer, meditation or a belief in a higher power. For others, in nature, music, art or a secular community, spirituality comes to life. Spirituality is different for everyone. One important attribute of spirituality is that it helps with stress relief. When we are in the grip of a psychological complex or under stress, we are not at our best.

Spirituality has many benefits including stress relief and overall mental health: It can help you

It supports feeling a sense of purpose. Cultivating your spirituality may help uncover what is most meaningful in your life. By clarifying what is most important, you can focus less on the unimportant things and eliminate stress. When you connect to the world, you feel you have a purpose in the world. This can lead to a valuable inner peace during difficult times. By using spirituality as a release control, you feel part of a greater whole. You realize that you are not responsible for everything that happens in life. You can share the burden of tough times as well as the joys of life's blessings with those around you.

Many find that by expanding support networks in a church, mosque or synagogue also strengthens other relationships. The relationships in your family can grow by taking time to be together, this sharing of spiritual expression can help build relationships. If you desire to lead a healthier life then consider how people who find spirituality important also appear to be better able to cope with stress. The essence of life appears as you discover your spirituality.

Uncovering your spirituality may take time and willingness to do some self-discovery. Here are some questions to ask.

What are your important relationships?
What do you most value in your life?
What people give you a sense of community?
What inspires you and gives you hope?
What brings you joy?
What are your proudest achievements?

Really, try to answer the questions above. The information you glean from the inquiry helps identify who the most important people and experiences are in your life. With this focus in mind, you draw on the right relationships and activities. You distinguish what is already working, and what needs improvement. Define your own spirituality in a way that reflects the person you desire to be along with who you are already.

Spirituality Fosters Positive Relationships

Spirituality also involves getting in touch with your inner self. A key component is self-reflection. Try some daily rituals that support a sense of inner wellness.

I engage in a variety of powerful practices such as centering prayer, insight meditation, and progressive relaxation techniques. These each help foster spiritual awareness. I relax my body, focus my thoughts, and enter a state of peace. The practice of centering prayer is part of any spiritual path. Many seekers pray and meditate in some way daily, such as on a sacred object, mantra, the rosary, or a prayer book. Some have a practice that includes channeling God's word, dancing to the psalms, or singing from the Scripture. Others have a very personal, idiosyncratic style through engaging silent prayer, ritual, and private devotion.

The practice of centering prayer employs the use of a "sacred word," Thomas Keating emphasizes that Centering Prayer is not an exercise in concentrating, or focusing one's attention on something (such as a mantra), but rather is concerned with the intention of connecting to God. The participant's single pointed focus is to establish and maintain the aim of connecting to God's presence and energy during the time of prayer.

Centering Prayer is more akin to the ancient practice in which the participant seeks the presence of God directly (aided by a sacred work) and rejects intrusive or interfering thoughts, and flights of imagination. Centering prayer is the vision of the divine light that emerges from direct communion with God leading to divine union, but this a rare experience understood as a gift of God, and must not be sought or fabricated.

Basil Pennington, one of the best-known proponents of the centering prayer technique, has delineated the guidelines for centering prayer.
- Sit comfortably with your eyes closed, relax, and quiet yourself.
- Be in the spirit of love and open to faith in God.

- Choose a sacred word that best supports your sincere intention to be in God's presence.
- Open to divine action within you (i.e. "Jesus", "Lord," "God," "Savior," "Abba," "Divine," "Shalom," "Spirit," "Love," etc.).
- Let the word be gently present as the symbol of your sincere intention to be in God's presence and open to divine action within you.
- Whenever you become aware of anything such as thoughts, feelings, perceptions, images, associations, simply return to your sacred word.
- Re-anchor yourself in prayer.

Ideally, the prayer will reach the point where the person is not engaged in their personal agenda or thoughts. Then centering prayer transports the devotional practice and one goes deeper than the habitual stream of consciousness. The goal is to bring the practitioner into a state of inner alignment.

Contemplative prayer arises in the 4th century writings of the monk St. John Cassian. He wrote of a spiritual practice transmitted from the Desert Fathers, the practice emerged again in the book *The Cloud of Unknowing*) from an anonymous work of Christian mysticism written in Middle English in the latter half of the 14th century.

The underlying message of this work proposes that the only way to "know" God completely is to abandon all preconceived notions and beliefs or "knowledge" about God. This is a courageous act where you surrender your mind and ego to the realm of "unknowingness." At this point, you begin to glimpse the true nature of God.

During phases of inner work on centering prayer, I keep a daily journal to help express my feelings and record my progress. I seek out a trusted adviser or friend who can help me discover what is important to me in this part of my spiritual life. Other people who have a centering prayer practice often have insights that I have not yet discovered. I focus on a centering word, such as God, Christ, Lord, love, forgiveness hope, or peace and later read inspirational stories and essays to help me evaluate different perspectives that arise from my meditation. I look at what works best for my value system. I talk to others whose spiritual lives I admire and want to emulate. I ask questions to learn how they found their way to a fulfilling spiritual life, one based on freedom from attachment and fear.

Nurturing your relationships

I nurture spirituality by prayer but also through my relationships with others. It is essential for me to foster relationships with people who share common values. Through a spiritual awareness, I deepen my sense of belonging to the human community. I see the good in people and in me. I accept others as they are, and so can nurture the relationship without judgment, and with deeper understanding.

A spiritual life is an ongoing process of give and take. I stay close to my inner spirit and respect those around me that walk this path. I also try to inspire those who are lost and desire to get back on the path. My concept of spirituality changes with age, but it always forms the basis of my holistic approach and helps me cope with stressors large and small, so I can deeply affirm my life purpose.

CHAPTER SEVEN:
Personal Development and Relationships

❧

You are here to express and share your creative gifts,
to give and receive love, and to be happy.

How do you grow as a conscious human being? This includes discovering and accepting my life purpose. When I am inspired, I naturally feel more motivated, energized, and passionate about the whole picture and everyone in it. Personal development promotes my capacity and desire to make a genuine contribution to humankind. I can finally experience the kind of life I have always dreamed was possible, the life I knew I wanted to live. I can feel the life force surging through my interactions. I discover this dynamic energy, call it love, wants to live in and through me.

To be a channel for divine energy requires a self-identity that is functional and intact. A person's self-image is a mental picture that is relatively resistant to change. Self-image displays particulars that are available to objective examination by others (height, weight, hair color, gender, I.Q. EQ score, etc.), and aspects the person has learned from personal experiences. A simple definition of a person's self-image is their answer to the question "What do you believe people think about you?"

Many individuals have a self-image which is markedly elevated. Self-worth becomes inflation by chronic indulgences in activities, convictions, and needs being special. These entitlements and needs demonstrate an exaggerated sense of self worth and feeling superior to others. Such feelings can lead to self-importance and self-indulgence, contributing to a narcissistic personality disorder. The person believes that they deserve extraordinary privileges, attention, and special treatment.

Other individuals have a self-image that reflects exceptional deflation, leading to self-pity, low self-esteem, and self-defacing actions. In terms of how self-image influences our relationships, we can consider self-image to fall under three types. Self-image results from:

1. How the individual sees himself or herself,
2. How others see the individual,
3. How the individual perceives others see him or her.
We all share these three types, and one style may not fully represent the person's overall self-identity.

Self-schema is the more technical term for self-image used by social and cognitive psychologists. Like any schema, the self-schemas is a way the brain stores information, retrieves the data, and influence the way we process information, construct thoughts, and accumulate memory. For example, research indicates that information that refers to the self is preferentially encoded and recalled in memory tests.

This phenomenon is known as "Self-referential encoding" (1996). The term self-schema refers to the belief in one's ongoing sense of self; the way we hold onto certainty and conviction of who we are. For example, the ideas and scheme people have about themselves. These beliefs guide, analyze, and organize information processing, especially when the information is significant to the self. Self-schemas are important to a person's overall self-concept.

Early in life, our parent's shape the idea of self from what they know. We begin to take on a very basic self-schema, which is mostly restricted to a "good child" or "bad child" schema (2008). We see ourselves in explicitly positive or negative terms. It is in childhood that we begin to explain our actions. Our capacity to reason creates the more intricate concept of the self. For example, a child will begin to believe that the self is a starting place of his or her actions. Then decide what impulse to offer as reason for acting in a certain way as justification for the behavior.

Self Identity as Portal into "the Other"

We are here to express and share our creative gifts, to give and receive love, and to be happy.

Our self-identity is the lens through which we view the world. It is a key portal into how we develop our views about other people and how they come to see us. We are not here to struggle and suffer. We are here to express and share our creative gifts, to give and receive love, and to be happy. As we make conscious decisions in our personal development, we gather resources that provide confidence that we can follow through on them.

What does this mean for you? This means having the maturity to take full responsibility for your health, your career, your finances, your relationships, your emotions, your habits, and your spiritual beliefs. It requires taking a deep look at yourself, consciously deciding what kind of person you truly are on the inside, and then getting your external reality to be congruent with your inner being. The goal is to help you achieve outstanding effectiveness while maintaining internal balance. Where your thoughts, feelings, actions, and skills are all working together to create the life you truly desire.

Personal development is hard work. It takes persistence, patience, and practice. If you are only here looking for shallow answers or quick fixes, then you are not interested in real, lasting change. That is not the right place to build relationships. If you are serious about personal growth and willing to commit to it, then this book is for you. You learn to build relationships from the inside out so to live more consciously with others. You summon the courage to face the unredeemed parts of your life. You solve the deeper problems you have not yet been able to face. You hit rock bottom to find the underlying cause of it all.

You must learn practical skills to make important changes in your life possible. You stop shirking your responsibilities and resist wanting to go over a million angles and approaches to the same problem. This is a way of not moving on and supports you staying stuck. Your self-identity does not want categorizing, or to be seen as having an ordinary problem. You feel that others do not understand the uniqueness or severity of the psychological situation.

Intense self-criticism reflects faulty self-perception of one's own body. The body itself becomes repugnant in some way. Some times the person holds onto an anorexic self-image and thinks they are fat, even when this is not objectively accurate. Anorexia is a symptom of negative self-image since not body is perfect. In the same light, they may sabotage a relationship since it is not perfect. Instead of considering, the intrinsic value of self, other, and allowing for imperfections.

We learn tolerance since no one is perfect. If you are in a relationship to control or manipulate another into perfection, this is not the point. The correct position is to work on your relationship within. This supports your ability to bring your attention to the present situation. You can note how you pay selective attention to negative or irrational aspects of yourself or relationship. You embark on a path of taking practical, growth oriented actions, rather than staying trapped or digging in your heels. If you build a relationship within, it is more likely that you will create a self-identity based on reality. This goes a long way in offering you a balanced personality.

CHAPTER EIGHT:
Positive Attitude

❧

I have more creativity and I am more effective.

It is hard for anyone to maintain a positive relationship with a loved one at all times, and under every condition. It is difficult no matter the circumstances. There are times when people may feel like the relationship with their partner is wide of the mark. Fortunately, you can learn how to build a positive relationship. This chapter provides information about the art of effective communication and self-development. Many people approach building a relationship much like an addict. They have a difficult time making a distinction between a healthy relationship and a co-dependent one; whether it is love or an addiction. You may need to inquire into the relationship to determine if you have a positive attitude concerning the relationship.

Begin by inquiring into what a positive relationship is for you. Consider what helps you to establish a positive relationship. Do you demand affection and approval? Do you seek love and appreciation by becoming indispensable to another? Are you manipulative and have many selves to show a different self to each person according to the situation? Do you seek love for performance and achievement? Are you critical of self and others? Are you attracted to people who are unavailable and focus on the absent lover? Do you relate by maintaining emotional distance, and not getting involved? Do you have trouble with commitment and like to keep your options open? Are you obsessively ambivalent, sending mixed messages to your partner? Do you see everyone's point of view, and readily replace own wishes with those of others?

We all experience difficulty in observing the nuances of our own personality. It is often easier for a friend, family member, or therapist to see our true nature. The best way to build a clear sense of self is to notice what maintains a positive sense of self. One way to make a relationship fulfilling is to take some time each day to appreciate the little things. When you tell someone, "You look great in that new outfit or that meal you prepared was delicious," it creates a more positive environment. When you do things that show that your appreciation, then the efforts you make for your loved one give you something wonderful in return. It is a good thing to make sure that someone understands that you love him or her. Demonstrate your love by doing things that will make them happy, even if it is just doing a domestic chore they hate, or taking them out for a special meal. The key to building a positive relationship is to making sure you both feel loved, valued, and trusted.

Positive intimate relationships

Be positive from the start. This may include discussing your relationship preferences. We teach another how to initiate a constructive relationship with us and take into account our own personality and notice the style we are accustom to use such as extroversion verses introversion. Awareness dawns and we see how many personality styles rub us the wrong way and thus we bring bias to our perceptions of others. There is an art to building positive relationships, but it is not always a one size fits all since we have to take into consideration "otherness." We need to learn the impact upon us of various personality styles, different ways of intimacy, to become fluent in our communications. When we are in touch with the power of positive feedback, we transform negativity into encouraging affection so the language of love grows in each relationship.

Affirmative styles of communicating intimacy offer relationships the added dimension of sexual contact. Many couples need clarity around sexuality, and this may require discussion. We may need to talk together about how we view the link between sex and relationships. Clarity of what works and does not work in the realm of intimacy requires positive self-regard. It is essential, since it supports you in difficult times, by giving you a set of principles and values that provide inner security.

You no longer sacrifice self-esteem to gain approval in the relationship. Self-confidence arises from within. Inner love provides a very clear idea of who you are and who you are not. At your core, you hold yourself in highest esteem. You are an individual person who wants the best out of life. This means that you are more likely to make clear decisions in your own favor and create good relationships across the board. Your clear choices have positive impact on the way you go about creating partnerships in both the bedroom and boardroom.

Here are some great ways to practice self-confidence

I have found in working with clients that had low self-esteem that some coaching may be helpful in building self-confidence. Strength based recovery of self-esteem is also very important. Holistic life coaching encourages the client to focus on building on his/her multiple capabilities, resiliencies, and talents. By establishing effective coping abilities, and honoring the inherent worth of the individual, the process of recovery moves forward. When we internalize hope, we share it with family, friends, peers, as a catalyst to deepening self-esteem and unconditional love. If you do not love yourself, then it is very hard for anyone else to love you. It affects family life, friendships, and work relationships as well. People who do not have high self-esteem tend to make bad decisions, and end up with people who do not respect them. These relationships are usually negative.

When we discuss how self-esteem affects relationships, trust is extremely important. People who trust their partners feel like they know them as much as they can, and that their partner will not intentionally hurt them. It also makes people feel like they have someone who will be there no matter what happens. This allows them to open up to each other, creating a new level of intimacy. To foster trust between partners, someone usually has to really open up to their partner, which will make the partner feel like it's safe to open up as well. What we need to be aware of is fear of not having a real self, or being a derivative, or imposter, and imitating others. This confusion betweens several serves leads to questions around self-confidence. The question may arise, which one is the authentic me?

If a couple finds that their relationship is suffering, there are ways to ask for clear definition of a relationship and recognize when you may replace real feelings with an excessive desire to control. You build a positive one again by trying to shift the attention away from "my way or the highway to your way as a real concern. The couple should devote more time to each other, even if it is only a small chunk of time each day. They should also make sure to pay more attention to each other, give compliments for no reason, and do something nice for their partner. The best way to make a relationship positive is to devote time and effort to it.

A key way to build intimacy and to establish a strong and positive relationship is trust. Positive relationships can be difficult to maintain, but you can do it with cooperation and love. People with low self-esteem tend to have less trust in the other and creates "lower quality relationships" than people with healthy self-esteem. Low self-esteem wrecks havoc on intimacy and causes less affection and security, and more conflict and ambivalence. People with low self-esteem are more likely to be in a relationship that is less stable (more likely to break up). Psychologists have developed influential models to explain why this happens.

Summary of Common Themes

Regardless of their self-esteem, people tend to assume that other people see them in a similar way to how they see themselves. For example, if I think I am special, warm, attractive, smart, and funny then I am likely to assume that other people also see me this way. So people with high self-esteem, who generally see the positive in themselves, tend to believe other people see them in a positive light. They typically think that people who do not know them yet will probably like them, and that people who already like them will like them. In contrast, people with low self-esteem tend to be less confident that other people perceive in a positive way.

They doubt whether strangers will like them, and they are not sure if the people they are close to will continue to like/love/accept/want them.

What is important to note about low self-esteem is that most people with "low self esteem" do not see themselves consistently negatively. Most people with low self-esteem actually have "unbalanced self esteem." Their self-esteem might depend on their mood or what has happened that day, or they might have OK self esteem in some domains and problem self esteem in other domains (e.g. they might be confident about their self worth in the work domain but not in the relationships domain or friendship domain).

Self-esteem is important because it demonstrates that the way we act towards other people depends on how we think others view us. If we believe, someone likes us we believe differently towards him or her than if we believe he or she does not like us. If we are not sure about whether they like us, or are not sure if they will like us, we will have more suspicion or doubt. It is difficult for people with low self-esteem to believe their partner unconditionally loves them. When we do not feel accepted by someone, we tend to hold back. We do not fully commit in relationships, make them vulnerable, or engage in other types of behaviors that are unhelpful for relationships (e.g. testing their partners' love).

One significant benefit of being in a relationship is you can practice increasing self-esteem or at least increase self-esteem in certain domains. For example, if your partner sees you as smarter, more talented, more attractive etc. than how you see yourself, then over time you will probably start to see yourself as more of those positive things. We start to "believe" our partners view of us – that we really are a bit more attractive, smarter etc. than we previously thought. Nevertheless, the problem for people with low self-esteem is that they often have trouble realizing and accepting their partners' view of them. This means that the people who most need self-esteem boost often have the hardest time getting this benefit.

What can people with low self-esteem do? Now that you know this model, you can be aware that these processes might be happening in your relationships or even in your friendships. Look out for times when you might be thinking someone is judging you more negatively than is the reality. Then you might want to see a psychologist and work on areas of self-doubt to help you evaluate what is correct or incorrect in the situation.

If you suffer from low self-esteem (or have been told you do), or treat people with low self esteem (or think you do), please read on. There are self-esteem myths that can block your progress. Scientific research helps form the facts you will find here.

Low Self-Esteem

People with genuinely low self-esteem, a poor self-image, and low confidence, have been thoughtlessly associated with bullies, narcissists, criminals, and child abusers. Popular assumption was that people did bad things to other people because they, themselves have low self-esteem. However, if you have ever asked yourself "Do I have low self esteem" fear not. The evidence points to the conclusion that low self-esteem is a distinct condition. Therefore, if you have low self-esteem, you do not have to feel that you are in the same group as bullies or abusers.

Research has found that people with genuine low self-esteem tend to treat themselves badly, not other people. Stopping people being bullies by trying to lift their self-esteem may be like trying to get an obese person to lose weight by feeding them more cake and ice cream. In the 1980's there was a movement to raise self esteem in schools in the belief that this would stop bullies bullying and prevent future crime in society. Nevertheless, peer reviewed research has shown schools trying to raise self-esteem do not prevent bullies bullying because low self-esteem was not causing them to bully.

Falsely and ineffectively focusing on lifting self-esteem does not raise academic performance either as the methods schools attempted to raise self-esteem may have even damaged the sense of self-worth in those suffering genuine low self-esteem. Low self-esteem is not to blame for nearly as many problems as has traditionally been thought. Many psychologists assumed that self-esteem could never be too high.

Too High Self Esteem Linked to Criminality

It is now clear that too high self-esteem or "High Self Esteem Disorder" is often more of a problem. (This is NOT merely a disguised form of low self-esteem, as commonly thought). If you are the victim of a bully then you can rest assured you do not have to feel sorry for them. Hundreds of pieces of reliable research now show that bullies and many criminals are much more likely to suffer from unrealistically high self-esteem, narcissistic disorder, and impulse control problems than low self-esteem. An exaggerated sense of entitlement - expecting much from many situations is more likely to lead to frustration and aggressive, antisocial, or even criminal behavior. If self-esteem can be too low, it can also be too high. It was a crazy and unwarranted assumption that all human behavior could be explained a way by low self-esteem.

Symptoms of Low Self-esteem

Characteristics of Genuinely Low Self Esteem

1. Social withdrawal
2. Anxiety and emotional turmoil
3. Lack of social skills and self confidence. Depression and/or bouts of sadness
4. Less social conformity
5. Eating disorders
6. Inability to accept compliments
7. An Inability to see yourself "squarely" - to be fair to yourself
8. Accentuating the negative
9. Exaggerated concern over what you imagine other people think
10. Self-neglect
11. Treating yourself badly but NOT other people
12. Worrying whether you have treated others badly
13. Reluctance to take on challenges
14. Reluctance to be first or get ahead
15. Reluctance to trust your own opinion
16. Expecting little out of life for yourself

So what is likely to cause very low self-esteem? Look at how to build self-esteem. However, one major factor is personal history.

Child Abuse Increases Likelihood of Low Self Esteem

People who experienced abuse, as children (physical beating, emotional torment, or sexual abuse) are more likely to suffer low self-esteem as adults. They have learned to be an object, and feel they are of little value in themselves. They have been "brain washed" by constant criticism or abuse that they are a certain way. When a person begins to question this former conditioning or indoctrination then a healthier and more accurate sense of self can emerge. This happens in a similar way to how people may break away from the psychological encoding as a cult or gang member. There are other forms of abuse. Undoubtedly, a history of negative criticism or unfavorably comparison to others can lead to low self-esteem. Parents unconsciously express favorites in subtle ways; "why can't you be more like your sweet sister?" "Why don't you suck it up like your older brother and stop crying like a baby?"

Former abuse may lead you to symptoms of posttraumatic stress disorder. You may try to maintain a sense of self-worth but the "damage" causes depression, anger, and self-harming behavior that erodes self-respect. Once a person can deal effectively with traumatic memories, the automatic negative emotions start to be comprehensible. When a person can accept the fact, that early loss was real, and that it needs mourning, they can finally set the upset aside and allow self-esteem to thrive. One can honor the ability to empathize with other's pain but learns to gain self-esteem by detaching and forming a bond within. As a result, better self-esteem naturally takes hold.

The 1980's drive to raise low self-esteem in schools backfired. Our aims to gain self-esteem will also backfire if we do not apply it to relationships in a correct manner. If we base self-worth on the idea that enhancing it with the daily use of positive affirmations, we may also be barking up the wrong tree. Inserting positive messages may not be effective, and can actually harm the recovery. If we still believe, we are not worthy, are a loser, and feel self-loathing then affirmations are a fabrication of our actual reality and interpreted as false.

Research demonstrates how positive affirmations actually worsen the mood of people who already have low self-esteem. It seems that mere positive thinking is too superficial an approach. The person with low self-esteem senses this. Telling someone they are great when they have nothing concrete to show for it, feels artificial and pretentious. Claiming a person is wonderful when they are constantly feeling shame, guilt, or are depressed will not work. Imagine if you really loathe yourself and someone tells you that you are lovely. You receive the positive compliment as fake and internalize it as a negative rejoinder. People with low self-esteem feel even less empowered by receiving disconfirming comments. Healthy self-esteem needs to emerge delicately, not as an abrupt result of hearing you are "really special" or extraordinary.

Paradoxically, when we are being "too nice" to someone with very low self-esteem, it can drive them away. People need to develop better self-esteem gradually, through "proof" in the real world. Just being repeatedly told (by someone who does not know you that well) that "you're fantastic" has never been found to work in lifting low self-esteem. Whenever we are highly emotional, we distort perception. When people calm down and are actually encouraged to get in touch with the "real self," the idea of a healthier self-esteem can emerge like a mountain range coming into view when fog clears. This provides self-awareness since it supports the individual feeling the illumination of real self-esteem that comes from accessing a relationship within.

Basic Human Needs

What else do those with low self-esteem need? Contrary to popular opinion, people with low self-esteem tend to be confident. That is the problem. This manifests in their conviction that they are worthless or inadequate. As you will know if you have ever tried to argue with someone who is negative with self-put downs, it is a losing battle. When someone with low self esteem starts to become less sure of their own opinion of themselves and therefore begins to appraise counter evidence regarding their insignificance, their self image begins to become more healthy. At first, the "ugly" duckling was certain it was an ugly, unsuccessful duck. That misdirected conviction had to come untied before its true worth and life direction could become clear.

Good self-esteem is actually a by-product of living in a healthy way. So rather than trying to raise it directly it is easier to focus elsewhere (such on what a person does) and let self-esteem rise as happy side effect of a change in living. What do we all need in life that will help us incidentally feel better about ourselves? For anyone to be psychologically and physically healthy then core needs must find an outlet. Being clear about what you need and making efforts to meet those needs constructively, means you will naturally have better self-esteem as a by-product of living well.

This is useful list of basic human needs:

1. The need to give and receive attention
2. The need to look after your body
3. The need for meaning, purpose and goals
4. The need for a connection to something greater than ourselves
5. The need for creativity and stimulation
6. The need for intimacy and connection to others
7. The need for a sense of control
8. The need for a sense of status and recognition from others
9. The need for a sense of safety and security

Of course, it is likely that at any one time, one or more of these may be somewhat wanting in your life, without awful consequences. Something else needs your focus, perhaps other issues rather than your own emotionality. You come together with others and have new experience so they increase the range of enjoyment you get from life. When you have a healthy level of self-esteem (not self-hating but not narcissistically self involved either) then you find it easier to actually forget about yourself. You will only think about your finger if it is in pain or if you are obsessively proud of it. Otherwise, it can take care of itself. It is the same with your sense of self. We all need to engage in activities which we enjoy and in which we can "lose ourselves" regularly.

Mental health and even, to some extent, physical health can be directly related to how self-referential you are in your conversations. As people become healthier they use the "I" word less, in the same way that when your finger stops hurting you do not need to rub it any more. People should be encouraged to focus their attention away from themselves and this becomes easier once they have met their own basic emotional needs in healthy ways.

We all amplify some parts of our experience and minimize others. Nevertheless, if we habitually do this by expanding the bad stuff and linking that to self-esteem whilst belittling the good stuff and distancing positives from self-esteem, then it does not take a rocket scientist (or even a psychologist) to see that low self-esteem will result. Low self-esteem requires a particular attitude towards success. Whenever you succeed at something, you must write it off as good luck, chance, or someone else's responsibility. To gain a more realistic view of yourself, you need to take appropriate credit for your successes.

This involves learning how to convert real successes into statements about your self. The other part of the picture is to view perceived failures as temporary and not evidence or statements manifesting your core identity. When you stop discounting things that go well, and magnifying stuff that does not go so well, you are less likely to be depressed or suffer low self-esteem. Low self-esteem treatment should consist of a balance between teaching new thinking, emotional, and behavioral skills. Ultimately a healthy balance should be encouraged as should the development of real practical skills such as how to be assertive and build a social life.

CHAPTER NINE:
Positive Thinking

⚜

*To change your self-image and improve low self-esteem,
you need to believe in an alternative opinion of yourself
through experience and real lived relationships.*

It is not just about Positive Thinking in the sense of leaving the body and retreating into the mind. Positive Thinking involves challenging the desire to not how easy it is to give up. As one client put it, "I tried once and it didn't work." Positive thinking can be useful in that it challenges you to form a different view of things. However, most of the time it just takes the form of arguing with yourself, and as we have seen from above, this does not work.

Low self-esteem may drive you to compare yourself to other people in negative ways. As self-esteem rises to a healthy level, you do this much less. Check this out for yourself and ask, "Do I have an inferiority complex?" You will discover that you will gain more ideas on how to stop negatively comparing yourself to others. You break the habit of detaching from your feelings when discussing personal vulnerabilities.

To change your self-image and improve low self-esteem, you need to believe in an alternative opinion of yourself through experience and real lived relationships. Just repeating platitudes about how great you are is not the answer. However, if you really espouse what you believe, what you affirm will be so! In the words of the wise: "If you are not for yourself then who else will be?"

The quality of our relationships make a significant difference in the way we feel. They have an enormous impact on how we respond to the peaks and valleys of life. We choose to surround our self with negativity that is what we encounter. Unhappiness, impatience with the flatness of ordinary feeling, and anger become the emotional state we bring to our relationships. This is the quality of our life. If we encircle our self with affirmative relationships then the reverse will be true.

Here is a brief example of dealing with negativity. I am on the subway and see my neighbor, Brenda. I hope that she does not see me, but she does. It is not that I do not like her. I just do not feel like dealing with her pessimism today. Brenda has the habit of focusing on negative details in a generally okay situation. She sees her husband as alternatively brilliant or unequally not up to par. In Brenda's mind, the world is a downbeat and harmful place. She acts as if the world was about to end with a surfacing of self-doubt which easily becomes projected. Brenda deals with her fear by sharing all the horrific and problematic details with who ever will listen. Her nonstop talking conveys negative memories are more available than positive ones and locks her attention on worst-case scenarios. I happen to be the one she has found this morning to share her negativity.

Brenda is full fear and suspicion and is a harbinger of bad news. I wonder, what is up with this behavior? I think to myself, I have a lot on my mind too. But I have come to a more encouraging view of my own psychology. When I discover that I am embroiled in negativity or what I call catastrophic thinking, I know I am getting off track. I practice relaxing into my inner space where I have an open minded view. I allow the positive flow of life to transport me. When I take an affirmative approach, I can deal with whatever on-going drama confronts me. I have more creativity and I am more effective. I can pay attention to negativity for just so long. Then suddenly it drains me and becomes a burden.

When Brenda opens her mouth, I wonder if it will be positive or negative. Will she greet me or dump on me? I silently hope that she will have something upbeat to say but she does not. Her workaholic husband is the negative force today. He is bothering her. What would help her deal with negativity? How can she bring positivity to the problems and relate more effectively? Brenda can learn to check out her fears against reality. She can note the habit of looking for hidden negative meaning in other people's behaviors. She can become aware of how her doubts and fears shut out potential help and support from her husband.

Positive Psychology

We have all been involved with people or situations similar to the one I just described. Let us challenge this attitude and look at some winning approaches to creating positive relationships. Positive psychology is a recent branch of psychology whose rationale was summed up by Martin Seligman and Mihaly Csikszentmihalyi (2000): "We believe that a psychology of positive human functioning will arise, which achieves a scientific understanding and effective interventions to build thriving individuals, families, and communities." Positive psychologists seek "to find and nurture genius and talent" and "to make normal life more fulfilling", rather than merely treating mental illness (pp.5-14).

This division of psychology complements the field of mental health. It does not intend to substitute a positive view of psychic distress that disregards traditional areas of clinical psychology. Positive psychology has an essentially different accent to the scientific method. It studies and determines constructive human growth. This area of psychology fits well with the investigation of how faulty personal development weakens overall psychological stability. Positive psychology believes that people are naturally creative, resourceful, and whole. This includes the ability to heal. Positivity gives us the capacity to seize opportunity since it supports growth, change, transformation, and revolutionizing human potential. However, positive psychology understands the difference between criticism and realistic self-evaluation. Moreover, it supports coming to terms with inner hierarchies such as "Where do I stand? What is my place? How are the others viewing me?"

In positive therapy models, the focus is on the upbeat attributes and strengths of the client you are working with. It is based on methods that support individuals building up encouraging relationships, community alliances, and empowering techniques since they tap into the source of deeper happiness. Psychotherapy based on a model of psychopathology elevates psychopharmacology and distances the individual from an inner source of natural healing. Medication only often results in an incomplete, and inadequate, understanding of a person's over all condition since it elevates the person's weakness and vulnerabilities rather than encouraging positive attributes and inner strengths.

Topics of interest to researchers in the field of positive psychology include achieving higher states of consciousness, happiness, energy flow, increasing values, building strengths, acknowledging virtues, honing talents, elevating inner worth, and encouraging spiritual attribute. These qualities promote pro-social personality structure and encourage positivity in educational, religious, and social institutions. Practitioners of positive psychology mainly work with four areas; including positive experiences, awareness of psychological traits, building positive relationships, participating in affirmative community structures, and wellness activities.

Positive Attitude

Convey Positivity

Positive relationships are mutual. If you find yourself in a continuously negative relationship, inquire more deeply into the situation and be willing to ask, what is my part in it? I ask myself, what is my role in the negative experience? Has one or both of us gotten into the habit of nit picking at every little thing? When you get together, do you complain and criticize everything that you do not like about each other? We all need to vent and find expression for our upset now and then. If it becomes a regular habit; it may be time to re-evaluate the relationship. Be willing to see what attitudes, behaviors, and beliefs need tweaking and then notice if you are willing to implement the changes and make adjustments.

See the Good

See the good in others. You will usually find what you look for in relationships. If you are always expecting the worst, then that is generally, what you will discover. Look for the positive in people and lift them up rather than putting them down.

Be Interested

Be genuinely interested in other people and their lives. Ask questions and find common ground. Step outside your own life and learn about the people around you.

Don't Jump To Conclusions

Try to give people the benefit of the doubt. Jumping to conclusions and thinking the worst about the other person have damaged many relationships. If a situation arises with someone else, be direct and give the other person the chance to set the record straight or explain his or her side of the story. We appreciate it when others do the same for us after all.

Be Giving

Be inspiring and fun to be around. Be there for others when they need you. People will enjoy being with you and naturally gravitate to you.

Like Attracts Like

If you have realized that, many of your relationships are negative, maybe its time for a change. Seek out positive relationships with like-minded individuals. You could try a new hobby or volunteer. Find places where you are likely to meet the kind of people with whom you enjoy spending time.

Compliment

A sincere compliment goes along way. Notice the good in other people. Witness what they do and let them know how they are engaging you.

Compliment the other when it seems appropriate. Watch the benefits this brings to the relationship.

Really Listen

In our busy world, the art of true listening is a rare but simple gift that we can give others. Practice being a good listener and really being there for others. Really listening to others has power. It can transform our lives and the lives of those around us.

If you practice these suggestions, I promise it will help you navigate through all your interactions. Since you are rooted in a strong inner connection within, you align with your Higher Self. Listening to others and applying good communication skills goes a long way in relationships. However there are aspects of our personal development that call for introspection, insight, and intuition.

We need a third eye to peer inside and illuminate what is hidden. Some are called to deeper self knowledge. As a person individuates and begins to live the life they were born to live, consciousness of the deeper meaning behind life moves to the forefront. Then we notice what makes us tick. The true purpose of our journey through life shines through all our encounters and endeavors. We begin to take a symbolic approach to the ups and downs of daily life. We allow a metaphoric attitude to surround us and we identify with the mystery at the heart of life.

CHAPTER TEN:

Carl G. Jung's Individuation Process

✤

Jung believed that the goal of psychological life is the development of the individual personality.

In our personal relationships, we grow with others, and develop a personality that seems to have its own agenda. The challenge of becoming an individual is to separate from parental influences, cultural norms, and move toward wholeness. This arduous and yet dynamic path is what Swiss psychiatrist Carl Jung referred to as the Individuation Process. According to Jungian psychology, the goal of the individuation process is psychological integration. Jung believed that the goal of psychological life is the development of the individual personality. For Jung individual beings form and differentiate from other human beings by the individuation process. He noted that in particular, it is the development of the psychological individual as a being distinct from the general, collective psychology.

In Jungian psychology, Jacobi (1959) explains that the symbols of the individuation process include archetypes such as the shadow, the wise old man, wise old woman, the anima (contra-sexual) in men, and the animus (contra-sexual) in women. The value of this process is that it puts us in touch with soul making, rather than merely individuating the ego personality. Soul making invites us to develop a conscious relationship with our shadow, and the unconscious motives that lurk within. In the individuation process, it is the soul which is our guide, ally, and collaborator. Soul making sensitizes us to something felt but unseen. We form a personal relationship to our soul and know by becoming receptive to the invisible pull to deeper self-understanding.

The first stage of self-understanding becomes soul making and includes an innate urge to go below appearances. We discover the hidden patterns, unconscious connections, and cloaked agreements we make with self. We recognize the field of interconnection as a chain of movement that forces us to face something from within. We are hit broadside by the necessity to deal with the outer ramifications of past decisions and choices. We encounter the darker realms of personal agency and try to plead insanity for our action.

In looking a relationship dynamics, self awareness helps both partners progress beyond limits and restraints of personality patterns. The ability to have self-awareness helps move us beyond our persona masks or ego shows. The way we present ourselves to others must include an awareness of a soul perspective. Without soul, the process of becoming a complete person is insignificant and empty.

The second stage involves working on letting go of the ego's exclusive grasp over our relational life and attendant emotions. This is perhaps the most difficult stage of individuation. Working on integrating the shadow into the larger personality encourages us to engage with sub-personalities, including the aspects of our character that we would rather not acknowledge. We often unconsciously project the shadow onto other people or groups we do not like or even hate. If we are resentful, desirous, jealous, or afraid of someone then they may be carrying our shadow. The shadow puts us in touch with the shameful aspects of our life, including sexual urges, fantasy, hatred, and revenge. Yet, the insignia of the ego is breath, rather than depth, appearance rather than substance. Letting go of the ego perspective is like a death, as it implies that we must travel into the unknown; we journey to out-of-the-way areas within our own being.

The anima and animus are archetypes in the human psyche that represent aspects of the contra-sexual. This is the most common of all relational archetypes and represents the role we give to the inner opposite. In our search for our other half, we experienced it through projection onto the opposite sex. We project onto the other the role of providing our completion, making us whole. Often beyond our awareness, there is an unconscious drive to merge with other. The face of the other, as our beloved, is but a remembrance of our original oneness. The Mother archetype supports the notion of a longing to return to the womb and oceanic oneness. In the process of letting go of the physical body in death, we join the Great Mother. What we retrieve in imagination is the forgotten realm of our soul.

The third stage of the individuation process we create an active and conscious relationship with the unconscious aspects of our psyche. We do this in a conscious way to bring these aspects of our total personality into awareness. We work to incorporate the split off parts into the universal intelligence which all humans share. This awareness comes from of living close to the archetypal realm. Here we are refueling our outer goals and aspirations by tapping into the power of creation within our imagination.

In the fourth and final stage of personality development, we meet our Higher Self. Some Jungian and transpersonal therapists would interpose psycho/spiritual exercises, such as active imagination, visualization, and embodied dream work to integrate core archetypes of divine wisdom gather by meeting with your inner wise old man and wise old woman crone. These are the two Great Parents and embody the spiritual archetypes prior to the last step of individuation conceived as the completed Self.

In addition to Jung's theory of individuation, he identified the concept of a "collective unconscious within the human psyche." Collective unconscious is a term that proposes a part of the unconscious mind that all humans share, much like we have two ears, two eyes, one nose, and one mouth. The collective unconscious is not literally a place but an attitude or common way of expression that is found in the psychic structure of all people, everywhere, and at all times. Jung believed that all life forms with a central nervous system inherit an innate structure that organizes experience in programmed and patterned ways. Jung distinguished the collective unconscious from the personal unconscious that Sigmund Freud had introduced psychoanalysis. The personal unconscious is a private storehouse of experience restricted to each person's unique and exclusive experiences. The collective unconscious gathers, organizes, files, and stores those personal experiences in a similar way with each member of the human race.

For Jung the collective unconscious is a transmission of unconscious processes that reveal encrypted meaning and symbol formation, much like activities from the creative realm of dreams and the imagination. Jung imagined the collective unconscious as a territory of images within the human mind, both sexual, and non-libidinous. This realm encompasses common personality types of extraversion and introversion, the compensatory and prospective functions of dreams, and the synthetic and constructive approaches to the configuration of fantasy and utilization of insight and intuition.

Individuation is a process of personal transformation whereby the personality is in dialogue with the images from the collective unconscious and brought into consciousness (by means of dreams, active imagination, authentic dance, automatic writing, bodywork, or free association to take some examples). The goal of this process is to assimilate these images into the whole personality. It is a completely natural process, but one that is not necessarily conscious for everyone. However, the process is a prerequisite for bringing conscious awareness to the integration of the psyche. Individuation has a holistic healing effect on the person. This must include fostering emotional, mental, spiritual, and physical well-being!

Personality as Relationship Tool

We each have a personality. Simply put, your personality is the foundation of your psychological being. Your personality is a gift from God, molded by many factors, over many lives, and perhaps even eons. How does karmic influence from our ancestors or "other lives" influence how our personality affects our relationships now? While our personality does many things for our relationships, its basic goal is to express our uniqueness.

There is no other personality like yours in the whole world, you are unique, you are matchless, and you are one-of-a-kind! Your personality helps you become the "authentic you" that you are intended to become.

Your personality is the "point of entry" for connecting to your Higher Self. Your personality enables you to work through a multitude of tasks and functions, it is the way you take in information and process your perceptions.

Here are some common personality functions that support this process of growing your personality. The ability to expand your personality means the ability to tolerate multiple points of view. When you stop looking at the world in black or white and refraining from wanting things to be either right or wrong, you have a better life experience. These are action words and include believing, perceiving, thinking, feeling, decision-making and conscious acting rather than unconscious reaction. You become aware when a one-right-way solution begins to limit the chance for compromise or options and pay attention to the worth and consistency of other people's value systems.

I have put these action words in the form of Relationship Affirmations:

I believe my attitudes and values are significant.
I know my glass is half-full rather than half-empty.
I perceive how I take in data from the world and trust my senses and perceptions.
I think and acknowledge my own principles.
I make meaning of what I perceive and am the creator of my life.
I feel my emotional reactions and acknowledge them in a positive way.
I make positive decisions from a sense of self-worth.
I consciously make consistent responses that display self-respect.
I am responsible for matching my words with my behaviors.
I make powerful choices that affirm a loving attitude toward self and other.

Each person's basic personality structure looks something like this.

Notice the flow of your personality from one function to the next. This flow forms the progression of your personality. No one performs the six functions exactly like you:
- No one else believes exactly like you.
- No one else perceives exactly like you.

- No one else thinks exactly like you.
- No one else feels exactly like you.
- No one else decides exactly like you.
- No one else acts exactly like you.

All this uniqueness adds up to something extraordinary ... YOU! You are a one-of-a-kind, intentional creation of God.

CHAPTER ELEVEN:
Personality Types

⚜

Discovering the preference of our personality style shows us how we and other individuals take in and process sensory data, and relate to the world

Personality type refers to the psychological cataloging of diverse styles of individuals. Personality types are sometimes distinguished from personality traits. Personality traits tend to have smaller representation in the grouping of behavioral trends. Types involve value differences among people, whereas traits might be construed as the number or range of differences. For example, introverts and extraverts are two different categories of people. Introversion and extraversion are part of a permanent facet of personality, with the majority of people falling somewhere in the middle.

Understanding the basics of personality types can be useful in building positive relationships. Knowing our own personality style helps us gain an appreciation of different personality styles of those we are relating. When we gain knowledge of how our personality type operates with other's types, we attain valuable insight into what fosters a good connection with that particular person. Discovering the preference of our personality style shows us how we and other individuals take in and process sensory data. This is how we interface with our relational world.

The knowledge of personality differences nurtures our relationships with others who may have similar or different styles of relating. As we gain self-knowledge of our personality style, we increase our ability to anticipate how others will experience us. It gives us pertinent information about other people, so we are better able to understand that not everyone experiences the world in the same way we do. We expand our relational approaches and increase our effectiveness with the individuals involved.

The Four Temperaments

An early appearance of personality type theory was the Four Temperaments system of Galen, based on Hippocrates "four humors model." Four temperaments is a proto-psychological interpretation of the ancient medical concept of four bodily fluids that affect human personality traits and behaviors. The temperaments are **sanguine** (pleasure seeking and sociable), **choleric** (ambitious and leader-like), **melancholic** (analytical and thoughtful), and **phlegmatic** (relaxed and quiet). The Greek physician Hippocrates (460–370 BC) incorporated the four temperaments into his medical theories. From then, through modern times, they, or modifications of them, have been part of many theories of medicine, psychology, arts, and literature.

Later discoveries in science and biochemistry have shown that the theory of bodily fluids does not exist. Nevertheless, complex systems of hormones do in fact help regulate emotion and cognition. Many personality type systems of varying scientific acceptance continue to use four or more categories of a similar nature. A current and widespread example of personality types is Type A and Type B personality theory. According to this theory, "Type A" people are classified as impatient, achievement-oriented, whereas easy-going, relaxed individuals are designated as Type B.

Several pop psychology theories have arisen to popularize personality typing in terms of relationship building. In his book Men are from Mars, Women Are from Venus, Gray highlights the difference between male and female personality styles, and corresponds to the polarity between thinking and feeling types. The book states that most of common relationship problems between men and women are a result of fundamental psychological differences between the genders.

Gray exemplifies by means of its eponymous metaphor: that men and women are from distinct planets – men from Mars and women from Venus – and that each gender is acclimated to its own planet's society and customs, but not to those of the other. One example is men's complaint that if they offer solutions to problems that women bring up in conversation, the women are not necessarily interested in solving those problems, but wants mainly to talk about them. The book asserts that each gender, (like other personality type systems), can be understood in terms of the distinct ways they respond to anxiety and stressful situations.

The Enneagram's model of nine distinct personality types is a classification of nine classically diverse types of people. The Enneagram uses numbers to designate each of the nine types because numbers are value neutral. They imply a whole range of attitudes and behaviors representative of each type, without specifying anything either positive or negative. Unlike the labels used in psychiatry, numbers provide an unbiased, shorthand way of indicating things about a person without being derogatory. The Enneagram has influenced the work of Carl Jung's significant ideas in the theoretical work published in the book Psychological Types. The MBTI assessment has roots in Jungian analytical psychology.

Jung categorized people into primary types of psychological function and proposed the existence of two dissimilar pairs of mental functions. The "rational" (judging) functions: thinking and feeling and the "irrational" (perceiving) functions: sensing and intuition Jung went on to suggest that these four functions find expression in either an introverted or an extraverted way. He proposed four main functions of consciousness: Thinking and Feeling functions are rational, while Sensation and Intuition are non-rational. According to Jung, rationality consists of symbolic thoughts, feelings, or actions. Objectivity, representing a point of view based on objective value, which is based on practical experience.

Extraversion & Introversion

Extraversion means "outward-turning" and introversion means "inward-turning."

People who prefer extraversion draw energy from action: they tend to act, then reflect, then act further. If they are inactive, their motivation tends to decline. To rebuild their energy, extraverts need breaks for time spent in reflection. Conversely, those who prefer introversion expend energy through reflection: they prefer to reflect, then act, then reflect again. To rebuild their energy, introverts need quiet time alone, away from activity. The extravert's flow is directed outward toward people and objects, and the introvert's is directed inward toward concepts and ideas. Contrasting characteristics between extraverts and introverts include the following:

The functions are modified by two main attitude types: extraversion and introversion. In any person, the degree of introversion or extraversion of one function can be quite different from that of another function. Sensation and intuition are the information-gathering (perceiving) functions. They describe how new information is understood and interpreted. Individuals who prefer sensation are more likely to trust information that is in the present, tangible and concrete; information that can be understood by the five senses.

Individuals who tend toward intuition trust hunches, which seem to come "out of nowhere" and prefer to look for sixth sense impressions and less to details and facts. Those who prefer intuitive style tend to trust information that is more abstract or theoretical, that can be associated with other information (either remembered or discovered by seeking a wider framework or blueprint for possibilities). They are more interested in future possibilities. They tend to trust those flashes of insight that seem to bubble up from the unconscious mind. The meaning is in how the data relates to the pattern or theory.

Thinking and feeling are the decision-making (judging) functions. The thinking and feeling functions are both used to make rational decisions, based on the data received from their information-gathering functions (sensing or intuition). Those who prefer thinking tend to decide things from a more detached standpoint. They measure the decision by what seems reasonable, logical, causal, and consistent.

Those who prefer feeling tend to come to decisions by associating or empathizing with the situation, looking at it "from the inside." They are apt to weigh the situation to achieve, on balance, the greatest harmony, consensus and fit, considering the needs of the people involved.

As noted already, people who prefer thinking do not necessarily, in the everyday sense, "think better" than their feeling counterparts and consider the opposite preference an equally rational way of coming to decisions. In any case, the MBTI assessment is a measure of preference, not ability. Similarly, those who prefer feeling do not necessarily have "better" emotional reactions than their thinking counterparts.

Four functions are used at different times depending on the circumstances. However, one of the four functions is generally used more dominantly and proficiently than the other three, in a more conscious and confident way. According to Jung, the dominant function is supported by two auxiliary functions. From the perspective of MBTI, the first auxiliary function is referred to as a secondary function. The second auxiliary function is usually called the tertiary function. The fourth and least conscious function is always the opposite of the dominant function. Jung called this the "inferior function" and Myers sometimes called it the "shadow."

Jungian Typology

Jung's typological model regards psychological type as similar to left or right-handedness: individuals either are born with, or develop certain preferred ways of thinking and acting. These psychological differences are sorted into four opposite pairs, or dichotomies, with a resulting eight possible psychological types. People tend to find using their opposite psychological preferences more difficult, even if they can become more proficient (and therefore behaviorally flexible) with practice and development.

Jung (1921) also identified two other dimensions of personality: Intuition - Sensing and Thinking - Feeling. Sensing types tend to focus on the reality of present situations, pay close attention to detail, and are concerned with practicalities. Intuitive types focus on envisioning a wide range of possibilities to a situation and favor ideas, concepts, and theories over data. Thinking types use objective and logical reasoning in making their decisions, are more likely to analyze stimuli in a logical and detached manner, be more emotionally steady, and score higher on intelligence tests. Feeling types make judgments based on subjective and personal values. In interpersonal decision-making, feeling types tend to emphasize compromise to ensure a beneficial solution for everyone.

We all have the fantasy that our relationships should be effortless. The allure of easy relationships sways most. The fantasy of a happily-ever-after marriage, friendships that last forever, or parent/child bonds which supplant the need to grow and mature are propagated through upbringing and the social media. We would all like to believe that our most intimate relationships are unconditional, and strong enough to withstand whatever may come. At some point in our lives, most of us need to face the fact that relationships require effort to keep them strong and positive. Even a wonderful, sturdy relationship can come to ruin by neglect and indifference.

Understanding our own personality type and the personality type of the other person involved in the relationship will bring a new dynamic to the relationship. Looking to improve a love relationship, familial relationships, friendships, or employer/employee relationships it is beneficial to know our personality type. This will allow better understanding and communication.

Different types of relationships have different characteristics and specific needs. Two basic areas are critical to all relationships and include communication styles and expression of expectations and needs. What do we expect from ourselves and the other person involved in the relationship? How do we communicate these expectations? How to we in confidence communicate our feelings and opinions to the other person in the relationship? How does our personality type affect our expectations of the other person? How does their method of communication affect us? Does our personality type negatively affect the kind of person whom we are attracted? How does it affect who our friends are, and who we work with best?

I am not prescribing a complete solution to your relationship problems, nor am I stating that there is any guarantee of improved odds with particular types of personality pairings. Statistics show that individuals who are most happy in their marriages are those who have the highest levels of inner peace, and those who have the most optimistic outlook.

Opposites Attract

That old phrase "opposites attract" has been around for ages. In truth, it is very accurate when it comes to love and intimate relationships. Through our research, we have noted that people are usually attracted to their opposite on the Extraversion and Introversion and Judging and Perceiving scales. We are naturally attracted to individuals who are different from ourselves because they are often unusual and exciting. It is not the only the exciting differences that attract us to our opposites but also a natural quest for completion. We naturally are drawn towards individuals who have strong point which we are lacking. When two opposites function as a couple, they become a better-rounded, working entity.

There is also the hypothesis that our natural attraction of our opposites is an unconscious way of forcing us to deal with the weaker aspects of our own nature. While we are highly attracted to our opposites, two opposites involved in an intimate relationship have significant issues and communication barriers to overcome. In a sense, our attraction to the opposite personality can be seen as our subconscious minds driving us to become a more complete individual, by causing us to face the areas in life that are most difficult for us. The same cannot be said for other kinds of relationships. When it comes to work colleagues, or friends, we are not interested in dealing with people who are unlike ourselves. We are most comfortable with those who have similar interests and perspectives, and we do not show strong motivation or patience in dealing with our opposites.

Birds of a Feather Flock Together

Although we are attracted to people who are different from us in the way we see the world, we are most attracted to those who have a similar worldview. Couples who have the same dominant function in their personalities seem to have the longest and happiest relationships. For example, an individual whose dominant function is Introverted Sensing (ISTJ or ISFJ) is attracted to partners with a dominant function of Extraverted Sensing (ESTP or ESFP).

We have noticed that people who take in information through the five senses seem to communicate best with other sensors, and that people with an intuitive personality seem to communicate best with other intuitive oriented individuals. There seems to have equal partnership between people who communicate on the same level, although there are successful relationships between people orientated toward sensation and others who prefer intuition. Two individuals of any type who are well-developed and balanced can communicate effectively and make a relationship work, but many people will communicate best with people who share their same information gathering preference.

It is no revelation to learn that research regarding Personality Type and Relationships, indicates that successful mates often share the same dominant function, and the same letter preference ("S" sensing or "N" intuition) for their information gathering function. That does not mean that people with different preferences cannot have a happy, successful marriage, it simply indicates that people frequently settle down with individuals who are on their same "wave-length".

CHAPTER TWELVE:
Relationship as Archetype

❧

Archetypes are identifiable prototypes that manifest throughout history and find expression in the arts, sciences, relationships and culture. Archetypes play out in all cultures and within all people.

Swiss Psychiatrist Carl Gustav Jung identified various archetypes that are part of the human psyche. He observed these differing but repeating patterns in the human repertoire of experience. Archetypes are identifiable prototypes that manifest throughout history and find expression in the arts, sciences, relationships, and culture. Archetypes play out in all cultures and within all people. Jung's main archetypes are not 'types' in the way that each person may be classified as one or the other, in the sense of personality type. Rather, we each have all fundamental archetypes within us. Jung's focus was on four of the main archetypes, Shadow, Anima, Animus and the Self, that provide the base of analytical psychology.

The Shadow is a familiar archetype that reflects deeper elements of our psyche. The shadow is an expression of dormant dispositions and latent characteristics in embryonic form within. It is common for the shadow to arise in everyone. Shadow elements in our personality reflect something that we have split-off from our awareness. Thus, the shadow is a defense mechanism we developed for survival. It was essential in our early self-organization and helped us build relationships with the people in our lives. The shadow often represents as a dark, unknown, and mysterious character that is not identifying with the ego. It is a potentially upsetting, and even dangerous aspect of self.

The Shadow

Shadow figures embody our personal pandemonium since it represents an inner figure that challenges the status quo. This aspect of us challenges authority and disobeys social rules. The shadow engages us in ways that embarrass and shame. In so doing, we may discover new domains of daily life, push things into turmoil, or disarray. The shadow is shadowlike and eye-catching. It evokes the out of the ordinary and exotic. Its alien nature can be as alarmingly as it is so seductive and strangely attractive. In myth and fairytales, the shadow often appears as the ogre, wild man or woman, spider-people, stranger, fighting gang, seductress, and dark enemies like monster, tyrant, giant, and bully.

It is rather obvious when the shadow arises in others. It is more difficult to admit that it also exist within us. We reject it in ourselves and project it onto others. The shadow in some people can be off putting to their ego. We cannot admit its presence and split if off from reality. The shadow is often a saboteur and runs rough shod over our hopes and dream while taking on a life of its own. It is common to experience the shadow archetype as something radically different from our customary self-identity. It is likely to be as if it is our other half or the hidden split-off aspect of the other, darker self within.

A prevailing goal of Jungian therapy is to facilitate shadow work. This therapy focuses on supporting the client along the uncommon path of personality development. Thus, individuation is the re-integration the shadow archetype by coming to terms with the unacceptable and secrets of our sinister side. We regain enormous power in the process of integrating the darkness within. We bring it into the light of our whole self. The process of integration of the shadow is a life long pursuit. We can become whole and complete once again. One vital way is to invite or "befriend" what was once split from us. Since we projected the unwanted or shameful aspects onto others, we find healing in taking it back into the whole of our self.

Our shadow may appear in dreams, hallucinations, fantasy, reverie, and musings, often as something or someone who is atrocious, wicked, horrifying, and fearsome. The shadow is most often something we consider loathsome in some way. It may be seduce in intimacy, outrage through fake friendship, intimidate with heartless words, or totally disrespect. Encounters with shadow, since it is an aspect of our subconscious mind, may expose deeper thoughts and fears. It may also take us over unswervingly. Some people in the grip of the shadow complex describe their bodily exploits automatically driven. They feel out of control that their mind has been co-opted by some alien force. They know when they are under the influence of the shadow self as they are confused, dazed, and feel drugged or on automatic pilot like in a trance.

Anima and Animus

Jung discovered a central archetype of love. He termed this anima/animus; these two words mean "soul" and "spirit" in Latin. He explored how these contra-sexual energies function as the drive to connect with soul since he understood soul to be a psychological term for the universal energy often used in religious language. The soul functions as the aspect within that performs in men as a feminine presence and in women and a masculine figure.

The next prevailing pattern Jung discovered in the inner lives of his patients is that of the Anima (male), Animus (female), or, more simply, the archetype of soul mate. The anima and animus are the contra sexual inner figures a man and woman meet on the path of individuation. These archetypes symbolize our secret, surreptitious, conflicting, and clandestine contact with the collective unconscious. The anima/animus represents our authentic self, as opposed to the persona or the masks we wear in public. The anima symbolizes for the man and the animus for the woman, the source of human sexuality and creativity. The anima/animus may appear as someone striking or unusual in some way, perhaps with amazing skills and powers. In fiction, heroes, super-heroes, and gods may represent these powerful beings and awaken in us the sense of omnipotence that we knew in that very early neonatal phase.

Anima and animus are male and female principles that represent the symbolic encounters with the opposite sex. In this dynamic dance we engage the opposite gender as different, unusual, weird, wonderful, and mysterious. Whilst men have a fundamental anima and women an animus, each may also have the other, just as men have a feminine side and women a masculine. Jung saw men as having one dominant anima, contributed to by mother and other females, whilst women have a more complex, variable animus, perhaps made of several parts. Jung theorized the development of the anima/animus as beginning with the infant's projection onto the mother, then replacing this projection onto prospective partners in later life.

Jung proposed in combination, the anima and animus are syzygy (a word also used to denote alignment of planets), symbolizing wholeness and completion. This combining brings great power and found in religious combinations such as the Christian Holy Trinity (Father, Son and Holy Spirit). A perfect partnership between man and woman can occur when the anima and animus, (as symbolic of the contra sexual and outer physical and common values) are shared and received as different and yet compatible. Thus, you might find your soul mate by finding your matching other half. This is love at first sight for a few and a lifetime of search for many. Hardly any succeed in this quest since love of the beloved must indicates a tangible, perceived, and authentic contact while also extending a hoped-for match with the anima or animus within, that in rare cases mirrored in the actual partner.

For Jung, the self is not just "the little me," but God in the largest sense, as the living spirit that yearns to connect. It is the universal aspect of self, since it is whole, and unifies both our conscious and unconscious psychic processes. Jung described formation of the self as a process of individuation, where all aspects of personality are brought together as one. Therapeutically, rebirth is returning to the wholeness of existence prior to physical birth, before we start to split our selves into many parts. Jung discovered from clinical practice that there is a large reservoir of archetypes that influence individuation. These common patterns overlap and becoming images within culture and many can appear in the same person, in multiple forms, and complex manifestations.

Examples of Family archetypes

Examples of Family archetypes are The Father: Stern, powerful, controlling and The Mother: Feeding, nurturing, soothing. The Child represents birth, beginnings, innocence, inexperience, salvation. Myth, fairytales and legends represent archetypes of the hero: Rescuer, champion and the maiden: Purity, desire. The wise old man embodies knowledge, guidance, the magician evokes mysterious, powerful, and Earth Mother represents the creative and destructive power of nature. Other archetypes display treacherous figures such as the trickster, saboteur, or rebel are characters of deception, and may hold hidden and secret qualities that bring new energy in its wake. Identifying helpful non-human or animal archetypes are also important in self-knowledge. The faithful dog highlights unquestioning loyalty. The enduring horse is symbolic of staying power and never giving up and also with basic instinct and erotic energy. The devious cat could be a quality of self-serving behavior, or a symbol of survival skills. The sly fox can represent qualities of being crafty and cunning.

A noteworthy attribute of Jung's archetypal view of the human psyche is the recognition that all humans have the capacity to recognize common prototypes of human imagery that evoke profound or powerful emotion. Archetypes exert intense influence on our spontaneous behaviors, thoughts, and feelings. This implies that they have deep and archaic origins within the human psyche. Thus, archetypes have a particular power over emotional and mental patterns. They hold immense potency and can wreck havoc for good or bad. The potential consequences of life altering choices erupt from the archetypal realm. Like all necessity these powers may be feared or revered as mysterious signifiers of things beyond our full comprehension or understanding.

In earlier work, Jung linked the archetypes to heredity and considered them as instinctual. Yet wherever he looked across cultures, he found the same archetypes and thus came to conceptualize them as fundamental forces that somehow exist beyond us but are apparent in latent form within all humans. They have existed in ancient myths as daemons, elemental spirits, or "gods." In psychotherapy, Jung sought to link his clients with this ancient region of experience.

The Shadow

As mentioned, the Shadow is not simply the psyche's dark side, but contains riches that transform our personality. Darkness is contained in the Shadow, but within the darkness of our personality, we often discover hidden light. We discover that the true goal is to uncover the gold of our individual life that is found within. But we share a common human imagination that gives us all access. Most often, we meet this realm in our encounters with our personal shadow, as a negative confrontation with our "shady self" or with a Dr. Jekyll within our Mr. Hyde.

It is incorrect to think that the shadow is about negativity. In truth, the shadow opens us up to our essential nature, including good and bad. We discover that some of the darkness within us actually holds precious light and renewed energy. As the storehouse of all that the conscious mind rejects, the shadow naturally frightens many people. You may notice your shadow by what you repress, deny, and displace onto others. Some may be so averse to facing shadow elements that it is impossible to even look at these attributes. The shadow is projected as a way of running from unredeemed personal issues. These actions strengthen and extend the shadow's power into our waking life where it is lives unconsciously, and builds in strength rather than diminishing its active potency.

It is unquestionable that the shadow is composed of some unwholesome elements. This is why we exile it into the unconscious. Individuals rarely recognize their own shadows. Instead we see tend to see the very traits we so abhorred inside our own psyche, and this is never a pretty sight. The mind is as capable of producing psychic projections much like reflections of the sun are capable of creating shadowy images. Ironically, it is projection that makes the faults of others so blindingly visible. An example of projection is the miser who, while taking back the dollar tip on a restaurant table, is simultaneously complaining about a sister's stinginess. The nauseating aspects of others may induce sickness because of their deep resonance within one's own psyche.

While it is true that the shadow contains some less than desirable elements, not all that is in the shadow is actually undesirable. To quote Swiss psychiatrist Carl Jung, "In the shadow is the gold." Shadow gold refers to those elements of the shadow that are actually quite precious, elements relegated to the shadow due to painful associations, societal judgments, cultural disapproval. For example, an extremely intuitive child might have a family of origin who saw intuition as evil or overt expressions of hunches or superstition as demonic. That child might suppress all intuitive urges. The child's intuitive abilities would still exist, but they would exist in the darkness of the shadow.

Similarly, a gifted artist who suffered abuse at the hands of an art teacher might sequester anything related to artwork into the confines of the shadow. Digging up elements of shadow gold, such as the recovery of one's personal imaginative power, can lead to life transformation. One's life can become a frightening prospect, since it involves leaving behind a life one knows how to navigate in favor of unknown waters. A survivor of abuse learned to cope with life in a certain way and the courageous act of leaving behind the only existence this individual knows, can feel life threatening but rewarding.

Abuse is at the extreme end of the spectrum of why shadow gold remains in psychic darkness. Some of us become dreamers in our comfortably numbed lives. You may notice how you will often run from anything, no matter how promising or precious, that threatens your dead end existence.

The Shadow elements of your personality are not all bad. Ironically, the shadow self is like a precious treasury that contains all your individual gold. The unredeemed value and worth of our true self resides within our psyche alongside our shadow self. Dragons in fairytales play the role of guarding our personal treasure. In such stories, the dragon is not evil since it is actually the protector of something precious and oftentimes vulnerable. Only the dragon's fierce energy and frightening image protects the treasure from theft or destruction. The same is true of our shadow.

The Shadow keeps the gold of the personality safe until the authentic self is ready and able to reclaim it. Ultimately, the only way for the psyche to be a whole self is to integrate and accept of all its parts, especially the aspects that seem unredeemable. Self-integration calls for ending projections by focusing attention inward, thereby illuminating the shadow with the bright light of our true and integrated self.

The ultimate goal of shadow work is to help us see our essence and unique brilliance. We stop projecting either negative or positive qualities onto others. Withdrawing our projections is the primary purpose of Jungian analysis because it clarifies our manipulations to uncover the authenticity or true worth. When you have self-acceptance, you regain the power of the redeemed shadow. The redeemed shadow provides each person with a sense of belonging, and leads to building supportive relationships that allow us to also embody creativity, imagination, and intuition in the various roles we play within our community.

Withdrawing Shadow Projections

Withdrawing our shadow projections means that we become aware of the ways we project unwanted, despised, or unclaimed aspects of our personality onto others. When we have awareness that we, and all humans, have the tendency to project our shadow, we can start to bring this awareness to our relationships. It is vital to notice that our projections are the way we project either good or bad onto "others." The need is to get rid of the things we harbor within. Awareness initiates a process of removing projections, and to stop always misplacing what we do not like onto others. We become more effective in dealing with the darkness in our world that is often caused by the violence that ensues from cruel and unusual projections.

The question arises: what is the difference between owning our shadow and withdrawing our shadow projections? It is different for each person, but requires the same attitude. We recognize, take ownership, and then withdraw our shadow projections. We notice that the feeling and thoughts are emerging from within and not necessarily from the outside world. We discern the ways we judge and condemn "others." We get in touch with the "other" inside of ourselves.

When you stop believing your preconceived notions and prejudices about the "other" who you imagine you are separate and disconnected from, you start withdrawing projection. It is difficult because it requires that you stop blaming others and start looking at your own actions. You take responsibility for the negative aspects of your own self. You stop assuming and maintaining erroneous views of others and look more accurately within you. Only then can you clearly see what you do not like, or are ashamed. You become acquainted with the "other within" who exists inside as you; a newly found and converted "other."

Although this is an intentional and conscious process, it is not subjectively driven. The experience is not under the control of your will power. To meet the other within is to discover that you are not the master of your own house. To conceptualize this other within yourself, think of your primary identity, of whom you imagine you are (a good, kind, spiritual person, for example). Then take the opposite side of this perspective. This is how the other within us sees the world. To paraphrase Jung, "...we discover that the 'other' in us is indeed 'another,' a real man or woman, who actually thinks, does, feels, and desires all the things that are despicable and odious.... A whole man or woman, however, knows that his/her bitterest foe, or indeed a host of enemies, does not equal that one worst adversary, the 'other self' who dwells in his/her bosom." To quote the cartoon character Pogo, "We have met the enemy and he is us." When you acknowledge the shadow is but an enemy within, you see that this aspect is actually just trying to be our ally, supporter, and friend.

The autonomous other within is symbolically related to the figure of the devil, who is the "other," and adversary, to God (one of the inner meanings of the word "devil" is the "adversary"). The battle between Christ and his adversary (the anti-Christ), seen symbolically, is a reflection of the dynamic that exists between ourselves and the "adversarial other" unconsciously residing within us. Commenting on this correlation, Jung said "..."the adversary," is none other than "the other in me." Yet, in some mysterious way, this adversarial other plays a crucial role in the actualization of our true nature. To quote Jung, "The shadow and the opposing will are the necessary conditions for all actualization."

This other within can really get in our way and mess with our best intentions, however. This other within can manifest in a way that is truly "devilish," thwarting us at every turn. Interestingly, one of the meanings of the word "Satan" is that which "obstructs." This other within can manifest so demonically and arouses such terror in us because it is a reflection and projection of our inner state of fear and denial. Ultimately this process is related to, an appearance of, something inseparable from us.

You may notice how you experience this "other" within you as alien and split-off from yourselves. You know it is not under your control, however, you feel fear upon meeting it. You experience the "other" as something foreign within and sense it is treacherous and unsafe. This is something that you have little control over. Whether in the outside world or within you, this stranger evokes extreme fear. Contact with the dark side simultaneously stirs up and reinforces the human proclivity to displace this negativity onto someone or something other than you!

CHAPTER THIRTEEN:
The Shadow and Autonomous complexes

༁

The split-off and disowned autonomous complexes appear to oppose us since they are aspects of ourselves that we have disassociated.

Jung relates the daemons or psychic forces as "autonomous complexes," and believed they are part of the psyche that has been split-off due to personal trauma or collective pain passed on from the ancestors. Thus, complexes develop a seemingly independent and quasi-life of their own. The split-off and disowned autonomous complexes appear to oppose us since they are experienced as aspects of ourselves that we have disassociated from our ego identity. So we experience the complex as something outside self.

This psychological process is similar to forgetting about a part of your physical body. Think of a part of your body; let us say your teeth. Imagine how your teeth will strive for stability and health by drawing attention to it when being ignored, for example tooth decay or needing dentures. The body seeks wholeness by trying to get your interest and wants you to take notice when something is amiss or you are in distress. It helps you to remember it. Therefore, if you do not get regular dental cleanings, you may harm the health of your teeth and mouth. It is similar in the psychological sense of bringing awareness to your psychic condition.

These autonomous complexes are your own energy appearing to you as if out-there, or outside of your. You project unwanted or unacceptable aspect of your own personality onto someone else. This is a common defense mechanism that compensates one-sidedness on your part. These autonomous complexes are genuine symbols that reflect your inner situation, while at the same time they hold the potential to be transformative. Complexes are an expression of the part of you that is one-sided, while simultaneously being the very doorway into wholeness. When you integrate your imbalances, you embrace the split-off inner "other" and actualize your intrinsic unity. How the autonomous other within you manifests – constructively or destructively – depends upon if you are able to recognize and implement this new awareness and what it is revealing to you into your daily life.

Jung said, "Individuation is an exceedingly difficult task: it always involves a conflict of duties, whose solution requires us to understand that our "counter-will" is also an aspect of God's will." This autonomous other, with its "counter-will," plays a mystifying, and yet essential role in the revelation of our true nature. Paradoxically, this "autonomous other" within ourselves, though seemingly separate, is concurrently no one but our self. When we disconnect from our true self, we imagine this part as the shadow since it feels unfamiliar, strange, embarrassing, disgusting, and even terrifying. We must get to know this aspect of our self in order to begin to develop a constructive and beneficial relationship with it.

When we are completely alienated from a part of ourselves, we project it outside of ourselves. The defense mechanism of displacement involves projecting unwanted aspects of self onto another person, place, or thing that may not be even remotely involved. This unconscious content actually belongs to ourselves and is fabricated in much the same way as we dream up characters in the form of an "other" within a fantasy or daydream.

If you can recognize the self-reflection that is being revealed to you in the complex, you begin the process of integrating the split-off aspect into your personality. This unconscious part of you needs to be welcomed into your conscious self-image. This is analogous to how Christ, who symbolizes God incarnate, had to fully incarnate in humanity. Jesus became human, that is to say completely unfamiliar and separate from God. So he could consciously reunite with God. In this mysterious relationship, Jesus became one with his Higher Self.

When you realize the "other" within you, it is a radical relationship, instead of trying to control and annihilate it; you begin to care for your shadow "conscientiously." You honor and respect this darker partner you share your life with. In this sense designing alliances with others is a spiritual activity and links us to ethics and honor. The etymology of religion "religio" derives from the word "religare," which means to link back and reconnects (to the source, God, our true selves).

In the context of building relationships, understanding autonomous complexes means careful consideration and observation of certain psychodynamic factors as originating from internal powers. This framework must not be confused with the contemporary derogatory use of religious fundamentalism, which typically refers to someone who is dogmatic, unbending in their beliefs, and holds a deep-seated attitude of self-righteousness and intolerance. Connecting to your true self and your Source entails something diametrically opposite to merely following a set of predetermined beliefs or laws imposed by an outside authority.

Our existential situation as human beings is to be in a state of curiosity, but there is a lot of miseries in our lives that stop us from bring an inquisitive attitude to our own personality. Curiosity encourages us to open to this new discovery. We find ourselves asking unanswerable questions that lead us directly into our own archetypal powers. For many the existential situation as a human is confronting existential fears. We fear that others are more powerful than us, and become apprehensive of what will happen if we withdraw projections. We feel exposed, raw, and defenseless in the face of the unknown within our own minds. Our existence and self-identity accompanies every urge, desire, and inclination for self preservation and yet we have given the complexes within us, the name of the mysterious other. We are compelled to ask, "Why do I see this relational situation the way I do?" Why do I have these emotional reactions when some people have completely different one? Why does my partner get angry at an event when I become depressed or manic?

It is interesting how the archetypal patterns play out on the spiritual stage of life. The Christian tradition speaks about this "other" as the "principalities and powers" that are always with us, but are mysterious and dangerous. We have no need to produce them, even if we could, since it is merely presenting us with illusions. These psychic distractions tempt us off the path of individuation. We must choose to be the master, if we wish to serve others. Our protection against being mastered by the "other" is to withdraw projections so that we bring awareness to how this force works within us for good or ill. Only then are we are in a position to decide, whether we know it or not, whether we become taken over by the "other" within ourselves. In a way, we unwittingly become its instrument, and relate to this power which is presumably greater than us.

You identify the kinds of actions you took in the past that led to negativity, compulsive, and addictive behaviors. This conscious awareness shines the light on essential choices to make if you desire to come to terms with your autonomous complexes since they enlighten you to relationship patterns that have been contaminated by projection. Contemplating your relationship to a power greater than you, (the numinous) is valuable, but it requires your participation and devoted attention. To relate to the "other" within, in a "spiritual" way, entails careful self-reflection. To paraphrase Jung, "Religion, as the Latin word denotes, is a rebinding to one's source as a form of luminosity or light consciousness. Rudolph Otto (author of "The Idea of the Holy") aptly terms the mystical component of religious as "the numinous."

A religious attitude helps us embody the dynamic of self-control. But we know that connecting to the numinous is not only an activity requiring strength of character, but one that necessitates special agency. It is not something we do with will power alone or by random and haphazard acts of personal force. On the contrary, the numinous grabs hold of us. Its power dominates, and controls us since we are always its target rather than the originator. The numinous, whatever its source may be, is always encountered as an extreme experience of an autonomous energy wrecking havoc to bring us wholeness. We each must reckon with this force for God that comes our way to instigate radical change.

The Move toward the Numinous

To treat things spiritually is to develop a more holistic attitude towards our life experiences. We realize that we are an inseparably amalgamation and one with our universe and each other. But this reality is not how most of us live. Many relate to the other as if they are merely objects, without intrinsic value, and for our own gain. Instead of relating to our experience in a literal, linear, and materialistic way, contact with the numinous has us experience what is most alive in the other. It provides a vision of how the "material world" is actually our creation mental construct behind which is infused with spirit. The consequence of cultivating a spiritual attitude is that we have a numinous experience in daily life. We get in touch with a relationship with the other within ourselves. The very cosmos in which we live transforms in the process of inner work. We encounter the magic of every moment, as our life experience is nothing other than a constant experience of the numinous power of life itself.

An Inquiry

Do we add consciousness to our experience of God or do we continue to experience the numinous indirectly as an unconscious and problematic aspect of life? The answer to this auspicious question plainly establishes your future relationships for better or worse. This is why Jung's main interest in analytic work was not merely concerned with the treatment of neuroses, but with the move toward the numinous in the lives of his patients.

The approach to building a spiritual life is the real thrust of depth therapy inasmuch as it encourages a connection to the realm of true behavior modification seen through the lens of mystical experiences. We release psychology and psychotherapy from a predominate focus on psychopathology. Even the very notion of human disease takes on a spiritual character as we see the numinous even at work in our physical and psychological symptoms. We encounter the numinous often when we hit rock bottom. The seemingly negative aspects of our life and relational experiences reveal itself to us as an aspect of the divine operating from within. An experience of this autonomous other within us can potentially show the way to a life-transforming experience felt as being genuinely in touch with the authenticity of our true nature.

People in contemporary culture often feel alone in the inner world. They assume that there is nothing inside or not much really there. They assume that it is all in the imagination, something fabricate or make believe. This is the best expression of our Source but is not to be confused with an unconscious identification with God, otherwise known as "inflation." We think we have made-up everything from our imagination and that nothing would happen if we did not do something. However there is a source of creation outside of our will and personal power.

At the root of many psychological problems is the fear that we are alone in an isolated universe. This is not true but this sense of deep loneliness is a replica for exactly how the Creator must have felt before the creation. The logic of creation is an act of reaching out and connecting with other. This is supported through psychological work and soul making that encourages you to ponder the other within. When you do this work, something unexpectedly changes. What happens is that you have a direct experience of the numinous. You reach a pinnacle where it becomes an experience of your Higher Self in relationship to your Source.

The Dark Other Within

When we become on familiar terms with and form a relationship with the mysterious other within us, we can directly experience the light of the numinous energy. As Jung emphasized throughout his work, it is when we bring the darkness to consciousness that we are enlightened. In fact, coming to terms with the dark other within us is enlightenment since illumination from within develops a strong sense of authority. We come to terms with who we are, embody our innate wholeness, and form a conscious connection with the divine. Developing an intelligence of our own innate wholeness sustains the relationship to the numinous through out life and into death and beyond. This act offers each person a direct connection to an inner power within without becoming overwhelmed by, identified with, or possessed by this powerful transpersonal power.

Paradoxically, the other within is ultimately an aspect of me, the facet that I need to embrace. I face up to the other within and naturally develop a perspective other than it. The other within teaches me how to say "no" and set a boundary. Like an extrasensory and intuitive workout that helps me to exert the very muscle, I need to develop. I engage with the other within to reinforce what is most empowering rather than projecting my weakness and fragility out onto others.

Relating to the other within is the most essential way you can participate in the transformation of your life via the archetypal power inside. You bring it into partnership. The more you engage with this part of yourself, the more you tend to experience the sacred marriage of alchemy that is only truly available within. At this point the "other" is no longer "other." You have become integrated, one with yourself and assimilate it into the wholeness of your being. In essence this is why you are here. This is you're your "Incarnation" is all about.

Often when darkness is dominant in life, there is hope. You discover some inner illumination. The light is potentially most accessible when inner sonar is available. What happens within me, the microcosm, is a reflection of the same process happening collectively, in the macrocosm and vice versus. When related to consciously, this shadowy figure awakens us to a more comprehensive state of wholeness!

Human unconsciousness plays out on the world stage from time immemorial. However, we each have the potential to activate the light of consciousness in our world. Thus, my individuation process serves as a vehicle for a shared advancement in both collective and personal relationships. Your individuation process parallels the choices you make when you become intimately acquainted with the dark other within. This conscious relationship within also empowers us to deal with darkness in the world, and notice how that influences our relationships for good or ill. The more we embrace the other within and bring it into our life in constructive ways, the more we are able to re-enchant our communities by creating positive relationships from the inside out.

SECTION TWO:
Family Relationships

CHAPTER ONE:
The Family Life Cycle

⚜

The family is the foundation of all relationships.

The family life cycle includes the emotional, relational, and intellectual stages we pass through from infancy into retirement, old age, and death. As a member of a family unit, we have our own individual passage through the life cycle. We also have a shared journey with our extended family and relatives. In each phase, we face the daily challenges of personal growth while engaging in our family's life circumstances. The family is the foundation of all relationships. Each member is an integral part of the family unit. Interconnections are strong, yet flexible. There is built-in resilience throughout the various changes in roles and responsibilities. We also need to build extra familial relations and friendships. These relationships help us face new challenges, build skills, achieve fulfillment, and manifest potential. The art is in the attention we give to each facet of our relationship. Love provides the inner strength to make it all worthwhile.

Not every person passes through these stages effortlessly or well. Circumstances like divorce, addiction, abandonment, severe illness, financial problems, or the death of a spouse can have an effect on the overall health of a family. Fortunately, we can develop relationship skills in spite of what has happened to our family, or what was lacking in our earlier development.

The basic phases we go through in the family life cycle are dependence, independence, and interdependence such as coupling, and if marriage, then parenting babies through adolescents and launching children into adult autonomy. We have our relationships with extended family, peers, co-workers, and then retirement, senior years, aging, and preparing for death. Family relationships that we can count on, give our life both breath and depth. We teach young people the craft of family solidarity by helping them understand the family life cycle. We encourage them to look at the reality and needs of each phase while educating the child on what it actually takes to create healthy family relationships.

Mastering the skills of each stage fosters successful passage from one age appropriate development to the next. If we do not master the skills, we may move on but life is tenuous at best. In the next phase, we are more prone to having ongoing difficulty with our relationships. If left unchecked negative behaviors lead to chronic relationship conflicts that persist throughout life. However, making good decisions helps us to face the future with hope and confidence. It is virtually impossible to have a positive relationship when there is on going disagreement and inconsistency. At each new juncture, negative attitude, dysfunctional patterns, and insecurities persist. When living under these circumstances we have trouble facing family difficulties. Research on healthy family bonds suggests that when there is a solid base successful transitioning occurs naturally. These family characteristics also help to prevent disease, stress-related disorders, and early onset of childhood obesity, addictive behaviors, and mental illness.

As a parent or child, brother or sister, husband or wife we are interconnected with our family. Our bodies and spirits linked by blood and united in love. Family and kinship bonds have an effect on all subsequent relationships. These family experiences influence who we are and who we will grow to be. We are predisposed to thrive during life transitions, if our family bonds have been positive. If the family foundation is solid then we are likely to develop independence while maintaining strong relations. This supports each person in the family and allows smooth passage throughout each stage, from dependence, to independence, and into the complexity of interdependence. There will be challenges. The better we understand the challenges, the more we can count on the family and they can count on us, when the going gets rough.

We discover that many disruptions in relationships are rooted in a problematic attachment to early caregivers. The dynamics we learn in childhood either help or hurt the way we handle other attachments. We undergo many changes through out the life cycle. The stress of daily living and coping with adversity can delay the usual changeover to the next phase of growth within the family. On the other hand, we may move on but continue to encounter disappointment, and difficulty. We flounder through life without the appropriate skills to succeed at interpersonal relationships.

Object relations theory developed out of the need to understand why humans struggle with interpersonal relationships and how this influences mental health. Psychoanalytic psychology describes the development of a human psyche in terms of the negative impact of upbringing. Often bonds to parents are problematic. As we grow up, to survive we must be in relation to care giving others in our surroundings. Theories developed around how object relations form. The studies demonstrate how people relate to others and situations in similar ways that they perceived being treated in childhood. This influences all subsequent relational experiences.

Thus, the basic tenant of object relations theory is that the behaviors and dealings of significant others towards us and how we received these messages are powerful and form our ongoing view of other people. For example, a grown person who experienced neglect or abuse in infancy will likely anticipate similar actions in future intimacy. If you were neglected or abused in childhood, other people you encounter as an adult, who remind you of the negligent or cruel person from your past, (frequently a parent), may cause you to assume similar treatment. These images of people turn into "objects" in the unconscious psyche. The image of the parent is a symbol of that negative person within the mind and becomes like a permanent, negative mirror-reflection. Thus, you may transmit onto adult relationships these internalized, harmful attitudes. This becomes the image used by your subconscious mind to predict how other people are likely to behave toward you in social relationships and intimate interactions.

Object relations theory provides a way to understand our relationships with others since it reveals the way we form attachment. This tells a lot about how we will engage in subsequent relationship, since the patterns we learn from the past become identified with the predominate influences that shaped us. The outlook we have toward significant others, according to this theory, are deeply rooted in our early attachments with our parents, especially our mothers. Objects refer to people, aspects of people, or corporeal items that symbolically represent either a person or part of a person. Object relations, then, are our relationships to those people and things associated with them.

The object relations theory is a derivative psychoanalytic practice as developed during the late 1920s and 1930s, and became all the rage during the 1970s. Karl Abraham, Margaret Mahler, and Melanie Klein are among those recognized with the original concept behind object relations theory. The early advocates of object relationships used it in psychoanalytic for the treatment of irrational fears and anxiety. This perspective is helpful in understanding blocks to intimacy since the difficulties that arise in relationships are principally those that center on important people and problematic connections with them.

Each person forms their own internal objects by the influence of patterns of behavior in early childhood. These patterns emerge from our repeated subjective experience of our home of origin. The family is our first relational environment. We all internalize our subjective experience of growing up in a particular family. However, what actually happened may or may not be a precise representation of the real, external others. In the theory, "objects" are typically internalized images of one's mother, father, or primary caregiver. Although they could also consist of parts of a person, for instance an infant relating to the mother's breast, or images inside one's inner world (one's internalized or fantasy image of others). Positive experiences with others in the future can reshape these early patterns.

Nevertheless, these internalized objects often persist. They exert a strong influence throughout life. "Objects" although sounds rather mechanical, is the term used in object relations theory for the people originally internalized as functioning within the infant's mind as the image of a "part object." For instance, the infant relates to the breast that feeds it when hungry as the "good breast," while the hungry infant who finds no breast is in relation to the "bad breast." The theory suggests that with a "good enough mothering" and a "facilitating environment" that serve as a "part object" in the infant's development functions in due course to transform the infants connection into a grasp of whole objects. This capacity dovetails with the child's ability to tolerate uncertainty and ambivalence when dealing with future relations.

Object relations theory understands that the child learns to deal with ambiguity by being able to see "part objects" since the child has the ability to see that both the "good" and the "bad" breast are a part of the same mother and her body. A whole object is a person, as she actually exists, with all of the positive and negative traits that she embodies. The aim of object relations therapy is to help the person move through the stages of development that were unsuccessful in childhood. When a person negotiates the developmental stages well they are more able to incorporate their whole of a person. This includes integrating the good and bad, to relate in a secure and confident way. The relationship is able to contain both good and bad feelings so the child comes to experience mother as a whole object.

An internal object is the psychological and emotional impression of a person we hold onto when the person is not physically present. The image is an internalized representation of how we come to remember the person. This image influences how we view the person in real life, over time. Consequently, the internal object greatly influences our relationship with the person that it represents. To grow in relationship to another, we must first develop what is termed "object-constancy." This is the mental capacity to hold a person in our mind when they are not with us. We learn to know that people or objects do not alter just for the reason that they are not present to us. We develop trust that when they are unavailable, or we cannot see the person or object we how the conviction that they are still there for us.

Infants begin to learn object constancy when their parent leaves a room, is absent for a moment, and then returns. As children mature, they begin to spend more time away from their parents. Separation anxiety, fear of neglect, and the trepidation of abandonment are universal emotions. These may often occur when the child is unsuccessful at mounting a sense of object constancy. Indeed, anything we do with another requires some dexterity in object constancy. The result of trusting another give us the added sense of confidence that arises when we have the capacity to hold an internal connection with another person when not immediately present. When we feel that these internalized objects match up with the reality of our external connections to the real person, we feel supported by this essential ability to trust our significant relationships.

Family Systems Theory

Family systems theory emerged from the belief that individuals initially learn to develop self-identity within the family. We discover our sense of self in community with those we live with. Here we either become skilled or not at dealing with emotions within our family. How it feels to grow up in a family is a personal experience, unique to each member since it provides the template for how we engage others. The family matrix is the crucible where we learn to function in future relationships. It is possible to learn to have a deeper understanding of ourselves when we look at the particular role we may have played in our family emotional system.

Understanding our family system supports healing energies in the home. Knowledge of each individual's role in the family offers a platform to express natural emotions in appropriate ways. We encourage expression of thoughts and feelings in an open and respectful system, since we can tolerate both negative and positive reactions to events. Under these conditions, the family dynamics are flexible, cooperative, and mutual. Positive family relationships lead to good friendships. Work, social, and community relationships benefit when growing up in a family system that is working well. The family systems approaches include many variations on strategically addressing the complex themes that arise in families. The root assumption of the model is that by working intentionally on direct communication and positive interactions within the family will influence the overall system.

Salvador Minuchin is a family therapist born and raised in San Salvador, Entre Ríos, Argentina. He developed Structural Family Therapy, which addresses problems within a family by charting the relationships between family members, or between subsets within the family. These charts represent power dynamics as well as the boundaries between different subsystems. The therapist tries to disrupt dysfunctional relationships within the family, and help them to settle into a healthier pattern.

According to Minuchin, the basis for family therapy is to address problems in the family system, and not the behavior of one individual. He believed that the family system is the problem and based his therapeutic model on this assumption since a family is a system that operates through "transactional patterns." The more a family repeats transactions the more they establish patterns of "how, when, and to whom, these patterns underpin the system" (1974).

The overall goal in structural family therapy is the reorganization of the family's relational patterns. The therapy involves creating an effective family chain of command with parents in charge, but working in tandem. This is the rationale for what brings about a sense of family interconnectedness. However, enmeshed families are encouraged to strengthen boundaries that allow for healthy limits such as the demarcation of where one individual begins and ends. This strategy highlights the needs of each member and yet set on firm guidelines that increase the clarity of boundaries. A family structure needs a solid base that fosters appropriate boundaries, supports intimate bonds, and provides a healthy structure to raise a family. This cannot happen when negative dynamics continue to occur.

Strategic Family Therapy

In the 1950s, therapists began to study the environment of a patient, not just the patient himself. The theory of strategic therapy states that the patient's symptoms are a result of attempts by family members to correct what they consider "problematic" behavior. Haley's strategic therapy focuses on short-term, targeted efforts to solve a specific problem. Jay Haley's (1984) strategic family therapy proposes that symptoms in an individual are an attempt at adapting to the family situation. Symptoms of dysfunction are purposeful in maintaining homeostasis in the family hierarchy, as the family transitions through various stages in its life cycle.

This adaptation is necessary, because it is the way each member learns to adapt and becomes accustom to living within a particular family system. These dynamics arise over time because of family relationship patterns and power struggles. In this model, the therapist must take on the role of director or authority figure, to develop strategies to intervene in the problematic patterns.

Haley's approach redefines the family's symptoms as unskillful attempts at communication or resolving conflict. In some cases, the symptoms are warning signs that an individual family member is in trouble. The family needs insight into the "symptom" to acknowledge it as an opportunity for creative problem solving that provides solutions and promote development of healthy patterns. Strategic family therapy is brief, and focuses on the present. The therapist thinks about the family in terms of units, items, and components rather than as isolated individuals. The notion of individuals embedded in an interconnected matrix replaces the literal and linear idea of cause and effect.

The Strategic Family therapist uses a number of techniques, such as directives, behavior modifications, and paradoxical interventions. Family therapy is advantageous because it challenges the family as a whole to experience new ways of interacting rather than blaming one person for the dysfunction. The family learns to have different experiences and to think about their life in the affirmative and creates improved interactions both in and outside the family.

Trans-generational Family Therapy

The concept of differentiation, the ability to make a distinction between self and other, is the formation of an independent self. The ability to recognize the difference between emotions and thought patterns supports each member of the family as they learn to react well to daily stress and sudden crisis. This premise is the foundation of Murray Bowen's trans-generational family therapy. He believed that people controlled by their emotions, and without boundaries, are not able to respond well or rationally in stressful situations. Bowen thought that the family emotional system reacts to what he considered a category of innate or chronic anxiety in humans. In families, this anxiety is a natural part of a struggle between individuality and togetherness. Bowen is best known for his innovative work on genealogy. He used the genogram technique, as a way of diagramming several (classically three) generations of family relationships.

Triangulation occurs when a dyadic relationship becomes too stressful or conflicted. A third person is involved as a way of diffusing the tension. This typically occurs in families, often with a husband and wife (or two partners) and one of the children. The more family members are interdependent, rather than co-dependent, the less likely they are to triangulate. Trans-generational therapy typically involves helping people learn to recognize emotional patterns that lead to triangulation, through better insight into how they inherited these patterns through generational transmission.

Attachment theory

Attachment theory describes the dynamics of creating and continuing relationships between humans. The key principle is that an infant needs to develop a relationship with at least one primary caregiver for psychosocial and emotional development to occur across a normal spectrum. Attachment theory emphasizes the importance of the child's early relationship with a significant other, the crucial role this plays, and the influence of the parent on the child's overall development.

Immediately after World War II, psychiatrists found that homeless and orphaned children presented many difficulties reconnecting to others and building relationship as they moved into adolescence and adulthood. The issue was so alarming that the UN asked psychoanalyst John Bowlby to write a pamphlet describing the negative consequences on childhood development when early bonding is not present. He was the first to discuss the growing concern of maternal deprivation from a clinical perspective. Attachment theory grew out of his subsequent work on the issues he raised around the critical phase of healthy attachment.

Bowlby's research found that attachment occurs in the child's experiences with caregivers in the first three years of life. Attachment Theory is the foundation for Object Relations Therapy and developed experiments to study this phenomenon. Bowlby used the "stranger situation" experiment with infants involving a methodical procedure of leaving a child alone in a room to assess the features of their attachment to parents. Infants only attach in positive ways to individuals who are sensitive and responsive in social interaction with them. When an infant begins to crawl and walk, they begin to use attachment figures, like parents, or familiar people, as a secure base from which to explore the world and a safe place to return.

Bowlby observed that positive responses from the caregivers lead to healthy patterns of attachment. These patterns foster internal working models that provide guidance and help create the individual's perceptions, emotions, thoughts, and expectations in later relationships. J. Cassidy (1999) suggests that separation anxiety or grief following the loss of an attachment figure is a normal and adaptive response for an attached infant. These behaviors may have evolved because they increase the probability of the child's ongoing survival since positive attachments result in pro-survival.

Experiential Family Therapy

All people are born into a condition where the struggle for continued existence is primary. The infant must reach out and forge a connection between themselves and their parents. The infant adopt survival techniques to protect them self from danger and life threatening situations. They must learn to attune to the communications from their mother and family.

Existential therapy helps the therapist alter the overt and covert messages between family members. Each member learns techniques that affect their body, mind, and feelings and promotes congruence. When the therapist validates each person's inherent self-worth the underlying mistrust or problematic patterns begin to surface. Virginia Satir is one of the few women family systems pioneers and believed that every human being has innate worth, and that all individuals and families have the potential to flourish. She had much in common with person-centered psychologist Carl Rogers, in her basic optimistic view of humanity.

Satir viewed any symptom or problem within an individual family member as a creative striving for growth in the family structure. Her approach was interested in not only what a family does to maintain a negative balance, but also challenged the family to take a new perspective toward the harmful dynamic. One ways was to help the family rethink the "family rules." She noticed that the family rules could be overt or covert. The essential aspect of her family therapy is to help the members clarify these rules, to examine how they affect individuals, and to bolster hope for the family in the midst of struggle.

Virginia Satir was legendary for her use of affection and employed touch as a way of promoting family growth. One of her favorite techniques was family sculpting. It involved her placing the family in different positions to facilitate an awareness of their feelings, roles, and communication styles. The field of family therapy and systems theory has developed many extremely useful approaches to a vast range of difficulties that arise in families. These include eating disorders, domestic violence, substance abuse, and juvenile behavior problems, to mention only a few.

CHAPTER TWO:
The Baby and Family

❧

*We are born with qualities such as affection, warmth,
tenderness, care and concern for our offspring.*

British child psychoanalyst, Donald Winnicott (1971) believed "There is no such thing as a baby, there is a baby and someone." Winnicott captures the actuality of the infant's genuine need for human connection. He noted this to be the essential psychological factor of future psychological health and happiness. Winnicott encouraged other therapist to understand the mother's primary role as the essential nurturing presence for her infant. Care giving and "good enough mothering" often require that he teach the mother positive ways to connect with her baby.

Mother, parents, and caregivers help infants mature by giving the infant full attention. He proposed that most mothers are incorrect to expect baby is to be a separate person from the moment infant takes his/ her first breathe. It takes time to secure a sense of self-identity and this forms slowly with the mother and then with other's within the family. When this transition happens successfully for the baby, the family will also feel secure with the infant's arrival.

Relating with the new baby is both rewarding and challenging since it requires patience, understanding, and putting the other first. As human's we are born with qualities like affection, warmth, tenderness, care, and concern for our offspring. Innate nurturing habits are human characteristics and emerged in our ancient ancestors before the advent of fire making or Stone Age tools. Since the human infant is so utterly helpless, these nurturing care giving qualities developed to insure the continuation of the species.

Most of the first year the baby is motionless and can hardly crawl, walk, or speak. An infant is limited in the ability to take action. The basic goal is for survival. The infant expresses a need for food, comfort, warmth, and affection by crying out or wriggling. The weakness of the human infant is vastly different compared to other primates who can fully grip onto the mother, at birth. The human baby cannot securely take hold of mother and this result in the caregiver having to hold and carry the baby for long periods. Seventy-five per cent of the infant's brain develops after delivery, resulting in intensive childcare. No baby can continue to live without the efforts of another person. We know from personal experience that it requires years of growth before a human infant can care for him/herself. A baby's defenselessness is a result of undeveloped growth and the inability to reason and make decisions.

To develop into the next stage, the child requires internalizing a sense of ongoing support and care so strength can flow from a fountain of knowing that tenderness and love is available. Life itself provides the mother as a starting place. This basic need is "good enough mothering" since it demonstrates that reliable caregivers can augment the love when the mother is absent. The Nurturing Mother is a profound physical and psychological archetype that is present in all cultures, at all times. Artists create images of the nurturing figure of mother and child with the intention of displaying this sacred act since it ensures the perpetuation of the species as manifested in the universal response of a mother nurturing her child.

Sally's Story

Sally, a woman in her mid-thirties and mother of an infant came for holistic life coaching. She needed guidance concerning managing her transition from a successful professional to a stay home mother. I asked how she would like to proceed with the session, she blurted out, "I want my baby to be better off than I was." Sally paused, "I want to know we can grow and be happy as a new family." Sally was anxious that she did not have the right stuff. She confided that she had suffered terribly as a young child during her parent's divorce. Sally was apprehensive that she might repeat the same dysfunctional patterns with her husband and child. I encouraged Sally to challenge this perspective.

Sally had doubts as to whether she had the right stuff. She reported feeling depressed and worried. She asked, "Do I have the self-control and resources that will allow me to nurture my baby? I had a good pregnancy, but now I feel down in the dumps. The real test is whether I will be a good mother. Will I be able to continue to support my baby's normal development? I did well during the pregnancy, but what now, after the delivery?"

Sally asked for help as she worked to develop a new kind of self-esteem. I suggested that she could learn new skills and advance her family's quality of life. Self-awareness, learning innovative coping skills, and building positive relationships in the present is a good place to start. Life coaching, spiritual direction and family counseling are avenues that I suggested might help her gain clarity on questions that arise with her new baby. These supports can help her deal with other problematic issues, from her past such as divorce, death of a loved one, losing a job, or being a part of a nontraditional family structure.

Sally came for coaching to get in touch with how she viewed her role as mother. She said, "As mother, I am a physical and psychological container for my infant. This role emerges out of love, but I also have fear and doubt. My purpose as mother is to nurture my baby." Sally was surprised that she had such strong conviction, even though she felt a bit unsure of this confidence within herself. Sally was shocked when she said, "I know every mother has everything she needs to give to her little one care and love." I echoed that she was on the right track for sure. Sally continued, "I have arms to hold, breasts with plenty of milk to feed and comfort. My body desires to share life, give warmth and offer care." Sally and I discussed the reality of motherhood and explored how as a mother, she and her infant is a couple. You and your baby Tina evolve together. The art of mothering is to help create a functional dance and partnership with your infant.

Still a bit unsure of this capacity within her, Sally asked, "If every mother has everything her little one needs, why should I still have doubts about nurturing my baby. I had a good pregnancy." Nevertheless, Sally continued to worry. She said, "I feel that the real test is ahead." I wonder, "Will I be able to continue to support Tina's normal development after the delivery?" Sally uttered a new belief; "My relationship with my baby does not evolve in isolation, but is an interconnected and mutually engaging process since we are life partners in a magical duet. Sally challenged herself to observe this dance between her and her baby in the life coaching process and became a confident mother.

The early bond between mother and baby provides insight into the baby's preferences. Mother learns how to dance with the baby, notices the shifting moods, physical needs, and relational styles, and responds accordingly. It is not possible to understand the human baby's developmental needs without considering the infant as a partner and not merely a separate human being. When the baby senses a disconnection with the "other" or mother, problematic attachment patterns arise resulting in troubles in future relationships.

No baby has survived without the help and support of another human. Perhaps the possible exceptions are few isolated and unproven reports of feral children raised by animals. Since the few individuals were abnormal in their development, it is safe to conclude that a baby who develops without the care of another human will be abnormal. When we speak about babies, or about their needs, we must also speak about the needs of the mother or the "other" who take her place as caregiver.

We all cross the threshold into the world with similar urges. The urge for positive attachments is essential if we are to get the emotional nurturing we need from others to survive. A baby needs to elicit tenderness and a caring response toward them from others, especially from their mothers. Without this capacity, the baby is in deep distress and potentially life threatening danger. Everything concerning an infant hopefully arouses a nurturing reaction from caregivers.

Sally reported that she felt these emotions awakening when she was breast-feeding her baby girl. She said, "Tina is tiny, soft, so vulnerable and dependent. Her head is wobbly, her smile so charming. Her need for my care and protection is palpable. When she cries, it causes me alarm but my anxiety is actually a call to give her my love."

Sally felt ready to trust since she knows when and why her baby is in distress. She observes that Tina may be in pain, hungry, wet, cranky, or disturbed. She reports, "I am a mother that is sensitive and uses suitable responses to Tina. My effort is to be of assistance to my baby."

Sally was encouraged to take a good look at her new role. All mothers must develop a relationship with their baby; it does not just happen automatically. The reality is that the mother carries her baby for nine months in her body. However, baby is initially a new arrival into the family, and causes upheaval since the family needs to make adjustments. As the coaching session ended, Sally felt reassured. She shared "my baby's life is part of me now." The take home message was that awareness of interconnection as an important person who makes it possible for her baby to have a secure life both during conception and as the child grows.

Non-Verbal communication

The mother must engage in the universal "forgotten language."

Shortly after birth, a baby begins to smile, to make pleasant and happy sounds, to recognize and to explore his/her mother, and then to laugh, reach out, touch, and hug. All of these responses increase mother's tender attachment to her infant. Mother indicates that she likes being with her baby and that baby likes mother and wants to be with her. Mother and baby bond naturally. Nevertheless, this does not work well if they act like strangers. Bonding assures mother is a friendly, social being, and that baby has human emotions. This provides a non-verbal sense of communion.

Mother and baby are structurally divided and without a placental attachment after birth, but they are not physically or emotionally separate. The art of mothering evolves to ensure continuation of life. Mother and baby is a nursing couple in close, physical contact day and night. This couple is reactive to each other's moods and feelings. A baby smiles when his/her mother smiles, laughs at his/her sounds of delight, becomes upset when his/her mother is upset, anxious, distant, angry, or not available when he/she wants her.

The mother-infant relationship, because of its physical intimacy, is by nature a powerful-shared reliance. The requirement for harmony in functioning, collaboration, understanding, and recognition may well be the most mutual of all human relationships. No other relationship, including that of adult intimacy requires the degree of patience and care needed to attune successfully to another person. Since it is first nonverbal, and then partially verbal for several years, a baby cannot inform you with verbal communication. The mother must engage in this universal "forgotten language." Those non-verbal ways of communicating with another human, that in infancy are the only way to communicate loving feelings to another. For a baby, the relationship with mother is instinctively communal. The baby's introduction to humanity, and the first human relationship, is with mother. This relationship sets the tone for all future relationships. For the mother, it is an opportunity to nurture and cherish the life of another.

Sally engaged life coaching to help her acknowledge how she shares and participates in helping to develop a firm foundation for another human being. The coaching encouraged her to see that by so doing, her relationships mature. A baby is unaware of either the positive and negative effect he/she may have on mother. However, the baby, without knowing it, relies on millions of years of human evolution. Baby needs to elicit the care giving response of mother in order to receive the tenderness and nurturing that ensures survival. The human mother evolved to provide her children just this security.

The Survival Skill of Connection

We nurture our infants to support the survival skill of building connection. Human DNA provides the basis of our instinct for self-preservation. It is in our hardwiring to support the continuation of the species. We are born to feel tenderness toward the life we create. The capacity to nurture this life, both before, and after birth is essential to the child's survival. Preceding the birth, unconscious nurturing procedures happens beneath the surface. For many conscious "mothers to be", nurturing can take on the form of self-care, giving up smoking, drugs or alcohol, diet, exercise, and stress reduction. This process of sustaining the new life within follows a natural track. The mother's body instinctively provides accommodation as well as required conditions that permit the growing embryo to develop and be ready for birth. Even unwanted pregnancies that go to full term can deliver healthy infants. For many individuals, the process prior to birth is crucial and may be the only time in their lives when they receive care in a positive way.

Human gestation does not end with delivery of the baby since a large part of the nurturing process must continue after birth. Although it is hereditarily and organically uninterrupted with the process prior to birth, it is regrettably not automatic or assured. The mother can choose, and be under the influence of others to suspend being a part of this succession. It is probable that in human's early development hormonal, instinctive, and reflexive processes in their reaction to their newborns guided mothers much more. As we developed our modern brain, the care of infants and young children became a conscious activity. This occurred as consciousness changed traditions, ethnicity and society's mores. The care of infants and children became a civilizing process prejudiced by socioeconomic conditions and regulated by cultural norms.

Many babies in modern society are no longer cared for in ways that meet their needs, instead in ways that make the baby adjust to the mother's world. We are a species that is genetically designed to nurture our young. Our capacity for consciousness and awareness in our care for infants is paramount in assuring a positive future development for humanity. We need to support our parents and caregivers so that they can better understand, value, and give primacy to the newborn's need for nurturing. We can encourage mothers to nurture their babies. However, awareness is a double-edged sword. Society conditions many parents to believe that biological mothering is inconsequential, superfluous, and an arduous and even inequitable interruption on women's lives and careers. Some even hold the belief that excessive nurturing "indulges" our baby and leads to spoiled child syndrome. The question remains, what kind of early care giving is most harmful or helpful to our child's development?

We can be certain that from time immemorial mother and child held a place of honor. For the basic continuation of the tribe, mothers, mothering, and a baby's need for care found respect as the main concern of the tribe or clan. If this had not been the fact, we would not have survived as a species that held mothering to be the primary task for survival. Mother and baby today cannot live alone without support nor could the primal mother and child have survived without the support of the community.

Ingrained in the mother is a capacity to be concerned about the life she generates from her own body. This response is the definition of a nurturing mother-infant interaction since it is love. This loving care is the model for all human relationships. As the underpinning for human civilization, it allows the infant to be born in an undeveloped condition, and to develop his/her functions and body in terms of relating to the care giving of the others. This nurturing process, based on the union of mother and child, helps create people who naturally function in harmony and accord with others. The human species would be sociopathic and even unrecognizably antisocial if we were born without the need to give and receive love through parental nurturing.

In our fast-paced culture, many a baby lives, and develops without his/her mother's attention. Much of the human affection, that only the love of a mother can give, is not available. This is often due to mother's hectic schedule or some other compromising factor in her situation. Some babies may respond in a negative way to such a lack of early nurturing, and not develop to be the kind of human they were intended. They must get used to and fit the surrogate that has replaced innate mothering from biological mother. Formula, pacifiers, cribs, playpens, security objects, and stand-in caregivers are not the same as the direct presence of the birth mother. Children raised in this kind of hands off environment become different from adults who grow up in relation to a nurturing mother.

Children raised with inappropriate and defective nurturing grow up devoid of the internalized ability to build positive, non-manipulative relationships. Kindheartedness is an attribute that contributes to the ability to give and receive love. We learn affection from the way others were affectionate towards us. As we give our tender feelings to our child, they learn to give love in return. They do not grow well without it since this kind of love is what makes us human.

CHAPTER THREE:
Creating Relationships with Infants

⚜

Babies are sponges and take in everything around them.

When needs are met with care, when significant adults respond immediately to infants' signals of distress, normal babies become "securely attached" by 12 to 18 months. Securely attached babies are more likely to reach out and call for an adult when stressed. They also tend to be more compliant and cooperative with adult requests as compared to "insecurely attached" infants (those who have received less sensitive and responsive care). Most securely attached babies grow up to play in friendly and accommodating ways. Insecurely attached babies may later become bullies, victims, or social misfits, or loners. Parents who are dependable and teachers who interact with consistent, quality care do make a difference in how a child will begin to bond with others and form attachments.

Babies are sponges and take in everything around them. Babies look to their special adults for social cues. If you, a special adult in the life of a 10-month-old, play the game pee-a-boo, you are supporting the development of attachments. Try this now. Stand in front of the child with a cloth over your face, and then suddenly reveal your face, a baby will look up and scan your face to see if he/she should crawl toward you or turn back and cry. Babies use this "social referencing" technique to figure out what is safe and what is scary.

Stranger Anxiety: Fear of strangers is a typical behavior for many babies as they near one year, though some feel this more intensely than others do. Your calm reassurance, close presence, and care in not forcing children to get close to or interact with strangers will help carry everyone through this social phase.

Tune in to Temperaments: Take time to learn the feeding and toileting rhythms of each baby, and then go with the flow. Some babies just get hungry more often than others do. Many babies need holding and carrying around for months after birth. Others do not. Some babies like bouncing while others prefer gentle rocking. Babies will adapt more easily to the social rules and regulations of your nursery, when you are able to tune in to their unique temperaments.

Building Toddler's Socialization Skills

The toddler who loudly says, "No!" when you call out "Lunchtime!" may well dash over to eat if you choose cheerful emphasis, "Yummy, good veggies!"

Socialization Struggles

Growing minds make toddlers very aware of the confusion in their lives. They go back and forth between wanting to be a "big person" and needing to be a "baby." Toddlers are ambivalent creatures. They fight for independence, show social awareness in playful interactions, and yet keep the loving caregiver within range when they need to check –in for safety, love, and security. The toddler scurries away from "mother" and then toward her, these darting moves between independence and connection are appropriate ways a toddler handles this stage of development. The child needs to run to you for comfort and cuddling, but they also want to be able to do things for themselves and to scamper about impulsively.

Rules are important for keeping toddlers safe. However, children this age may react with great resistance and indignation. Let toddlers know you are there for them. We support toddler's social skills by becoming aware when our toddler is on an emotional seesaw. We support our toddler finding balance especially when oscillating between obeying rules and deciding whether to disobey them. Use soothing and loving touches often circumvents the need for verbal battles. The toddler who loudly says, "No!" when you call out "Bath time!" may well dash over to the tub if you choose cheerful emphasis, "Warm water with lots of bubbles and a rubber ducky!"

Keep Rules Simple for toddlers

Set fair, firm rules about personal rights by making your home safety-proof. This helps avoid fusses over safety rules. When plying with another child, set the boundaries right away by allowing no hitting or grabbing a toy from another child. Also, set sensible rules so that each child gets a few minutes with a well-liked toy or activity. Remember: Toddlers need a lot of practice, and many reminders, as they are learning the social skills of sharing!

Help Toddlers Focus

Gain children's attention before asking them to do something. For instance, you might say, "Look at the big ball, Rick! Now roll the ball to Bobby." When you help a child focus first, he will be more likely to understand and comply. When you tune into children's needs based on observations of each child's unique personality, your reward will be a more cooperative, friendly, and peaceful child.

Be Patient and Supportive

Most toddlers are strong on will and wants, but weak on skills and patience. Try to stay positive when children seem to defy suggestions and rules. Encourage toddlers to cooperate. You might to encourage cooperation when a child is picking at her spaghetti by saying, "I bet you can twirl your fork and pick up lots of noodles!" Most important, never shame toddlers for eating with their hands or pressure children into early toileting.

Do It Myself: connection, independence and flexibility

Parents who want to encourage good decision making in their children must also encourage one of this skill's important components: individual autonomy. How does one proceed? When we raise children to have positive relationships, we do not push them to succeed at all cost. By stepping back and letting out children "live their lives" and by not shielding them from every possible hurt, fosters confidence and the ability to build relationships. Some have characterized current trends in childrearing as espousing the opposite style of childrearing.

The recent overflow of parenting books, blogs, and information sites often confuses the real question of what is good enough parenting. Even the experts cannot come to a definitive explanation. Of course, we cannot really blame the authors. To sell a book, authors have to convince publishers that they have something unique and important to offer. This often means they need to stand out from the competition. They do this by emphasizing their dissimilarity and confuse what is best. Some do this by overstating the obvious or even obscuring what simply works.

Many young parents are in the dark about child rearing. I know that my husband and I certainly were perplexed! Rigid identification with one view on the subject of parenting is not always the best way. No way is always right. We may find a different strategy that works by using common sense and establishing a firm foundation from which children can find root and yet fly.

Parenting Styles

Parents discover that the advice they are given is often opposite from what they are sensing from within their own set of values and beliefs. This causes the parents to be in conflict about what to do. Especially if they cling to the assurance, that one or another approach is the only "right" one. Discussing conflicting views on parenting is emotional. Conflict creates difficulty in parental relationships but paradoxically can also help a family to grow beyond the difficulties together.

Let us consider parenting from a more fundamental perspective. Digging deeper than culture and opinion, what are the basic elements that the human brain needs to mature into adulthood? What external qualities help a child develop the capacity for autonomy and good decision-making? These capacities, say researchers, stem from secure attachment with early caregivers. Ironically, our ability to act responsibly and autonomously is rooted in our early dependencies on caregivers and the security of knowing someone was attuned and responsive to our needs when we were utterly dependent.

Of course, there are genetic factors involved in our ability to build up these healthy skills. Even if we have, contradictory parenting approaches or differing styles the common denominator is always that the child has the promise of the parent's love, presence, and concern for their well-being. If this were lacking in the parenting style then any of these approaches would not work. This is not to say that variations in parenting approaches might not produce certain differences among our children. We may recognize these differences as more or less preferable, depending on our culture. For instance, some cultures may encourage lesser or greater degrees of individual assertiveness. As a baseline for mental health, we all need the ability to connect with other human beings and to form healthy relationships. This capacity stems from secure attachment.

Researchers, go so far as to say that there are certain core "competencies" that support lifelong psychological resilience, maintain healthy life choices, and protect children from risky behavior. These include good decision-making skill, a positive sense of self, self-control, delay of gratification, and a moral system of belief, sociable concern, and empathy for others (pro-social skills). It is conceivable that we agree that all parents want these skills for our children. Sure, it is appealing, even amusing to muse on the cultural differences between us as we teach these competencies to our children. Nevertheless, there are human needs that transcend culture. The need for secure attachments includes relationships that encompass love, understanding, attunement, and connection. These basic qualities are vital to any life. It is the central "competency" that provides a secure attachment since it is as real as the need for air, food, and water.

CHAPTER FOUR:
Sibling Relationship

❧

*Because siblings often grow up in the same household,
they have a large amount of exposure to one another, but
this relationship is not always on equal footing.*

Siblings play a unique role in one another's lives since it is often the first peer relationship and mirrors the degree of companionship and personal significance allowed in the home while also influencing extra familiar friendships. Because siblings often grow up in the same household, they have a large amount of exposure to one another. However, this relationship is not always on equal footing. Furthermore, sibling relationships often reflect the overall condition of health and interconnectedness within a family.

Sibling rivalry is "the aggressive response to the new baby is so typical that it is safe to say it is a common feature of family life." Researchers today generally endorse this view, noting that parents can ameliorate this response by not playing favorites or taking appropriate preventative steps when imbalance in parenting arises. In fact, researchers say, the ideal time to lay the groundwork for a lifetime of supportive relationships between siblings is during the months prior to the new baby's arrival.

Difference in Parental Treatment

According to observational studies by developmental psychologist, children as early as one year of age may be able to exhibit self-awareness. Children perceive difference in parental treatment between themselves and siblings almost from the outset. These early impressions can shape a lifetime relationship between the younger and older sibling. Siblings can understand family rules, know how to comfort another, and be kind to each other. Children have a sophisticated grasp of social rules, can evaluate themselves in relation to their siblings, and know how to adapt to circumstances within the family. The drive to adapt, to get along with a sibling whose goals and interests may be different from their own, can make the difference between cooperation and conflict within the home.

The content and context of sibling relationships varies in different cultures. In industrialized global cultures, the nature of sibling relationships is normally optional. People are encouraged to stay in contact, and cooperate with their brothers and sisters. However, this is not an obligation. Older siblings in these cultures have a responsibility to watch over a younger sibling. This is only occasional, with parents taking on the primary role of caretaker. In contrast, close sibling relationships in non-industrialized cultures are often obligatory. Strong cultural norms prompt cooperation and close proximity between siblings. These cultures also extend care-giving roles to older siblings. It is common for siblings to assume the role of "watching over younger siblings."

In infancy and childhood, a relationship begins with the introduction of two siblings to each other. Parents make older siblings aware of their soon-to-be younger brother or sister during their mother's pregnancy. This may help facilitate adjustment for the older child, and result in a better immediate relationship with the newborn. Early in development, interactions between older siblings with younger infants, can contribute to the older sibling's social and cognitive abilities since it stimulates the younger sibling. Older siblings adapt their speech to accommodate the low language comprehension of the younger sibling. Similar to what parents do with baby talk.

Attachment theory describes an infant's relationship to a primary caregiver as similar to the bond with siblings. If an infant finds an older sibling to be responsive, and sees him or her as a source of comfort, a supportive bond may form. On the other hand, a negative bond may form if the older sibling acts in an aggressive, neglectful, or harmful manner. Sibling attachment escalates in the absence of a primary caregiver. Since the younger sibling must rely on the older sibling for security and support.

Sibling Relationships Change

As siblings age and develop, there is substantial solidity in their relationships. This occurs from infancy through middle childhood, during which positive and negative interactions remain steady. This time also marks great changes for both siblings. An age gap of only a few years marks the time when the older sibling is beginning school, meeting peers, and making friends. This shift in the family milieu reduces both children's contact to each other and lessens the older sibling's reliance on the younger for social support.

The nature of sibling relationships changes from childhood to adolescence. Young adolescents often provide each other with warmth and support. What often marks this period of development is an increase in conflict and emotional distance. This effect varies based on the sex of the siblings. Mixed-sex siblings often experience significant change i.e. drastic decreases in intimacy during adolescence. It is more common for same-sex siblings to experience a small increase in intimacy during early adolescence, followed by a slight. In both instances, intimacy once again increases during young adulthood. This trend may be the result of an increased emphasis on peer relationships during adolescence. Often, adolescents from the same family adopt differing lifestyles that further contributes to emotional distance between one another.

Siblings may influence one another in much the same way that peers do, especially during adolescence. These relationships may compensate for the negative psychological impact of not having friends, and provide individuals with a sense of self-worth. Older siblings can effectively model good behavior for younger siblings. There is evidence that communication about safe sex with a sibling may be just as effective as with a parent. Conversely, an older sibling may encourage risky sexual behavior by modeling a sexually advanced lifestyle. Younger siblings of teen parents are more likely to become teen parents themselves.

Research on adolescents suggests that positive sibling influences can promote healthy and adaptive functioning while negative interactions can increase vulnerabilities and problem behaviors. Intimate and positive sibling interactions are an important source of support for adolescents, and promote the development of pro-social behavior. When the quality of sibling relationships provokes conflict and aggression, they promote delinquency, and antisocial behaviors among peers.

When siblings reach adulthood, it is likely that they will not live in the same place. They will become involved in jobs, hobbies, and romantic interests that they do not share. They will find it difficult to relate to each other. In this stage, the struggles of school and family dynamics are not a significant factor. When the authority of parents ends the bonds that keep siblings together may break up. Despite these factors, siblings often maintain a relationship through adulthood and old age. Physical proximity and emotional closeness are large factors in maintaining contact between siblings. Those who live closer to each other are more likely to visit more frequently.

Gender also plays a significant role. Sisters are more likely to maintain contact with each other, followed by mixed-gender dyads. Brothers are likely contact one another less frequently. Communication is especially important when siblings do not live near to one another. Communication may happen in person, over the phone, by mail, and with increasing frequency, by online communication. Often, siblings will communicate indirectly through a parent, a mutual friend or relative. Between adult and elderly siblings, conversations tend to focus on family happenings, and reflections of the past.

In adulthood, siblings perform a role similar to that of friends. Friends and siblings are often similar in age, and any age gap seems even less significant in adulthood. Both relationships are often equal in nature. However, unlike sibling relationships, we chose our friendships. The specific roles of each relationship also differ, especially later in life. For elderly siblings, friends tend to act as companions while siblings play the roles of confidants. It is difficult to make long-term assumptions about adult sibling relationships. They may rapidly change in response to individual or shared life events. Marriage of one sibling may either strengthen or weaken the sibling bond. The same is true for a change of vicinity, the birth of a child, and other life events. However, divorce or widowhood of one sibling or the death of a close family member often results in increased closeness and support between siblings.

Sibling Rivalry

Sibling rivalry describes the aggressive relationship or hostility between siblings, whether blood-related or not. Competition is often the result of a desire for greater attention from parents. Even the most reliable and consistent parents can expect sibling rivalry. It plays out in all siblings, as children are natural competitors with each other. They vie not only for attention from parents, but also for recognition in the larger community.

Siblings spend more time together during childhood than they spend with parents. The sibling bond is complicated and complex and is created by factors like parental treatment, birth order, personality, and other people in the home. Sibling's experiences outside the family also become significant influences. According to many child psychologists, sibling rivalry is strongest when children are close in age, of the same gender and when one excels intellectually, socially or physically. Sibling rivalry can involve hostile actions; however, it is not the same as sibling abuse, where one child victimizes another.

There are many things that can influence and shape sibling rivalry. According to research in sociology, each child in a family competes to define who they are as individuals. They want to show that they are separate from their siblings. Children may feel they are getting unequal amounts of their parents' attention, discipline, and responsiveness. Children fight more in families where there is no understanding that fighting is not an acceptable way to resolve conflicts. Siblings learn that there is no alternative way to handle conflicts except to fight. Stress in the lives of parents and children, can create more conflict, and increase sibling rivalry.

CHAPTER FIVE:
Autonomy and Independence

✤

You discover the ability to take care of many of your own needs and to support yourself emotionally, physically, socially, and financially.

Self-determination is the ability to step securely into the phase of autonomy. It is a significant stage of the life cycle and moves beyond childhood into puberty. We enter youth, adolescence, and progress toward young adulthood. During this stage, we begin to separate from our family, disengage psychologically, and become emotionally distant from our family. This is an interlude where we go to the upper limits to turn our self into something that is different from our identity as a child. We discover the ability to take care of our own needs and to support our self emotionally, physically, socially, and financially. We set in motion the maturation process and begin to build up distinctive traits and characteristics that differentiate our personality and self-identity.

Independence is critical to deepen any relationship. To acquire an intimate relationship requires that we have an aptitude for independence while still under the protection of the family. This helps us to extend our independent living skills and brings us endurance for the long haul. Independence grows out of positive attachments. It gives the young person a solid foundation to stand on as they move into the adulthood.

Intimacy grows with the ability to develop and maintain close relationships, that can endure tough times and other challenges. In an autonomous and yet interdependent relationship, we learn about commitment, commonality, and compatibility with others. We develop skills that support interdependence on another person who is not in our family. We also learn who we are outside of our family identity. Our ability to develop an intimate relationship depends on how successful we were at developing our individual identity earlier in life.

To live successfully away from our family, we must develop financial and emotional independence. We also become aware of personal agency and taking care of our own health and responsibility for our diet choices, physical care, and medical requirements. Developing healthy habits at this time, like good nutrition, regular exercise, and safe sex practice, is imperative for wellbeing and happiness. We expand our comprehension of what it requires to gain independence as we move through our youth and into adulthood. Even when we have moved on to another stage of life, such as coupling, we continue to practice self-care. During the autonomy stage, we anticipate seeing our self as a separate person in relation to our biological family. We learn to grow intimate peer relationships outside the family by establishing our self in our schoolwork, extracurricular activities, or career.

During the adult phase, we explore other important relationship qualities like trustworthiness, moral character, inventiveness, work ethics, and self-identity. We become who we are in the larger world as part of the human race. The specific goals for this stage are courtship, romance, sexuality, and intimacy. We make life-changing decisions, i.e. form a new family with a partner, realign our relationships with our family of origin, and our friends must now include our spouse or significant other. During this phase, making the decision to have a baby of your own together is center stage. At some point in your relationship, you and your partner will decide if you want to have a baby. Some couples know when going into a relationship that they do not want children.

Parenting is one of the most demanding and taxing periods of family life. The decision to have children is one that affects your individual development, the identity of your family, and your relationship. Children are so time-consuming that skills not learned in previous stages of development will be difficult to learn at this stage. There will be unseen challenges. Your ability to weather the vicissitudes of childrearing, to communicate well, and preserve your relationships will come to the forefront.

CHAPTER SIX:
Having a Baby

☙

As new parents, your individual identities as a couple and partnership change along with how you relate to each other and to others.

Bringing a child into the world and into the dynamics of your family has dramatic consequences. Inviting an infant into your life is a major change in responsibility for you and your partner. Each parent has three distinct and demanding roles: as an individual, a partner, and a parent. The individual identities of couples change with the arrival of a child along with accommodating how each person relates to the adjustments. If you have not learned to give and take as a couple, have not established loyalty in the earlier phase, you may not have the skills you required to changeover into this demanding and yet rewarding stage of family life.

In conjunction with the delight that comes from having a child, you may feel nervous and notice apprehension about these changes. A woman might have concerns about being pregnant, going through childbirth, and becoming a mother. Men tend to keep their fears and anxiety about the responsibilities of becoming a father to themselves. This can cause physical illness and mental health problems. Talking about your emotional or physical concerns with your family physician, obstetrician, psychotherapist, or spiritual counselor can help you and your partner deal with these concerns.

Parenting young children while simultaneously helping your child build other relationships is a key emotional process of this stage. You will take on the parenting role and transition from being a couple to being a parent. This is an exciting and often challenging time. You are still evolving as individuals; you and your partner are also becoming decision-makers for your family. You express your autonomy as an individual. While performing effectively as a couple, this dynamic dance of partnership parenting is the result of a well-built marriage.

Your child's healthy development depends on your ability to provide a safe, loving, and organized environment. Children benefit when their parents have a strong relationship. Caring for young children reduce the amount of time, you spend alone or with your partner. If there are skills, you did not learn in earlier phases, i.e. cooperation for the good of the family, the relationship suffers. Divorce and extramarital affairs often occur during the raising of small children if the parents have not learned proper life skills. For those who have the appropriate tools, this can be a very rewarding, happy time. Optimally, you grow as an individual, as a couple, and as a member of a family. Specific goals when young children join your family are adjusting your marriage to make space for children; taking on parenting roles, realigning your relationships with your extended family to include parenting and grand parenting roles.

Parenting teenagers

Parenting teenagers can be a rough time for your family and can test your relationship skills. It is also a time for growth and creative exploration for your family. Families that function well during this period have strong, flexible relationships that have developed through good communication, problem solving, mutual care, support, and trust. Most teens experiment with different thoughts, beliefs, and styles, which can cause family conflict. Your strengths as an individual and as a couple are critical as you deal with the increasing challenges of raising a teenager. Strive for a balanced atmosphere in which your teenager has a sense of support and emotional safety as well as opportunities to try new things. An important skill at this stage is flexibility, as you encourage your child to become independent, creative, resourceful, and whole. Establish boundaries for your teenager, but encourage exploration at the same time. Teens may question themselves in many areas, including their sexual orientation and gender identities.

If we developed our individual identity in earlier stages of our life, we will be more secure about the changes our child is going through. If we did not gain the needed skills at earlier stages of life, our children's changes will make us to feel anxious, resentful, angry, or helpless. Some parents feel powerless and out of control with these new developments. We sense the bodily changes and psychological mood swings in our teen that may trigger unresolved issues from our teenage years.

Flexibility in the roles each person plays in the family is a valuable skill to develop at this stage. Responsibilities like the demands of a job or caring for someone who is ill may require each person in the family to take on various, and sometimes changing, roles. This is a time when one or more family members may feel some level of depression or other distress. It may also lead to physical complaints that have no physical cause (somatic disorders such as stomach upsets and some headaches) along with other stress-related disorders.

Nurturing our relationships and our individual growth at this stage is imperative. Toward the end of this phase, a parent's focus shifts from the maturing teen to career and relationship. Neglecting our personal development and our relationships with growing teen-age children can make this shift difficult. We also may begin thinking about our role in caring for aging parents. Making our own health a priority in this phase supports us as we enter the next stage of the family life cycle. Specific goals during the stage of parenting adolescents include shifting parent-child relationships, which includes allowing the child to move in and out of the family system, shifting focus back to your midlife relationship, and career issues.

CHAPTER SEVEN:
Empty Nest

⚜

Free from the everyday demands of parenting, you may choose to rekindle your own relationship and possibly your career goals.

The stage of launching children into adulthood begins when your first child leaves home. This phase ends with proverbial the "empty nest syndrome." When older children leave home, there are both positive and negative consequences. If your family has developed significant skills through the family life cycle, your children will be ready to leave home, and ready to handle life's challenges. Free from the everyday demands of parenting, you may choose to rekindle your own relationship and possibly your career or vocational goals.

Developing adult relationships with your children is a key skill in this stage. Challenge yourself to accept new members into your family through your children's relationships. You may focus on reprioritizing your life, forgiving those who have wronged you (maybe long ago), and assessing your beliefs about deeper life values such as forgiveness and gratitude. If you have not moved through the phases with the appropriate tools and attitudes, you may not have taught your children the skills they need to live well on their own. If you and your partner have not transitioned together, you may no longer feel compatible with each other. Remember that you can still gain the skills you may have missed. Self-examination, education, and counseling can enhance your life and ensure a healthy transition to the next phase.

This is a time when your health and energy levels may decline. Some people diagnosed with chronic illnesses have symptoms that can limit normal activities. Health issues related to midlife may begin to occur. This can include high blood pressure (hypertension), weight problems, arthritis, menopause, osteoporosis, heart disease (coronary artery disease), depression, and stress-related illnesses. You may also be caring for aging parents in this phase, which can be stressful and affect your own health.

Specific goals at this stage include refocusing on your relationship without children, and shifting the focus to developing adult relationships with your grown children. You may want to realign relationships to include in-laws and grandchildren when your children begin their own families. This is a time when codependency issues arise. Co-dependency is a psychological term for a person who is unable to separate the needs of the other from one's own. People in co-dependent relationships often have low-self esteem. They have an incessant need to give to others, control the relationship, or take responsibility for everything. This person may tend to people please, and to be a doormat, when they cannot say no. They may be the kind of parent in a situation where a grown child is having difficulties, and the codependency arises in negative and harmful ways to all involved. When we build relationships on faulty foundations, we fuel the relationship by chronic reactivity, emotional disturbances, and excessive fighting. We play the blame game since we feel burdened by the desires or needs of the other. In the stage of retirement and ageing, we must take responsibility for our own needs as well as those of our children and grandchildren.

Jenny's Story

Here is an example of multi-generation issues that affect the overall health of a family. Jenny, a smart, extroverted perky woman in her mid-fifties came for coaching on how to deal with an aging mother while also taking care of a six-year-old granddaughter. Her thirty-year-old adult daughter's alcohol and drug addiction had caused Jenny and her second husband to take in the six year old. Jenny's desire to fix her daughter and to take control her granddaughter, while also taking care of her elderly mother was driving her to the brink of insanity.

Jenny tried to take control of it all, but it actually ended up controlling her. She had started to drink too much herself and had developed an obsession to ease her stress. She had become a hair puller, diagnosed with trichotillomania. Jenny found she was embroiled in her own problems due to nervous tension and constant worry. She found a stress relief in pulling out her hair. This compulsive urge to pull out her hair was leading to noticeable hair loss, pain, social alienation, embarrassment, and functional impairment in her job as a receptionist. Trichotillomania is a classification in DSM-IV the diagnostic and statistical manual use in psychiatry to determine mental disorders manifesting as an impulse control disorder that is associated with obsessive/compulsive disorders that are often chronic and difficult to treat.

Jenny is not alone in feeling overwhelmed by her relationship responsibilities. We all have times in life when we feel called to help another or to be the responsible one because of duty, concern, or love. If we grew up in a dysfunction family where boundaries were unclear and co-dependency was the norm, it is difficult not to be fixated on every detail of another person's life. This preoccupation can borders on obsession and become unhealthy, unproductive, and part of the problem if we cannot monitor the need to rescue a family member. Nevertheless, when our own urge to control the problematic behavior of someone else we find that our own self-care spirals out of control. It initially did for Jenny when she tried to care for both her aging mother and granddaughter. Interdependence within our family must be balance with taking care of our own needs. Otherwise, the care giving becomes co-dependent. Jenny needed assurance that she could find balance amidst the chaos. She came to coaching which took great courage, she new that she needed to ask for help. Only then did Jenny begin to stop neglecting her own life, health, marriage and sanity.

Jenny's daughter was a causality of sexual abuse, raped by her father's employee, as a pre-teen. Jenny had been working in a different part of the country when this awful event occurred. She blamed herself for her daughter's victimization that resulted in substance abuse, alcoholism, and the inability to care for her child. When asked if she believed her daughter, Pam, was responsible for her own life. Jenny paused and said not now. Pam is helpless from her addiction; this prevents her from taking care of herself and her daughter.

Jenny began to stand up for her own life and identified her role in her daughter's abuse. Even though Jenny says that she does not approve of her daughter's lifestyle choices, she feels that she has to do whatever she can and has done everything she could do such as providing money, support for rehabilitation programs, and medical/psychiatric services. Jenny started her own healing when she could accept her daughter's situation and challenge the negative. Jenny slobbered through her tears, "No one can change this, even if Pam fails terribly and never recovers." Jenny's awareness of her own illness with hair pulling was a stress reaction to feeling powerless. Jenny's new awareness had her make the confession, "I must let go of trying to control what I can't control and must set limits with Pam, so that her behavior stops controlling me." Jenny obtained professional psychiatric support to help with her own psychiatric destabilization. Once Jenny started to challenge her issues with multi-generational co-dependency, her troubled daughter began to get back on track as well. In working on the issue with Jenny's aging mother, she said, "I need to find her a retirement community where I can visit." Jenny considered taking her mother in as well, but realized she needed a different outlook. The issue Jenny faced with her aging mother was a dilemma that many of her friends shared. In this area, she did not feel as alone, helpless, or ashamed.

Today there are almost 50 million American caring for aging parents. One thing they all share is how stressful it is. Caring for healthy children and parents is taxing enough. Nevertheless, with the triple whammy of raising a granddaughter, caring for an aging parent and the ongoing stress of dealing with an alcoholic daughter was too severe. Jenny began to work on reducing her stress by acknowledging the tendency toward co-dependency in her family relationships. Jenny set in motion a more effective style of being with her family. This new approach made the negative situation with her daughter granddaughter, and aging mother workable. Jenny left the life coaching session determined to ask other people in her family for support and to seek appropriate profession help, social services, and community agencies.

CHAPTER EIGHT:
Retirement & Senior Stage

⚜

Exploring new family and social roles providing emotional support for your adult children and extended family members is a positive goal for this phase.

During the retirement phase of the family life cycle, many changes occur in our life. Welcoming new family members or seeing others leave our family is often a large part of this stage as our children marry, divorce, or we become a grandparent. This stage can be a great adventure but tricky. We are free from the responsibilities of raising our children and can simply enjoy the fruits of our life's work. Challenges we may face include being a support to other family members. Since we are still exploring our own interests and activities or focusing on maintaining our relationship. Many people are caring for elderly parents at this time. We feel challenged by their emotional, financial, and physical needs while trying to help them keep their independence.

We may experience declining physical and mental abilities or changes in our financial or social status. Sometimes you must deal with the death of other family members, including your partner. The quality of your life at this stage depends on how well you adjusted to the changes in earlier stages. It also depends on how well we have cared for our own health up to this point. Normal aging will affect our body, resulting in wrinkles, aches, pains, and loss of bone density. The chance of having a mental or chronic physical illness does increase with age. However, aging does not mean you will automatically experience poor health.

Retirement can be a fulfilling and happy time. Becoming a grandparent can bring you great joy, without the responsibility of raising a child. Those who are without adequate support systems or not well off financially, though, may have a more difficult time in this phase of life. Specific goals at this final stage of your family life include maintaining your own interests and physical well-being, along with those of your partner. Exploring new family and social roles, providing emotional support for your adult children, and staying in touch with extended family members help maintain a positive outlook during this stage.

You have the need to share life stories, impart wisdom to the younger generation, and support older family members in life transition. You are able to provide support for the older generation, by giving back to those who supported you. You have time to give to others since this helps you deal with the loss of a partner, siblings, and peers. Reaching out to help another, such as volunteering at a hospital or connecting with hospice, are ways of preparing for your own death. This is a precious time to review your life. This is often when the rubber hits the road; a spiritual practice supports inner reflection, self-understanding, and inner peace. Retirement is anything but retiring in the sense of inactivity. It is a time of enhanced inner work that brings joy as you look back on all you have learned and experienced during your life.

Healthy Family Relationships Enrich Retirement

Satisfying relationships and strong family bonds are essential elements in achieving and maintaining good health, a longer life, and greater resilience during illness and aging. By cultivating and renewing relationships with immediate and extended family, we can strengthen kinship bonds, minimize our differences, and find meaning and purpose in sharing time together during retirement.

Take advantage of your retirement years by devoting more time to your partner, children, grandchildren, or other close relatives. To make sure your family relationships stay happy and healthy, you may have to rebalance your life at home. You must be flexible with other people's schedules and sensitive about becoming over-involved with your children's lives, and work at reconnecting with extended family that may have become distant during our busy mid-life.

It takes time to readjust

Retirement has a major impact on your entire family, not just you. The transition to retirement provides both opportunities and challenges in family relationships. It is natural to want to be helpful and involved in your children's lives. However, we know this can be a delicate balance. Let your children know your limits around boundaries in time and financial commitments; such as agreeing to activities like babysitting, childcare responsibilities, or lending money. This need to be straightforward and fair since it is important to keep your boundaries as well. Visit only when welcomed, so as not to disrupt your children's lives. Remember you have more free time in your schedule now and that your children might not have the same luxury. Your children have their own methods of dealing with life. This is the amazing part of raising children to maturity!

If you are part of a couple, you need to make conscious, clear, and healthy adjustment to the new reality of being together 24/7. Allow yourselves an adjustment period by keeping communication open and honest. Here are pointers for a smooth transition. The honeymoon period will be short-lived if you rigidly hold to your previous patterns and routines. Be flexible with each other and sensitive to your partner's needs. If your partner wants to cook but never had the time, work out a meal schedule, and help with recipe hints. You need to find the right balance of shared and independent activities. Feel free to keep up your independent interests, but take time to explore hobbies you can share. Joining a book club, taking up photography, or speed walking together will help keep your mind and body active, and strengthen your relationship. If you feel claustrophobic and need your own space, consider organizing a spare room into an exercise haven, art studio, hobby room, or reading retreat.

Keeping It in the Family

If you live far away from your family, this may be the ideal time to develop new family traditions like organizing an annual family vacation or reunions. Now you may have more time for an extended visit to help with a new grandchild by giving the new parents a hand with childcare, cooking, and cleaning. This is the time to reconnect with brothers and sisters, or nephews and nieces. Renting a cottage together, going on a family cruise, and just stepping out to a ball game or the theatre are ways to spend time together and have fun. Retirement is your chance to do things you have always wanted to do. So get out there and get involved, stay active, and keep learning.

Today more people than ever are beginning a new phase in life. Now that children have grown and gone, and a lifetime of work has ended, it is time to move on to retirement. Often people dream of retiring only to feel overwhelmed by their newfound time and freedom. However, retirement is a wonderful opportunity. It is your chance to do all those things you always wanted to do, but just could not find time. After decades of rushing around, meeting deadlines, and never stopping, you finally have the opportunity to slow down and decide what you really want to do with your time. Take advantage of it, and start living life to the fullest.

Be a change agent by considering volunteering your time and energy for a cause you believe in. Many organizations and grassroots efforts can make real differences in the world. Now is a great time to lend a hand. Whether you are concerned with the education system, environment, or politics, you will be able to find a group attempting to make positive changes. Taking your mind off your own problems and focusing on issues bigger than yourself is a great way to give your life increased meaning and purpose.

Working your mind and staying active is key. You are never too old to learn something new. Now that you have more time available you are in the perfect position to learn. Take a sculpture class, learn chess, or start playing an instrument. Having a new challenge to mentally focus on is very rewarding. Have you ever checked out the continuing education courses available at the local college? You might be surprised at just how many affordable classes are out there. Enrolling in a class or two is a great way to keep the mind sharp and to meet new people.

Consider mentoring others. There are many opportunities for you to mentor and share your vast experience and knowledge with someone less experienced. Children who have the benefit of a positive role model have a distinct advantage in life. Look into local mentoring groups and get involved in volunteerism. Maybe coaching a sports team is more your style or tutoring children at risk? Whatever you decide to do, providing guidance and assistance to a younger generation is truly rewarding. It allows you to make a lasting impact on the world.

Meeting New People

Meeting new people keeps us socially active and relationally informed. Take the time to make new friends. Socializing is a good way to spend time and learn new things. Call up relatives you have not seen in awhile, or reconnect with old friends. Many people lose touch with friends while working every day. Now that you are retired, you can socialize all you like! Perhaps you would like to join a local club or group. Visit your library or search online to find what clubs are in your area. Joining a book club or bird watching club can be a great way to meet new people.

Being on the move is essential to keeping relationships active. Whether you like to dance, bike, run, hike, swim, or walk, keep on moving! Exercise will help your body feel fit and healthy, and it will elevate your mood and keep you feeling youthful and at your best. You do not have to overdo it. Just make sure you move. Go out for dinner and dancing once a week. Go for a morning walk. It does not matter how you chose to keep moving, just make sure you move. Spending time each day rocking in your favorite rocking chair to music that soothes your soul, water your garden to notice natural beauty, light cleaning to care for your home all will have a positive effect.

Travel is a common activity of retirement. Many have time and money to see the world. Are there places you have always wanted to visit but have still have not seen? Why not plan a trip, and see the sights you have always dreamed of seeing. There are so many amazing things to see in this world, and now is the best time to see them. If you are not sure about traveling alone, then look into a travel group. Traveling with a group is a great way to see new places and more affordable. If you are not sure about traveling the world, then simply see new sights in your own country, state, or town. You do not have to go far just to see something new.

Caring for a pet keeps many people happy and engaged. You may have an affinity for animals then now may be a great time to get one. Whether you consider yourself a dog person or cat person, spending time with an animal will give your life additional meaning. Look in a pet store or better yet go to the local animal shelter to see the animals in need of a home. You might just fall in love with a new furry friend.

These tips are just suggestions to help you enhance your happiness and well-being. However, there is so much more you can do! This really is your chance to do things you have always wanted to do and to make a real difference in the world. So get out there and get involved, stay active, and keep learning.

CHAPTER NINE:
The Family as Foundation

꒞

As the bumper sticker says "It is never too late to have a happy childhood" meaning, that you do not have to let anything or anyone control your life forever!"

The family unit, its belief system, and attitudes to life, form the foundation of all other relationships. We carry our ancestor's experience in the way that we link to a particular family's values transmitted in DNA. Networking with the power of our inheritance leads us through life passages that translate ancestral dreams into physical life. For us to have enriching embodied experience, our eons of conditioning have given us a proclivity to soak up information from the environment in idiosyncratic ways.

We inherit both positive and negative attributes; attract helpful and harmful behaviors that bring good or evil into the field of human interaction over time. These patterns cause positive and negative situations in family and community relationships. On the other hand, we are recipient to many brilliant and precious qualities from past kin.

You do not need to let your programming and the negative family attitudes undermine your relationship to your higher source and to your fellow travelers. As the bumper sticker says "It is never too late to have a happy childhood." This means you do not have to let anything or anyone control your life forever. The unconscious attitudes received from your family legacy; do not have to stop you from bringing new awareness to possibilities. You can tap into conscious change since you know that transformation is possible.

Negative and positive transmissions from childhood can affect you for your entire life if you allow unconscious family patterns to smolder. The particular conditions of your upbringing influence you for the rest of your life; ancestral linage, like the seeds of your conditioning, bud into your personality. Tribulations felt in early life may well impinge on future success and spoil later stages of development. They may manifest as depression, anxiety, panic attacks, and a host of adjustment disorders resulting in chronic mental illness. It also manifests as physical disabilities and may lead to social phobia, problems with peer groups, inability to feel secure in social settings, and problems at work. When things get out of control, the family's state of mind suffers, often through many generations.

In her influential book, "You Can Heal Your Life" Louise Hay (1984) coaches that there is no value in holding other people responsible for acting in a harmful manner towards us. They are also sufferers of their individual conditioning and problems with lack of personal development. The people we often blame the most, hurt us the most. In addition, when someone hurts us, it is often because he/she is in anguish. It is healthy to forgive, forget, and shift your perspective to view the glass of life as half-full rather than half empty. Hay House announced in 2011 that You Can Heal Your Life had reached 40 million sales, so her wise counsel reaches many and remains an inspiration to us all.

The nuclear and biological family is symbolic for the first tribe and represents the security of the human kinship bond. Thus, the family is the crucible of all relationships. Since we emerge into a particular family culture, we receive specific acculturation; that manifests in particular behaviors and attitudes that we receive, and then model. Upbringing powerfully sways the way people relate to all other groups of people. We can witness this progression, when relatives, spouses, children, or close friends that are accustomed to getting away with a narcissistic style of behavior discover that peers, teachers, and the general culture will not accept or allow this conduct.

The person faced with this predicament is not totally at fault. Since they do not recognize their off-putting behavior, the negative actions often get no acknowledgement. This behavior, within the family, creates a situation for the individual where another coping strategy is not accessible and they are stuck in negative relational styles. It is problematic when a family member is in the grip of negative programming and tries to reach out to another person for help but do not know how. We all need trusted role models. Skillful mentors are important in rites of passage since they support us with positive role and mirror a value system during the agonizing passage of adolescence. However many individuals undergo repeated set backs on their way to deepening a relationship with others.

Our conditioning significantly influences how we go about building a healthy intimate relationship. There are some ground rules that may help. In the first stage of any relationship, benefits and challenges are both present. The early months of a relationship can feel spontaneous and exhilarating. When you and your partner are in cooperation early on in your relationship, you are able to build stamina for the long haul. It is important to encourage constructive expression of emotions when situations are both working or when change is required. A practical way to approach this activity is to center your attention on the thoughtful things your partner says and does. Contented couples make a point of noting tiny opportunities to say kind words, i.e. "I love and appreciate you," "thank you" and "you make my world shine." Rather than focusing on slip-ups and errors.

When you augment your need for self-knowledge with being conscious of what makes the other person tick, accelerates the path to know the other person in a genuine way. This can be challenging, thrilling, inspiring and yet maddening! Exploring mutual interests provides a long list of things to take pleasure in together. Try new things together to develop common interests. Partners that have the ability to establish a pattern of forgiving and forgetting tend to have lasting relationship and this extends to the family. Are you able to apologize if you make a mistake? Saying "I'm sorry" may be tough in the moment but it goes a long way towards repairing an unintended hurt. People will respect you if they know that you will take responsibility for your actions.

As time passes, new issues arise, that force you to recognize important things in your relationships. During this phase, it is vital to remember that relationships change and evolve over time. The ebb and flow of life will influence what you require in your relationship from moment to moment. Adjustment, adaptation, and revision are unavoidable! Staying open to change is more productive than stopping it from happening. Occasionally, all relationships require a check-up! It is necessary to set aside an occasion to make certain that both parties are on the same relationship page. Periodically check-in with each other, renew the intention of the relationship. Reflect on shifting expectations and goals. This is crucial to the health of any relationship. If a couple closes their eyes to thorny topics, their relationship is liable to become a source of pain and upset. The same is true with our family relationships where ongoing, open communication is imperative.

Divergences in a Relationship

Difference of opinion is useful a relationship, since we all the same. When we meet divergences, we know that this is not only common, but in fact, variations reinforce the connection. Complexity is inescapable since there will be times of heartache, pain, unhappiness, anxiety, or out-and-out animosity in most enduring relations. The origin of conflict arises when one or both partners make irrational demands or "my way of the highway" attitude. Resolving conflicts in this case requires honesty and a readiness to consider your partner's point of view, even if you do not agree with it. Be willing to have on-going open contact with your partner that allows for diversity within unity.

Strong communication is paramount, particularly when there are challenging decisions concerning sex, matrimony, children and money. The following are some guidelines for communication and conflict resolution. It behooves a couple to understand each other's family patterns and cultural identity. You discover how your partner's family dealt with conflicts and how your family may had a different approach can be extremely significant when dealing with divergent styles. Knowing the other's family background provides a helpful way to understand and work with a range of differences.

This open style helps move the relationship along. It is common for couples to discover that their families had ways of expressing anger, and resolving differences that were miles apart. If your family was not good at communicating or resolving conflicts, give yourself permission to do so in a more effective manner. When you and your partner can both experiment with new ways of managing conflict, you will discover that you process fear, anxiety, and conflict with some of the most difficult issues with amazing ease.

Timing Counts

Timing Counts when working with intimate relationship issues and the impact of family. Contrary to prior beliefs, the peak time to resolve a conflict may not be in the moment. It is normal for one or both partners to call for a time out. A time out can help you circumvent saying insensitive things in the heat of the moment. This will help the situation cool down! Partners can then clearly identify what changes are most important. Keep in mind; if you are aggravated or disappointed with your partner but do not know why, it will be impossible for your partner to figure it out. Remember they are not mind readers. If you can establish an attitude of emotional idling, that is half the battle. Emotional support involves accommodating your partner's differences, and not insisting that they meet your needs, in the way that you want them met. Find out how your partner shows love to you, and do not set unconditional demands.

This on-going dynamic process includes agreeing to disagree and then moving on. Most couples will bump into issues upon which they will not agree. Rather than continuing a succession of repetitive fights. Agree to disagree and negotiate for cooperation. Discover an approach that works around the problem. Try to differentiate between things you would like versus things you need. For example, for security reasons, you might need your co-worker to lock-up on time after dark. However, calling him numerous times a day may only be an obsessive want and not a need. Your partner may not want you to call several times a day as a reminder that he is going to pick you up after work. Your demand that he calls or texting him twenty times, that is a bit obsessive!

Whether conflict is on the agenda, or the relationship is experiencing smooth sailing, it is essential to clarify your communication. An unambiguous message delivers a respectful but direct expression of your wants and needs. Take time to identify what you really want before talking to your partner. Work on being able to express your request in clear, observable terms. For example, you might say, "I would like you to snuggle on the sofa, talk in an affectionate tone, and kiss more often" rather than, "I hoped you would be more intimate."

Moving toward intimacy is a delicate dance. Discuss one thing at a time, and try to stay on the topic at hand. It is enticing to catalog your grievances, but doing so will prolong on extend a disagreement. The conflict naturally subsides, when you do your best to focus the center of attention on the core issue. You and your partner can only resolve one conflict at a time.

Really, listen! Being a good listener requires the following: (a) don't interrupt, (b) focus on what your partner is saying, and (c) check out what your partner said. You might start this process with, "I think you are saying…" or, "what I understood you to say was…" This act alone can avert misunderstandings. It is always best to restrain yourself. Research has found that couples who "edit" themselves are typically the happiest. When we revise and amend our verbal expressions, we do not burn bridges.

Relationships built upon understanding, more easily adopt a "win-win" position. A "win-win" attitude means that your objective is for the relationship, rather than for either partners "win." Ask yourself, "Is what I am about to say (or do) going to increase or decrease the likelihood that we'll work out this problem?" Every one goes into romantic relationships with ideas based on childhood conditioning. What we have learned from society, from social media, and in our own past relationships causes us to hold on to idealistic expectations of what a relationship is supposed to be. This can cause an intimate relationship to not meet up to the phantom lover or to fantasy images of the ideal partner. Thus the relationship begins to feel monotonous, and dull, partners act tentative, and become unresponsive to the actual partner. This sense of unreality can create tension in the family, leading to psychological disorders if unresolved.

The following will help you to distinguish between healthy and unhealthy relationship expectations.

What you want from a relationship in the early months of dating may be quite different from what you want after you have been together for some time and have a family. Anticipate that both you and your partner will change over time. Feelings of love and passion change with time. Respecting and valuing these changes is healthy. Love literally changes brain chemistry. For both physiological and emotional reasons, a mature relationship will have a more complex, and often-richer type of passion than a new relationship.

When you respect change and are able to allow differences, it is a sign that the relationship is healthy. It is fitting, to admit that there are things about our partners that will not change over time. No matter how much we want them to. Unfortunately, there is often an expectation that our partner will change in the ways we like. We may also hold the unreasonable hope that our partner will never change. It is imperative to express true wants and actual needs. While it is easy to expect that your partner knows your wants and needs, it is not the reality. Inappropriate expectations can be the source of much anxiety in relationships. An improved style is open communication with your partner. Respect your partner's rights, in strong relationships, there is value in each other's right to have their own feelings, friends, activities, and opinions. It is not fair to require that he or she have the same priorities, goals, and interests as you.

Be equipped to roll with the punches. Couples, who do so, are better prepared to make it in the end. If you see conflict as a threat to the relationship, and something to avoid at all costs, the relationship is already on a slippery slope. If the relationship breaks down it is often the result of accumulated and unaddressed conflicts. The real threat is not when couples fight but when they "fight unfairly." When we can admit when we are wrong, and seek the middle ground, then the need for fighting diminishes.

Maintain a Meaningful Relationship

There is an art to maintaining a meaningful relationship. Most of us know that keeping a vehicle moving in the preferred direction requires not only ordinary refueling, but also ongoing maintenance. A similar situation applies to long-term relationships. While we may work hard to get the relationship started, expecting to cruise without effort, typically leads the relationship to stall or crash. Though gifts and romantic getaways are important it is often the small, acts of kindness for each other that keep the relationship satisfying.

Outside pressures arise due to differences in background. Even partners coming from very similar cultural, religious, or economic backgrounds can benefit from discussing their expectations about how a good friend, co-worker, partner, or spouse behaves. What seems evident to you may astonish your partner, and vice versa. If you are from different backgrounds, be sensitive that you may need to spend more time and energy attending to your differences. Take the time to learn about your partner's culture or religion.

The time you spend together and apart is a common relationship concern. If you interpret your partner's time away from you as, "he or she doesn't care for me as much as I care for him or her," trouble may be brewing. Check out what time alone means to him or her, and share your feelings. Demanding what you want, regardless of your partner's needs, usually ends up driving your partner away. Work on reaching a compromise. Some people find dealing with their partner's family difficult or annoying. It can help to take a step back and think about parental good intentions. Families may offer well-intentioned guidance about your relationship. It is important that you discuss and agree on how to respond to conflicting family values, and support one another.

This also applies to friendships. Some people assume that "I have to give up all my friends unless my partner likes them as much as I do." Giving up friends is not healthy for you or the relationship. At the same time, keep in mind that your partner may not enjoy your friends as much as you do. Negotiate which friends you and your partner spend time with together. You might ask, "Which friends do you like seeing and which ones would you rather I see by myself?"

CHAPTER TEN:
Benefits of Positive Family Relationships

⚜

In a supportive and healthy family matrix, happy mutual relationships naturally grow.

Effective communication within the family can lead to better relationships between the members of the family. Communication is a key ingredient; all relationships thrive on a foundation of trust, listening, and understanding. The more effective your family can communicate with each other, the better for all. Share your thoughts and feelings, encourage expression from your family. It will promote a safe home environment. All parties will feel at ease, safe, and secure in their foundational relationships.

Effective Family Communication

Building relationships outside of the home is based on how we communicate who we are to others. Communication is best when you express your thoughts, feelings, and opinions to someone else, while they listen and reciprocate. In the home, communication takes on a much more personal tone. When you communicate with your family, you can expect a listening ear. Healthy family support is one that can soothe pain or provide an honest opinion that directs you to your true path. Taking the time to make sure that you and your family work on communication skills ensures that your family remains tightly knit. Communicating effectively within our family fosters ongoing awareness of both the shared and individual needs of each member. We learn how important it is to recognize the intrinsic worth of each other and encourage open and honest communication at all junctures.

Self-Esteem

If we come from families or living situations where we do not feel valued it lowers our self-esteem. We often feel we are not worthy of love, that we are incapable of intimacy or beneficial relationships. If the relationship style in a family is overly critical, it can create an atmosphere of control where interactions focus on having power over another, rather than self-control. Low self-esteem arises when we feel we must meet high or impossible standards. This often results in a family member feeling guilty that they are not doing it right, fearful that they are letting the family down, and should be ashamed. This causes a negative atmosphere in the family home that is based on stress, upset and isolation. Everyone at times feels the pressure to live up to unrealistic expectations, but if the family dynamics become a burden due to unrealistic demands, perhaps compromise is in order.

In families where children are encouraged to develop self-esteem, there is a natural sense of give and take. In a supportive family, healthy, happy, mutual, and joyful relationships naturally grow. Research demonstrates that parents who teach their children to express feelings, thoughts, and opinions, have higher self-esteem. Self-esteem flourishes in an environment where thoughts and opinions are valued and recognized. The child is more likely to go to school, head to extracurricular activities, or participate in social events, with balanced self-esteem. This enables the child to be more outgoing and less inhibited when expressing their true self.

Emotional Expression

Expression of a wide range of emotions is crucial to ongoing security and the well-being of a relationship. Many people are afraid to express negative feelings such as anger or sadness. According to one definition, anger is "an emotional state that varies in intensity from mild irritation to intense fury and rage." According to psychologists who specialize in the study of anger, like other emotions, anger causes physiological and biological changes. When you are experiencing anger, your heart rate and blood pressure go up, as do the levels of your energy, hormones, adrenaline, and noradrenalin. The cause of anger may be both external and internal. Anger can express a broad-spectrum of concerns or it can be exact and specific. For example, you could be angry with a particular person (such as a friend, coworker, or spouse) or an event (traffic jam, a cancelled flight, etc.) or caused by worrying or fixating on individual troubles. Angry feelings can be triggered by memories of trauma, disappointment, and hurtful events or catastrophic circumstances. The upset can be difficult to process.

Practice active presence, listen between the lines, and encourage the expression of a broad range of feelings. It will give spaciousness to the range of communication. Expressing resentment or other complex feelings in a positive manner will yield positive results. Expression of emotion will reduce combativeness in a home, as well as encourage the sharing of both good and bad feelings. When a family communicates effectively, all of the members are better able to practice conflict management, problem solving, and share intimacy. A family is not afraid to express their thoughts and feelings through sharing in creative and inspiring projects.

Reactivity is often the automatic way we express anger. It is to act in response to another in a hostile or antagonistic manner. Anger, or acting out, is an innate and adaptive reaction to fear, intimidation, and threat. We all need the capacity to engage our anger since it inspires powerful emotions and destructive behaviors which allow us to protect ourselves when we are assaulted or under attack. A proficiency to mobilize anger is fundamental to survival!

However, our conditioning in early life makes us either skillful or not at expressing our rage and fury. Think back on childhood tantrums. We receive training in how to express emotions in different ways, for example in nursery school, than we learned from our family. We learn or do not learn that we cannot strike out at others, who frustrate or annoy us. Building relationships within the family is crucial to establishing how we relate to social norms, and how we abide by laws. This enables us to use common sense. To place limits on how far we allow our emotional responses to go, and to what degree, we allow them to control us.

Some children learn to act out, create problems, or to push others buttons. They do this to seek attention. They want to shock! When parents and siblings foster better communication, there is no need for children to act out. Children then have time and space to communicate their feelings and needs. When parents are overly critical of their children, they operate by perfectionism. The desire for the family to look perfect and appear successful on the surface is more important that the expression of real needs or concerns. This kind of communication can lead children to seek attention in negative ways. Shift the emphasis so that the child feels loved based on their efforts rather than being perfect.

Home is where we begin to learn and practice relational skills such as anger management. Effective communication helps to inform children how to move effectively through the many stages of life and transition successful outside the home. Basic communication skills such as emotional expression, deep listening, and conflict resolution will affect their school, social, and professional life. We learn how to effectively communicate in the home, but when this does not occur we may have set backs.

We establish a platform to launch from that includes the attitude, mind-set, and outlook in our home environments. To create a happy life we must learn to listen well, reserve judgment, understand, accept, and empathize with another. Children learn the correct words to use when communicating with others and most of all; they develop skills that will affect all of their future relationships. Good listening skills are vital to healthy relationships. Whether you are strengthening a relationship, resolving a conflict, or offering support in a crisis, good listening skills can provide you harmony and relational accord.

Follow theses 9 steps to learn how to be a supportive listener. You will find yourself surrounded by others who do the same with you.

9. Steps to Develop Good Listening:

1. Listen, Listen, Listen. Ask your friend what is wrong, and really listen to the answer. Let them voice their fears, frustrations, and other feelings. Maintain eye contact and show that you are interested in what they have to say. Resist the urge to give advice, and just let them speak.

2. Reframe What You Hear. Summarize and repeat back your understanding of what they are saying so they know you are hearing them, and focus on the emotions they might be feeling. For example, if your friend is talking about family problems, you might find yourself saying, "It looks like things are getting pretty hostile. You sound like you're feeling hurt."

3. Ask About Feelings. Ask them to expand on what they are feeling. Asking about their feelings provides a good emotional release, and can be more helpful than just focusing on the facts.

4. Keep The Focus On Them. Rather than delving into a related story of your own, keep your center of attention on them. You can reference something that happened to you if you bring the focus back to them quickly. They will appreciate the focused attention, and this will let them know they are cared for and understood.

5. Help Brainstorm. Rather than giving advice in the beginning, wait until they have gotten their feelings out, and then help them brainstorm solutions. If you help them come up with ideas, they are likely to come up with a solution that causes them to feel good. On the other hand, after feeling heard, they might feel better.

6. Stay Present. Sometimes people feign listening, but they are really just waiting for their friend to stop talking so that they can say whatever they have been rehearsing while they have been pretending to listen. People can usually sense this, and it does not feel good. They tend to be unfocused and miss what the other is saying.

7. Don't Give Advice. It is a common desire to immediately give advice and "fix" the problem. Unless you get a specific requested, do not! While you are trying to help, what works for you might not work for them? Advice can also feel condescending. Unless they ask you directly for advice, your friend desires you to listen and probably

just wants a sounding board or an open ear. They can find their own solutions.

8. Trust The Process. It might feel a little strange to listen to feelings before offering solutions. Hearing your friend talk about upset feelings might make you feel helpless. Usually offering a supportive ear and sitting with your friend is the most helpful thing you can do. Once you can sort out the feelings, the solutions start coming.

9. Let Things Even Out Over Time. With all the focus on your friend's problems, it might be difficult to focus equal time on your own. Relax in knowing that, when you need a friend, your friend will be a better listener. If you are consistently doing all the giving, you can re-evaluate the dynamics of the relationship. Nevertheless, being a good listener can make you a stronger, more caring person, and bring a supportive angle to your relationships.

Good Decision Making

Parents who want to encourage good decision making in their children must also encourage individual autonomy. Do parents do this? Some take the approach by pushing children to succeed at all costs as in the typical "Super Mom." Others may do so by stepping back as the "Back Seat Parent" and allow their children to "live their own lives." Other parents try to strike a balance, by setting limits and not shielding them from every hurt.

It seems the latest wave of parenting theories has muddied up the question rather than clarifying it. You cannot blame the authors! To sell a book, authors have to convince publishers that they have something unique and important to offer. This means that they need to stand out from the competition. They do this by emphasizing their differences and even exaggerating them if necessary. Readers identify with one author or another, friends and family become polarized, especially if they cling to the conviction that one or another approach is the only "right" one. Views on parenting are emotionally charged. This can create rifts in family relationships.

Let us consider parenting from a more fundamental perspective. Dig deeper than culture and opinion. What are the basic elements that the human brain needs to develop the capacity for independence, autonomy, and good decision-making? These capacities, say researchers, stem from a secure attachment to early caregivers. Ironically, our ability to act responsibly and autonomously is rooted in the security of our relationship with someone who was attuned and responsive to our needs when we were dependent.

Of course, there are genetic factors needed for consideration. UCLA researcher, Daniel J. Siegel (2007) explored in The Developing Mind, the importance of being aware of the significant and very real contributions of genetic and constitutional factors to the outcome of development. Nevertheless, he also raised the point that it is equally crucial to examine what we know about how personal experience shapes development. Siegel suggests that such a balanced view enables us as parents, for example, to have a sense of responsibility for the experiences we provide our children, without the unnecessary burden of guilt generated by the belief that our actions are solely responsible for the outcome of our children's development. Siegel explores a position that takes into account both nature and nurture, and has authored several books on parenting and child development with this in mind.

Lifelong Psychological Resilience

If we are concerned enough about our success as parents, we should expect to care for and respond to our children as infants. If we have different parenting styles, the common denominator is that each child has the reassurance and guarantee of the parent's love, presence, and concern. If this underlying sense of security is not apparent, the approach will not bear good fruit. This is not to say that variations in parenting methods might generate positive differences among our children. We may identify these variations as preferable, depending on our culture or social situation. For instance, some cultures encourage lesser or greater degrees of individual assertiveness. As a baseline for mental health, we all need the skill to connect with other human beings and to form healthy relationships. This ability stems from secure attachments in early life.

Researchers are finding that there are certain core "competencies" that support lifelong psychological resilience and protect children from high-risk behavior. This pro-social proficiency includes good decision-making skills, a positive sense of self-identity, self-control, and the ability to delay gratification. When a child is guided by a moral compass, has a system of belief, and demonstrates outgoing concern/empathy for others, you can say they will likely act in pro-social ways.

It is plausible that all parents, no matter what there parenting style is, want these skills for their children. It is motivating, even humorous, to muse upon the cultural differences between us. There are human needs that transcend background and ethnicity, including the need for safe and non-intrusive attachments. This is as real as the need for food and water and encompasses a wide range of actions like love, understanding, attunement, and physical connection.

As we have seen, there are many ways to characterize a family. However, they all have one universal initiative: love. The nature of a family that communicates the core sense of unconditional love is by its very nature warm and caring. Whether a family is a nuclear family, a stepfamily, blended, a single-parent family, or an empty-nest family, it consists of related people who love and care for each other. Regardless of a family's style or approach, all families need appreciation and understanding at various times.

CHAPTER ELEVEN:
Strong Family Relationships

☙

**Loving families share activities and express a
great deal of gratitude for one another.**

Many things influence building strong family relationships. The
foundation of powerful, effective, and well-built relationships starts
with the capacity to love. The seven characteristics that contribute
to strong family relationships are love, laughter, loyalty, faithfulness,
communication, time together, and a spiritual foundation. Love is the
cornerstone. When people say, "I love you" they can mean very different
things. How would you personally define love? Is love is at the heart of
your family?

All humans have the need to love and to be loved since this is what
it means to be part of the global family. Love is the secure amalgamation
of a spiritual, physical, and mental connection with self and others. This
mutuality arises from the interaction between the two people. It includes
privacy, intimacy, sharing, belonging, and caring. The atmosphere of
real love is one of honesty, understanding, patience, and forgiveness.
Love does not happen automatically; it requires constant daily effort
by each family member. Loving families share activities and express a
great deal of gratitude for one another. Love takes time, affection, and
a positive attitude.

We learn relational skills and behaviors from within our family.

Strong families manage and control their learning experiences. They establish a pattern that begins with a positive home life. The parent's reflect wholesome values and select appropriate media access. They guide their children into the world outside the home. They do not let social forces rule their family life. They involve themselves in their neighborhood, school, government, church, and business in ways that support their family values. Strong families teach by example and learn through experience.

Strong families have a sense of loyalty and devotion toward each other. The family sticks together. They stand by each other during times of trouble. They stand up for each other when attacked by someone outside the family. Loyalty grows through sickness and health, want and good fortune, failure and success, and all the things the family faces. The family is a place of shelter for individual family members. In times of personal success or defeat, the family remains a cheering section, a shoulder to cry on, or a space for mourning. We also learn a sense of give and take in the family, which helps prepare us for the necessary negotiations in our other extra family relationships.

Laughter is good family medicine. Humor is an escape valve for family tension. Through laughter, we learn to see ourselves honestly and objectively. Building a strong family is serious business, but if taken too seriously, family life can become very tense. Laughter balances our efforts and gives us a realistic view of things. To be helpful, family laughter must be upbeat in nature, laughing with but not laughing at. Laughing together builds up a family. Laughing at each other divides a family. Families that learn to use laughter in a positive way can release tensions, gain a clearer view of things, bond in safety, and feel part of a family.

Leadership & Commitment

Leadership is essential. Family members, usually the adults, must assume responsibility for leading the family. If no one accepts this vital role, the family will weaken. Each family needs its own special set of rules and guidelines. The base of these guiding principles is the family members' understanding of one another. These guidelines pass from the adults to the children by example, with firmness and fairness. Strong families work together to establish their way of life, allowing children to have a voice in decision-making. However, in the initial stages and in times of crisis, adult family members must get the family to work together and set the boundaries.

In studies conducted around the world, several characteristics of well-developed families were established. Strong families are devoted to the well-being and happiness of the other members. They value family synchronization and harmony. Commitment serves as a firm foundation for strong family relationships. Loyalty means that we consistently demonstrate that we are dedicated to each other. When push comes to shove, we put the family unit first. We take our work and social activities seriously, but they come second to family. We honor each person and act with intention that every family member is precious and has unique gifts. We know that hard times or difficulties will not destroy our family relationships because we show that we truly care.

Commitment includes faithfulness and closeness to each person. The partners must set the stage for commitment within the family. We acknowledge that mistakes happen, but know that forgiveness is always available. Priorities help maintain clear boundaries and must be set to insure that relationships are healthy. At times, we make some sacrifices but they need to support mutual goals. Commitment takes into account the traditions and rituals that the family recognizes as important. Members of strong families show their appreciation for one another and express the need for love. With love comes one of our most vital human needs, the call for positive reception. We work hard in life to receive and give love.

Many families find motivation in acquiring money, power, or position or need acceptance and approval at all cost. It is the obsessive desire to feel appreciated and the way we seek approval that causes much of our suffering. Appreciation is vital in healthy families. We enhance each family member's self-esteem when he or she feels cherished, loved, and valued. Appreciation is the sweetness that encourages all members to act positively toward one another. Enjoyment in families requires that we look for the positive instead of the negative. We treat our family members like our best friends, and show our love in small, but affirmative ways. Expressing affection and physical connection means having the assurance to say, "I love you" when needed. Praise is important and expresses the need for giving and receiving positive feedback.

Members of strong families work at developing good communication skills. They talk about the small things as well as the deep, important issues of life. Communication is the lifeblood of the family. The way we express love and other emotions helps us build the strong relationships we desire. We experience the other through communication, and it is up to us whether the communication in our families is successful or not.

Effective communication means that we are open and honest. Communication involves listening carefully without distraction or interruption. When we listen and communicate, we check-out the meaning and clarify messages that are not clear. We avoid mind reading and other projections that result in forming preconception or acting unfairly. We are willing to walk a mile in the other family member's shoes. This requires that we work on trust building and avoid criticizing, evaluating, and acting superior to others. We communicate effectively by dealing with one issue at a time, and contract with the specifics, rather than generalities. We support each other and refrain from attacking, since we pursue the problem not the person.

Spending Quality Time Together:

Time together is important in all relationships. Strong families spend quality time with each other. Some families may say, "We don't spend much time together as a family, but the time we are together is quality time." Studies conducted on strong families indicate that both quality and quantity are necessary for good relationships. Time together filled with bickering, internal strife, and contention do not make for a strong family. Neither will infrequent high-quality time. Nurturing family relationships takes an abundance of good times. We build our family memories around family activities, time spent together. Time spent together helps eliminate isolation, loneliness, and distancing. Time together helps the family develop an identity; a sense of a group union and a sense of family history. It helps avoid the "fizzle and die" of some marriage relationships. It enhances the communication process by allowing other occasions to build up the family foundation.

Spiritual Wellness

Spiritual wellness is a key ingredient to happiness in families. It does not matter if they attend formal religious services or not. Family members have a sense of a greater good or higher power in life. This conviction gives the family direction, potency, and purpose. We define spirituality as a force, power, or energy that helps us reach beyond our ego self to become part of something bigger. Spirituality encompasses our superior nature and includes the aspects of our lives that are upright and honorable. The majority of people consider human beings as having a soul or partaking of a spiritual dimension. Despite the description of our spirituality, we have a need to accept and care for our spiritual life. For many of us spiritual principles give us the tools to deal with life's most perplexing questions. "What is life about?" and "Why am I here?" "What is my purpose?"

The spiritual dimension in families provides many additional benefits. The advantage of having spirituality and a guiding principle is that it assists family members in maintaining an affirmative stance in life. It provides guidelines for living well since a spiritual practice provides access to meaningful faith, ritual, and tradition. Participating in evocative sacraments and ceremony provides a spiritual heritage endowing the family with core values. Spirituality is consciousness of a divine presence that fuels the energy of life and relationships and helps provide coping skills during times of trouble or change. Spirituality encourages a sense of awe and reverence for life itself. We have confidence in a higher power to work out the larger mysteries of life.

Coping Skills

Coping abilities provide families with a constructive view of demands and stress. We learn to treat crisis as an opportunity to grow and learn since good problem solving increases our confidence. We can deal with most things that come our way. We find a variety of coping strategies in strong families. Spirituality provides the ability to find something positive, in any situation and to focus on that affirmative element.

Counselors refer to this as "reframing." It is the ability to see the glass as half-full rather than half empty. A positive perspective allows us to cope with bad situations without becoming overwhelmed. Family members unite and pull together when things get tough. No one individual within the family has to bear the total responsibility for resolving the situation. By sharing the responsibility, every family member can focus on the things he or she can do to help solve the problem.

Strong families get outside help when needed! While many problems or crises can be resolved within the family, strong families are wise enough to know when they are in over their heads. They are not hesitant to seek the assistance of outside resources, such as their church or synagogue, friends, neighbors, extended family, or helping professionals. Some crises may seem so overwhelming that it takes a person from outside the family to help put things into perspective so the family can get their lives back on track.

Many families rely on their spiritual resources to get them through times of crises. Spiritual beliefs can help sustain people in times of trouble by providing a philosophy of life. A spiritual foundation provides a positive perspective by offering hope, comfort, and a sense of peace. Open channels of communication make problem solving easier. Crises are times of change and uncertainty, and family members may feel angry, anxious, fearful, depressed, or guilty. Effective communication allows members to express their feelings freely, which is an important part of surviving the crisis. Flexibility is another important strategy that strong families use to help get through crises. Strong families bend, change, and adapt, and when the storm is over, they are still intact and see the rainbow.

Keep a Family Strong

Each feature of a strong family is important in and of itself; one does not work in isolation from the rest. All positive qualities interact, overlap, connect, and reinforce each other in multifaceted ways. For example, a person who is not committed to the family is not likely to give much time to those relationships. They may not feel the need to pull together with others, in a crisis. Families who spend time together reinforce commitment and clear communication. Achieving these things within our family system may well take the rest of our lives. The ancient Chinese philosopher Lao Tzu said, "A journey of a thousand miles must begin with a single step." So get started!

Let us consider the family's first step from a more fundamental perspective. The human brain needs to develop the capacity for self-sufficiency and quality decision-making. When we have secure attachments to early caregivers, we are ahead of the game. Our ability to act responsibly and appropriately in various situations is accessible. Autonomy is rooted in the security of our relationship with someone who was attuned and responsive when we were helpless or in need. During our early years, we need love and care. Otherwise we cannot flourish. We end up with a vulnerable self-identity and susceptible to mental illness, addiction, adjustment disorders, and posttraumatic stress syndrome. Poor upbringing results in difficult transitions into adulthood and can result in sociopathic relationships that lead to incarceration, institutionalization, mental illness, or social isolation.

If this is the case, here are some exercises to practice to help you let go and move on. You may have been "away" and spent some time "inside." During that interlude, you had time to muse over your earlier life; had a chance to reflect on slip-ups and achievements. You may have said to yourself, "If only I could do ____ (insert situation) over again, I would." It is never too late to begin working on building the relationships you desire. Now is your chance to get started!

What insight can you bring to make different choices in future relationships?

Take a minute and write down all of those would have/should have/could haves! Is there anything you can correct from the past? What mistakes can you make right? Who are the people that you have offended? What insight can you bring to make different choices in future relationships? What character traits do you have now that will allow you to respond in a different way? Turn this list into a "do true" list and check off each item as you move through your past and make amends. If there is a situation that you can correct attempt to do so. If there is some situation you cannot correct, cancel out that action by being a positive force in someone's life now.

There is an old saying, "don't cry over spilled milk." You are on your way. It is the time to do it in a new way now. Take a stroll through your old neighborhood and notice how much things have changed. At the same time, make this the occasion to remember those changes you have already made, and are determined to make in your life. You have noticed growth in your neighborhood and if you take a close look, you will notice that you have grown too.

If you want the same result you have had in your earlier life, you will do the same things you were doing in the past. If you want a different ending, you must choose a new beginning. You are no longer inside a cell (whether literal or figurative). You are free and less confined to certain spaces and mandated activities. As you look up in the sky, you will notice that there is nothing blocking your view of the heavens. Close your eyes and imagine yourself flying high. Fly high above your circumstances, high above those negative influences, high above the fear in your heart.

Begin to visualize your perfect life. Do not limit yourself! Your expectations for your life's happiness will manifest immediately. If you imagine loss and struggle that may be exactly what you will receive. Change your intentions and you will begin to see things line up with your expectations. If you continue to expect people to reject you or judge you, you are looking for signs of rejection and judgment. Any expression you interpret in this way will be faulty. When you learn to expect the best, you will receive the best! Although this may seem like hot air, you will not know if it works, unless you try.

Life Lessons

There are certain life lessons that you will only learn by experiencing them. Share your knowledge with someone who has an open mind and is receptive to what you have learned from your mistakes. This supports positive choices in the future. If you truly believe that the confined life was a negative experience, you will do whatever you can to ensure that those who head in that direction will make different choices. You made it through that situation and you have the responsibility to guide others away from it. Be a mentor by offering to teach younger teens about the pitfalls of their lifestyle through coaching or tutoring.

Allow your life to be a warning signal for others. Proudly become the role model -you always knew you were. The positive energy that you send out into the world returns to you more abundantly than you could ever imagine. Do not let that spark smolder by allowing the world and its issues to bring you down. Sometimes we sabotage our own self-love because we stop being true to our self. Avoid these pitfalls and start celebrating the beauty of you. Share the wisdom you have gained. You will reap the benefits of being a valuable resource to others. Even if we had a difficult time, growing up we can still develop positive and healthy relationships!

Sometimes a family system is damaged and malfunctions in ways that derail the growth of the individuals. In working with various family systems, Bert Hellinger describes age-old "Orders of Love," which are deeply embedded in the unconscious of family groups. Awareness of how this ancient history influences present family patterns is a powerful tool for healing dysfunctional family systems. Knowledge of the role of our ancestors and rediscovering our roots in the family tree refurbishes the family identity in ways that revolutionize people's lives.

Instability to the "Orders of Love" in previous family members in past generations will inescapably affect the lives of both concurrent and future generations. Healing occurs when a family understands the profound pressure of such a deep influence. The family torment and personal anguish reveals life in a completely fresh light. Deep healing of past wounds confirm how love, even when broken, lost or forsaken, can transform into a force for therapeutic gain.

In counseling a family at risk, it is imperative to have them understand that their family system is unique. Family Constellation technique is used to help demonstrate this with practical application since an individual or the entire family may have the opportunity to observe their own family constellation represents family members. /

when family members interact with other participants' constellations this method of family therapy brings new awareness and provides a powerful experience of peering inside the hidden dimensions of a particular family system.

Initially imagine that you are in synchronization and accord with all of your family relationships. Envisage what it would be like if you felt serenity with yourself and synchronization within the family. Discover how within this visualization of simplicity and ease you can relax and use inner vision to see the various roles you are playing. All the fighting, hostility, and aggressiveness within the family may cause conflict and unresolved issues to remain stymied. When you are able to create a map that identifies the various roles and games being played, you can determine to revalue the roles you are playing. Then the family can see how in certain ways each member is already creative, resourceful, and whole. Trust that you have all of the resources within you to bring about a new perspective. Believe in your family, trust that positive experiences are possible, and respect how this affects your world.

The rich tapestry of Family Constellation work will help you discover the power of functioning with the help of your ancestors or relatives from the past. This is a potent exercise for a family to connect to ancient traditions and customs. Working with these forces empowers an innate drive to transform what you see both manifest and hidden in your life. The unsettled inner dialogue or unresolved "family ghost" starts to have less negative control. The harmful patterns of behavior, thinking, and lament inherited from certain ancestors can be reframed in a new light and embraced in an affirming manner. The ancient ones no longer leave a residue of embarrassment or pain since we discover a trace of hidden gold in the stories of our ancestor's defeats and triumphs. A new perspective supports the family breaking the unconscious spell of the past. New family members challenge the actions and stress inherited from such a difficult legacy. The shift in perception of the family tree can be brought to the family table since undisclosed elements can now be celebrated and healed.

I tried this activity by tapping into the world of my family's hopes and dreams. I started a practice of active imagination, began meeting characters from my family in fantasy, and used my inner vision to embark on a journey to meet with my ancestors. When we start to dig into past family history we start becoming curious and ask for stories, myths, and memories. This helps me discover a safe route to imagining a deeper sense of belonging where I am one of the branches of a powerful tree. My heart flows freely like a powerful river of grace taking me home to my primordial family

Some say that ancestor work is beyond conventional therapy. It is more than personal development as it puts us in touch with a deeper tribal pattern. This prototype manifests as a vision of participating in a shared presence as the totality of our particular family. It is a way of reunion with individuals within our family that we have not consciously ever met before. After I participate in this ancestral communion, I often leave the session with a life-altering understanding of my deeper linage to the ancient ones who have paved the way and gone before me. The power of enduring love courses through particular blood lines to demonstrate the depth of human belonging as a unique member of a tribe. The force that governs true relationship emerges from this ancient ground of being.

Family Constellation therapy requires creative explorative work for individuals and couples seeking novel ways to work with troubling features of their family history. Some clients come to look at family constellations when their family dynamics manifest in physical illness, financial trouble, or in disturbing or difficult life patterns such as suicide, murder, rape, addiction, mental illness and criminal behavior. In almost every family, there are things that have happened that can disturb the unity, well-being, and overall health of the family.

A family constellation gives each member a lens to looks at various roles a family member plays out on the family stage. The critical issue in this work is for participants to remember and include forgotten individuals like the "black sheep" of the family. On every level, there is a need for balance between giving and receiving (between individuals, families, and larger groups such religious, racial, or national identity).

Children are born into a particular role in the family constellation. This influences both negative and positive functions. When there is predominantly trauma, the child adopts the suffering of other members of the family. A child may mimic the patterns as if they were his or her own issues or imitate negative relational patterns throughout life.

Moreover, certain events cause profound distress in any family. These destructive spirits and shadowy characters are part of much family history causing residual impact on family members.

The following list includes:
An early death of parents or grandparents
Tragic accidents where a member of the family has died
Divorce
Miscarriages, Stillbirths, Abortions, Death of a Child
A member of the family forced into the role of "Black Sheep"
War
Holocaust Survivor Guilt/Loss
Descendents of Jewish Pogroms
Descendents of African slaves
Adoptions
A mother that dies during childbirth
Kidnapping
Torture
Cult survivor

Family Constellation Therapy Session

A Family Constellation session involves a leader working with each client or workshop participant to identify, discuss, and represent various family members from his or her perspective. The participant places each family member in a position on a diagram or intuitive chart. This also includes an individual that represents you. As you begin to place each family member within the constellation you will be amazed! The family constellation comes to life, as if stars making recognizable patterns in the sky.

I encourage clients engaged in family therapy to look sincerely at the individuals they have included in the family constellation. Your particular family constellation comes alive as you notice how you represent those who symbolize a specific family member. You begin to feel their emotions, fears, and desires as if they were your own. You look at the family from the other's point of view and try to imagine how life feels from their observation.

Through this process, I see the underlying conflicts in a fresh way. I find this to be an amazing approach since I see more clearly the various roles played in the family story. We see our place in the family, notice the roles being played. The first time I experienced working on my family constellation chart, I was surprised. It confronts me with how it must feel to play a role that is different from the one I chose to play or was assigned. I clearly see how I chose family members to represent various roles in my configurations. I identify how my unique role is a role I take part in that radically influences how I choose to view the roles played by others in my family.

The goal is to bring awareness to how, why, and who plays the various roles within the family. It is beneficial to notice the roles others have adopted, the character one exhibits, the responsibilities or lack thereof. We become conscious of the underlying patterns of how our particular family constellation works, so we can activate ongoing awareness of the task, purpose, and position of each member.

The experience of working with family constellation gives me a change of perspective. It is a deep process since it helps me understand the particular role each member of my family is playing out in our distinctive constellation. Clients who participate in this exercise commonly report that it helps them better recognize the position they embody within the family. However, they are also astonished at how powerful the experience can be. Many report that as a child within their family, they wanted more than anything else to feel secure and a sense of belonging. Working with the constellation helps each individual to find happiness and harmony within the family by reimagining how they fit in.

Codependency

After investigating our family constellation, we often discover that we are in some form of codependency, based on the role we play within our family. Codependency is a psychological condition that often manifests in a relationship based on control or manipulation by another. One person's behavior (co-dependency) is in the control of a pathological condition (typically narcissism, abusive behavior, or drug/alcohol addiction). Simply put, co-dependency refers to the dependence on the needs of, or control of, another.

Codependency also commonly involves placing a lower priority on one's own needs, while being excessively preoccupied with the needs of others. Codependency can occur in any type of relationship, but is most common in family, but arises in work, friendship, romantic, peer, or community relationships. Codependency has the characteristics of extreme denial, low self-esteem, excessive compliance, or control patterns. Narcissists are natural magnets for the codependent as are dependent personalities with addictive behaviors.

Historically, the concept of codependence comes directly out of Alcoholics Anonymous. This system is part of a dawning realization that the problem was not solely the addict, but also the family and friends who constitute a network for the alcoholic or addict. It later broadened to cover the way that the codependent person is obsessed, engrossed, and absorbed in another person. They seek approval, sustenance, security, and so on. Some would maintain that to actually be co-dependent would requires one person to be physically or psychologically addicted, such as to drugs or alcohol, and the second person to be psychologically dependent on that behavior.

In terms of the family, codependency describes behaviors, thoughts, and feelings that go beyond normal kinds of self-sacrifice or caretaking. For example, parenting is a role that requires a certain amount of self-sacrifice and giving a child's needs a high priority. Although, a parent could nevertheless still be codependent towards their own children if parental sacrifice reaches unhealthy or destructive levels. Normally, a parent who takes care of their own needs (emotional and physical) in a healthy way will be a better caretaker, whereas a codependent parent may be less effective, or may even do harm to a child. From this perspective, the needs of an infant are necessary but temporary whereas the needs of the codependent are continuous.

People who learn codependency in childhood often take on the role of martyr; they constantly put others' needs before their own. Others may take on the role of the superstar or the saint and in doing so forget to take care of themselves or others. This creates a sense that they are "desirable." They cannot stand the idea of being alone and no one needing them seems a cruel punishment. Codependent people are constantly in search of acceptance. When it comes to arguments, codependent people also tend to set themselves up as the "victim". When they do stand up for themselves, they feel guilty or ashamed.

Codependency does not refer to all caring behavior or feelings, but only those that are excessive to an unhealthy degree. Indeed, from the standpoint of Attachment Theory or Object Relations Theory, to learn healthy co-dependency or interdependency is the goal of healthy development. The risk of the overly self-reliant person is becoming dependent and is a positive step forward. The person who is compulsively independent and always has to be autonomous may need to be more dependent as a psychological move toward interdependence. It is not about only depending on a source outside oneself but finding a thriving, tolerable, reliance on others.

In a family system it is helpful to look at the patterns of codependence.

Here is a list:

Denial Patterns:
I have difficulty identifying what I am feeling.
I minimize, alter, or deny how I truly feel.
I perceive myself as completely unselfish, dedicated to the well-being of others.
I lack empathy for the feelings and needs of others.
I label others with my negative traits.
I can take care of myself without any help from others.
I mask my pain in various ways such as anger, humor, or isolation.
I express negativity or aggression in indirect and passive ways.
I do not recognize the unavailability of those people to whom I am attracted.

Low self-esteem patterns:

I have difficulty making decisions.

I judge everything I think, say or do harshly, as never "good enough."

I am embarrassed to receive recognition, praise, or gifts.

I do not ask others to meet my needs or desires.

I value others' approval of my thinking, feelings, and behavior over my own.

I do not perceive myself as a lovable or worthwhile person.

I constantly seek recognition that I think I deserve.

I am jealous of the relationships between others I would like to have as my own.

I have difficulty admitting that I made a mistake.

I need to appear to be right in the eyes of others and will even lie to look good.

I perceive myself as inferior to others.

I look to others to provide my sense of safety.

I have difficulty getting started, meeting deadlines, and completing projects.

I have trouble setting healthy priorities.

Avoidance patterns:

I act in ways that invite others to reject, shame, or express anger toward me.

I judge harshly what others think, say, or do.

I avoid emotional, physical, or sexual intimacy as a means of maintaining distance.

I allow my addictions to people, places, and things to distract me from achieving intimacy in relationships.

I use indirect and evasive communication to avoid conflict or confrontation.

I diminish my capacity to have healthy relationships by declining to use all the tools of recovery.

I suppress my feelings or needs to avoid feeling vulnerable.

I pull people toward me, but when they get close, I push them away.

I refuse to give up my self-will to avoid surrendering to a power that is greater than I am.

I believe displays of emotion are a sign of weakness.

I withhold expressions of appreciation.

Compliance patterns:

I compromise my own values and integrity to avoid rejection or others' anger.

I am very sensitive to how others are feeling and feel the same.

I am extremely loyal, remaining in harmful situations too long.

I value others' opinions and feelings more than my own and am afraid to express differing opinions and feelings of my own.

I put aside my own interests and hobbies in order to do what others want.

I accept sex and/or sexual attention when I want love.

I am afraid to express my beliefs, opinions, and feelings when they differ from those of others.

I make decisions without regard to the consequences.

I give up my truth to gain the approval of others or to avoid change.

Control patterns:

I believe most other people are incapable of taking care of themselves.

I attempt to convince others of what they "should," think and how they "truly" feel.

I become resentful when others will not let me help them.

I freely offer others advice and directions without being asked.

I lavish gifts and favors on those I love and care.

I use sex to gain approval and acceptance.

I have to be "needed" in order to have a relationship with others.

I demand that my needs be met by others.

I use charm and charisma to convince others of my capacity to be caring and compassionate.

I use blame and shame to exploit others emotionally.

I refuse to cooperate, compromise, or negotiate.

I adopt an attitude of indifference, helplessness, authority, or rage to manipulate outcomes.

I have obsessive, compulsive thinking patterns and cannot focus on daily activities.

I use terms of recovery in an attempt to control the behavior of others. I pretend to agree with others to get what I want.

Role of Narcissism:

In family dynamics if there is co-dependency, there is also narcissism. A family member, who is in the role of the narcissists, has the uncanny ability to seduce others to adopt their vision of life and the family. Narcissism helps them make it a reality since they are an innate magnet for the co-dependent person. Narcissists need the co-dependent and rely on their tendency to put others' need before their own. Among the joint security device of the interacting pair, are the way the narcissist has an overriding need to feel center stage and special. The co-dependent has a well-built need to help others feel that way. The narcissist exaggerates self-caring and demands it from others, while the co-dependent diminishes or may even allow for no self-care or personal preferences.

In psychoanalytic terms, the narcissist manifests such all-powerful and unstoppable behavior and is especially self-governing and self-determining. They exert a particularly captivating effect on all dependent persons since they struggle to participate in the supreme and invincible narcissist's power. Narcissist and codependent participate together in a form of an ego-defense system called projective identification. Projective identification differs from simple projection in that projective identification can become a self-fulfilling prophecy, whereby a person, believing something false about another, relates to that other person in such a way that the other person alters their behavior to make the belief true. The second person is influenced by the projection and begins to behave as though he or she is in fact actually characterized by the projected thoughts or beliefs, a process that may happen outside the awareness of both parties involved.

Alan Rappoport (2005) identifies codependents of narcissists as "co-narcissists." The codependent narcissist gives up his or her own needs to feed and fuel the needs of the other. In everyday family life, recovery means the ability to recognize the self-destructive elements in one's character structure, and to expand strategies to reduce the harm to family members.

There are various recovery paths for individuals and families who struggle with codependency. For example, some may choose behavioral psychotherapy, such as Dialectical Behavioral Therapy or Cognitive Behavioral Therapy sometimes accompanied by (psychopharmacology) chemical therapy for accompanying depression, anxiety, and obsessive/compulsive disorder.

There are many harmful effects of unaddressed codependency. Unresolved patterns of codependency can lead to serious problems like alcoholism, drug addiction, eating disorders, sex addiction, and other self-destructive or self-defeating behaviors. People who grow up in a family with codependency are also more likely to attract further abuse from aggressive individuals, more likely to stay in stressful jobs, or relationships, and less likely to seek medical attention when needed. Codependent personalities are less likely to get promotions, and tend to earn less money than those without codependency patterns.

For some, the social insecurity caused by codependency can progress into full-blown social anxiety disorders like social phobia, avoidant personality disorder, or painful shyness. Other stress-related disorders like panic disorder, depression, or PTSD may also be present. Many therapists maintain that finding a balance through healthy assertiveness (which leaves room for being a caring person and engaging in healthy caring behavior) is true recovery from codependency and that becoming extremely selfish, a bully, or an otherwise conflict-addicted person is not.

In family dynamics, a common image emerges of victim mentality. Developing a permanent stance of being a victim is not representing true recovery from codependency. A victim mentality is a part of one's original state of codependency. It may arise in childhood due to lack of empowerment causing one to feel like the "subject" of events rather than being an empowered agent or actor or one's life story. A family that helps all members truly recover from codependency empowers the family and brings new life-affirming dynamics into play. The individual feels like an author of life and takes action rather than being at the mercy of outside forces.

Building a relationship within becomes the source of true recovery. The perspective of moving beyond victim-hood requires the capacity to forgive and let go. There are certain cases (with exception of very cruel abuse) where forgiveness seems impossible. Nevertheless, this could be a sign of real recovery from codependency since it demonstrates a willingness to stop further abuse. Returning to codependency and allowing the abuse to continue would not be a sign of healing.

Choosing to care for an individual with a physical addiction is not necessarily a sign of pathology. Before naming the caregiver, a co-alcoholic/addict look at the role the individual takes. Who is responsible for the continued existence of the partner's alcoholism? If for example, it is the enabling pathology of care giving behavior then something is amiss. To be skillful at being a caregiver may only require assertiveness skills. The ability to stop being responsible for the addiction, and put the responsibility on the other is key.

Not all mental health professionals agree about codependence or its standard methods of treatment. It is not listed in the DSM-IV-TR. Stan Katz & Liu, in "The Codependency Conspiracy: How to Break the Recovery Habit and Take Charge of Your Life," consider codependence as over-diagnosed. Many people find help with shorter-term treatments or basic self-awareness instead become dependent on long-term self-help programs or co-addicted to 12 step programs.

Some believe that codependency is not a negative trait, and does not need treatment, as it is more likely a healthy personality trait to the extreme. Codependency has some links with characteristics of family functioning or dysfunction. The language of pathology is frequent used of the codependent personality. The word is an alternative to the concept "dysfunctional family," without statements that classify it as an illness.

Not everything promoted by the self-help, recovery, or pop psychology industry is a definite scientific fact; some of it arises from a cult craze or faith alone. Families dealing with issues of co-dependency must examine the problem from multiple perspectives before jumping to conclusions about where the issue really lies and with what family member(s).

There also exists support groups for codependency, such as Co-Dependents Anonymous (CoDA), Al-Anon/Alateen, Nar-Anon, and Adult Children of Alcoholics (ACoA) based on the twelve-step program model of Alcoholics Anonymous. Although the term codependency originated outside of twelve-step groups, it is now a common concept in many of them. Often an important result of a Family Intervention is to highlight codependent behaviors of various family members. This often requires a great commitment to love and forgiveness when encouraging the codependent person to accept help. The capacity to work through codependency has powerful ramifications for future relationships and especially with deepening true intimacy.

Now you have some of the skills to create positive family relationships. You have a toolbox that helps you clearly design the family relationships that you yearn for and deserve. Throughout this section on the family, we learn that the best predictor of a successful future for your family is appropriate behavior in the earlier period of development and childrearing. This is a great burden for parents raising children today and is an immense responsibility since co-dependency is an obstacle to the child's future success in all fields of endeavor.

The behavioral patterns and habits we adopt from childhood upbringing become engrained in our psyche causing habitual thought pattern. These patterns are unconsciously transmitted into all adult relationships. The child's training is apparent in their personality since they receive it via the parent's feelings, emotions, values, sense of worth, and behaviors. These unconscious patterns by definition are automatic since we are not aware of them. The flow of the family's emotions, and the lifestyle created within the specific matrix conspires to suck the life out of further relationships if the unconscious patterns continue unchecked.

Nevertheless, we know that the family can win this battle. We can challenge ourselves and those we work with to distinguish ways to build effective relational skills. We do so by supporting each member to move from codependency to interdependency. Following The Golden Rule provides the opportunity to fulfill our unique destiny. I strongly believe the human capacity "to do unto the other, as we would have them do unto us" must begin and end with the recognition of the Golden Rule within the family. When we imagine we are part of the human family we move the whole closer to adopting a widespread universal moral code.

An Initial "Declaration toward a Global Ethic" from the Parliament of the World's Religions (1993) proclaimed the necessity of following the Golden Rule. They stated, "We must treat others as we wish others to treat us" as the common principle for many religions and offered it as an attitude for the human family. One hundred and forty three respected leaders from all of the world's major faiths signed the Initial Declaration, including Baha'i Faith, Brahmanism, Buddhism, Christianity, Hinduism, Indigenous, Interfaith, Islam, Jainism, Judaism, Native American, Neo-Pagan, Sikhism, Taoism, Theosophist, Unitarian Universalist and Zoroastrian. Again, this highlights the value of a establishing a firm foundation in family values. These values help us all deepen our relationship to our deeper self within. This supports the human community aligning with a higher power so we can strive to embody the attitude proposed by the Golden Rule.

The dictionary of philosophy contains the following exact quote under the entry for "The Golden Rule": The maxim "Treat others how you wish to be treated." Various expressions of this fundamental moral rule are in tenets of most religions and creeds through the ages, testifying to its universal applicability. Walter Terence Stace (1937) argues that the Golden Rule was much more than simply an ethical code. Instead, he posits, it "expresses the essence of a universal morality." The underlying principle for this important distinction has occupied much of this book. I argue that this "universal morality" emerges from deepening our relationship within.

SECTION THREE:
Intimate Relationships

CHAPTER ONE:
Romantic relationships

❦

In romantic love, there is an emphasis on emotions, especially those of love, buoyancy, thoughtfulness, positive reception, and attraction rather than physical intimacy.

The opening step of an intimate relationship is like falling down the rabbit hole into wonderland. This initial theater of romance is more involved with the feeling of being in love than love itself. The primary sensation of this stage is feeling as if your heart is a rushing whirlwind of agony and ecstasy. Rapture sweeps you up, but you also oscillate between suffering and seventh heaven. There is the fear of suddenly being taken over or entrapped by the other. The other becomes an obsession that ensnares you in a furtive, hush-hush of yearning and desire.

In romantic love, there is an emphasis on emotions, especially those of love, buoyancy, thoughtfulness, positive reception, and attraction rather than mere physical intimacy. The attributes of love in the early stage is uncertainty, nervousness, and emotional apprehension since the vulnerability of falling in love could lead to betrayal, rejection, or other kinds of negative responses. Love stirs up vast questions about our very ability to be loved. It spins us around like a tether ball on a tent pole of insecurity while simultaneously it launches us on an unknown course where we meet new desires, longing for wholeness, and discover completion within another.

Romantic love is always a conversation between two and requires a special language particular to intimacy. Often courtship marks the early stage of intimacy since it focuses on emotional closeness, and trust rather than mere physical passion and sex. This is not to say that sexual intimacy is to replace romance as an expression of affection, adoration, and dedication. The opposite is true. Intimacy and romance comingle and become the subtext of our life drama. "He loves me he loves me not," goes the old rhyme game of plucking the daisy petals. Every girl hopes to land on he loves me! The boy hopes against all hope that the girl will say yes. Therefore, we are like the birds, the bees, the flowers, and the trees, we keep insisting on union of opposites, conjoining, and perpetuating our self by procreating.

Everyone remembers his or her first love. Some may carry this to an extreme and go through life feeling a deep longing for someone they loved in the past but could not have a relationship. They may pine for someone they never consummated a relationship but the fantasy of union endures. Many have shared stories of such events in their own lives that still haunt them. Others have memories of initial adoration and bliss but wonder for years what went so wrong. The premature lust for union we feel in courtship, puppy love, and early forms of closeness linger around our minds and pull at our heartstrings. The first flame of intimacy continues through out life as an enduring presence.

In the book *The Transformation of Intimacy: Sexuality, Love and Eroticism in Modern Society,* Anthony Giddens (1992) suggests that romantic love was first explored as an art form in early literature. Initially it appears in the romance novel as a personal expression of a secret passion for another. Love as an outward appearance of personal infatuation first became the inspiration of clandestine love affaires portrayed in novels. Romantic love emerges from the erotic imagery of our personality and how it plays out in the world of fantasy and flights of the imagination. As such, romance is a worthy subject of the narrative since it taps into the unconscious psychic realm of dreams, hallucinations, hypnotic states, and orgasmic rapture.

As romantic creatures, we all have a fantasy life that is very imaginative to begin with. We need to court and spark this aspect of our creativity and bring this fervor into our daily life. However, this can be tricky business for the novice. The focus of romantic love is on the virtues, rather than the shortcomings, of the beloved. When you are in love, you are afire and all a glow with your passion. Even though your needs are important, in romance you tend to put the other first.

The importance of the other becomes tantamount since your ability to act correctly toward the beloved helps you telegraph your romantic desires and this enhances your personality. You feel invincible, and this is the key to passionate love. Your innate confidence opens the door to sexual intimacy. You may be holding the trump card on all the romantic power, but you are not likely to use this influence unjustly. Your romance will flower because your partner admires and appreciate both your restraint and your ardor.

Do not be surprised if you become infatuated. You derive unexpected feelings of love from thinking about your love. This fascination happens when you are away from your beloved. Use this feeling to extract even more juice from an already valuable situation. In romance, outward appearances are important in the initial attraction field. It might affect how your partner views things, but not you. You will know how to dig deep beneath the surface. You will figure out a way to romance your significant other without compromising yourself.

The value of being able to communicate your truth to another and share the deepest and darkest areas is crucial. When we can tell our stories, even the most embarrassing and venerable aspects with another, this is romance. After all, the term "romance" in Early English connotes the activity of storytelling. Who does not enjoy a good, juicy love story? The swell of romantic love as a challenging aspect of society coincides with the emergence of the novel. Through the art of writing, romantic love became associated with the tenet of love as freedom of self-expression.

The ideals of romantic love are everywhere from literature to art and music and creates a unique attraction field for each person. Memories of love arise from times in the past when someone special has rallied round us or were there when we needed to feel adored or special. Our compassion is easily aroused when we are in the romantic mood, and we do not take advantage of our partner. We get the most satisfaction from indulging in our charitable instincts. We begin to tell our own romance story and engage in an activity that draws us into a deeper dance with another where we are aware of both autonomy and interdependence.

Romantic love is the relationship that has particular forms of betrayal and abandonment. Here the green eyed monster of envy often rears it's ugly head in the forms of coveting one's neighbor's wife or going after another woman' husband. These common stereotypes attempt to reduce the archetypal urge to control or own another. This increases in frequency in romance when we blindly blame another for our unhappiness. The potential to project our unconscious desires for intimacy onto another lead to extremes, like acting out negative behaviors when we are rejected. These actions are often associated with domestic violence such as changes in marital status or mid-life crisis, leading to being consumed or fixed on unavailable romantic partners. For many the preoccupation may lead to harmful encounters.

Our society strives to treat others as fairly as possible by right of law. We also know that romantic feelings are often not shared or mutual resulting in sexual crimes. Sexuality is a powerful force that can get out of control. With human rights and gender choices, more people live in a time of sexual revolution or evolution. In current society romantic life is in transition. Intimacy is under scrutiny and our erotic contact feels the challenging effects. With the growth of technology our social relations are changing, including family structure, marriage, and partnership. The meaning of marriage has undergone significant alterations. Women have more socially acceptable options than ever before and are utilizing their power. However, more than ever, men and especially women are less willing to tolerate unhappy relationships. Consequently, divorce rates are persistently on the increase; now to over 50%.

The stage of relationship that we call "romance" is as real today as it was in ancient times. The perennial question remains, how do we appropriately romance and get together sexually? What is the chemistry that causes us to fall in love? What does it really require to maintain intimacy, during courtship, as well as after the "honeymoon"? In part, romance offers exciting relational activities, exploration, and adventure. It is a rare time where we consent to engage another person intensely in emotional and physical revelation. During these displays of affection, we desire to know every aspect of the beloved since we find them irresistible.

Instinct tells us to shine and be adorable so we are attractive. Strut your tail feathers and display all your fluff since this flaunting opens you to the possibility of attracting your ideal mate. This seems so easy and direct for some. Nevertheless, for many people, intimacy offers deep contact that is scary and out of the ordinary. In romantic companionship, sharing profound intimacy interweaves our diverse romantic experiences into tapestry that makes sense and has meaning for both partners. Romantic love is an extended, eternal dialogue. It is a constant conversation with the other, since what we see in the other is actually a mirror of our deepest self. We romance our soul. We seek the beloved one in the outside reflection of the beloved other. Most think we discover this in an outer romantic relationship, but actually, it is the longing for a relationship within.

Romance in time-honored terminology means "court as lover." The concept of romantic love originates in the late nineteenth century, primarily from French culture. This idea spurs us to examine the connection between the words "romantic" and "lover." Love may include, but is not limited to, the idealistic, rapturous feeling that accompanies the intense emotional aspect of "falling in love." Romantic love feels amazing as well as unpredictable, erratic, infuriating, and changeable. It is a roller coaster ride that consumes time, energy, and drains due to the emotional intensity. It can get out of control because there is always the lurking possibility of "falling out of love." Nevertheless, the eternal flame burns on!

Love Styles

Love styles are the various modes two people use to come together. It is the modus operandi of how people love. Originally developed by John Lee (1973, 1988) where he identified six basic love styles, also known as "colors" of love that people use in their interpersonal relationships. He described these styles as *eros, ludos, storge, pragma, mania* and *agape*.

1. Eros is a passionate physical and emotional love based on aesthetic enjoyment; stereotype of romantic love.

2. Ludus is a love one plays as a game or sport and loves conquest. One may have multiple partners at once.

3. Storge is an affectionate love that slowly develops from friendship.

4. Pragma is love driven by the head, not the heart; restrained, phlegmatic, and unemotional.

5. Mania is obsessive love; experience great emotional highs and lows; very possessive and often jealous lovers.

6. Agape is selfless altruistic love.

John Lee compared styles of love to the color wheel. Just as there are three primary colors, Lee suggested that there are three principal styles of love. These three styles of love are: (1) Eros, (2) Ludos and (3) Storge. Continuing the color wheel analogy, Lee surmised that, similar to combining the primary colors to create complementary colors, these three primary styles of love when combined create nine different secondary love styles. For example, a combination of Eros and Ludos results in Mania, or obsessive love.

Six Styles of Loving

Three primary styles:
1. Eros – Loving an ideal person
2. Ludos – Love as a game
3. Storge – Love as friendship

Three secondary styles:
1. Mania (Eros + Ludos) – Obsessive love
2. Pragma (Ludos + Storge) – Realistic and practical love
3. Agape (Eros + Storge) – Selfless love

Triangular Theory of Love

Psychologist Robert Sternberg proposed a triangular theory of love that suggests that there are three components of love: intimacy, passion, and commitment. Different combinations of these three components result in different types of love. For example, a combination of intimacy and commitment results in compassionate love, while a combination of passion and intimacy leads to passionate love.

Sternberg suggests that human's build relationships on two or more elements. He used the term consummate love to describe a combination of intimacy, passion, and commitment. While this type of love is the strongest and most permanent, Sternberg implies that this type of love is exceptional and uncommon.

Intimate relationships require attention

As long as the health of an intimate relationship remains important to You, it is going to call for Your attention and effort.

Many people fall in love, become a couple, and only focus on their relationship when there are specific, unavoidable problems to overcome. Once the problems have been resolved, they often switch their attention back to their careers, children, or other interests. However, intimate relationships require ongoing attention and commitment for love to thrive. As long as the health of an intimate relationship remains important to you, it is going to call for your attention and effort. Sometimes problems in a relationship may seem too complex or overwhelming for a couple to handle on their own. In that case, it is important to reach out together for help.

Most relationships will undergo stress and conflict at some time, resulting in low functioning. When we are not connecting in the best possible way, both parties produce maladaptive patterns and engage in negative interactive cycles. There are many possible reasons for this, including insecure attachment, ego, arrogance, jealousy, anger, greed, poor communication, or problem solving skills, not to mention ill health, third parties entanglements, and family conflicts.

Changes in situations like, physical health, employment, economics, and the influence of trauma, and violence can exert intense pressure. Automatic negative reactions and hurtful responses contribute to the break down in communication in a relationship. Frequently, the rupture is the result of a crossing point between two or more important personal value. Disagreement drives a wedge between two people. Common problems are a result of faulty communication in the field between two people. We are aware that it is never only one person that creates negative qualities or lack of enthusiasm. Relationship pressure is by no means one-sided.

A workable solution is more likely when we address the problem in a positive way. We are more likely to catch flies with honey, so sweetness helps put romance back on the path. One practical answer is to fine-tune customary responses so they do not become habitual. Each individual has sensitivity and feelings about how to approach an intimate relationship. The relationship must encompass the reality and perceived truth of each party. We each assume we know what is happening within the relationship, but rarely stop to ask what is stirring in the other. We respond to problematic situations and experiences the best way we can. Perceptions of, and emotional responses to, a relationship are encoded within our memory and brought to the surface during tension and conflict. We each co-create an unconscious mental map of the relationship, also called a "love map."

John Gottman (1999) identified love maps as a therapeutic way to help couples explore creative solutions to conflicts so they can join forces in love. He found that when couples work together with a love map they stop sabotaging the relationship. His research found that we tend to build intimate relationships around common values. We discover the specific encoding of our partner's deeper issues. We are aware of areas of conflict, what causes unhappiness, and move away from difficult patterns. Love maps then are altered, adjusted or changed. When attitudes and activities no longer suit relationship, there is open discussion. This involves each person taking equal responsibility for the difficulty. The relationship work centers on accountability for how each person's behavior contributes to the conflict.

Couples counseling can reveal the degree to which hopelessness has taken over. The therapist is aware of the inner dynamics and provides for both parties to freely share. The couple is encouraged to look at what hurts and what helps. The therapist sheds light on what is vital and what intolerable. Each can endure looking at how they are involved in the suffering that the relationship undergoes. The process of working on a love map supports each party in looking clearly at how he or she contributes to the problem.

Awareness of the role each person plays guarantees new strategies will emerge. The individuals need to foster fundamental changes by rewriting their love map. One significant way is to reimaging what a revolutionized relationship would look like. When you know how your partner views you and brings value to your character this helps you design artful and shared intimacy. The couple evaluates the value of these changes they have identified and come back to reevaluate the changes over time. This supports interdependence and builds a flow between self-sufficiency and dependence, so the two are separate yet equal partner on a journey to a deeper relationship within.

CHAPTER TWO:
Fundamentals of Couples Counseling

❧

When the couple sees conflict as potentially positive, it revolutionizes the relationship.

The focus of couples counseling is primarily to help conflicted partners center attention on the process of communication. The most commonly used technique is active listening, utilized by the late Carl Rogers and Virginia Satir. More recently, a method called Cinematic Immersion by Warren Farrell (1999) emerged to help couples learn a method of effective communication.

Farrell's Cinematic Immersion is a way to create a safe environment for each partner to express feelings and to tolerate hearing the feelings of others. Farrell's observations led to noting that active listening enhanced the work of creating a safe environment for the criticizer to criticize, and for the listener to hear the criticism. The listener, often feeling overwhelmed by the criticism, tends to avoid future encounters. Farrell's hypothesis suggests that we have biological programming to respond defensively to criticism. Therefore, his form of counseling includes mental exercises to help the partners understand how they often interpret criticism as the result of omitted or misplaced expressions of love. Disapproval results in negative feelings such as anger, suspicion, and fear. The absence of condemning words creates devoted partners since both partners feel safe to be real and effectively to communicate conflicting feelings.

After three decades of delving into what makes for an enduring marriage, John Gottman (1999) found that healthy couples almost never actively listen or mirror each other's feelings as might be expected. Gottman's research illustrates that whether unhappy or intensely joyful, couples said what they thought about an issue. Gottman's research reveals that the couple said they got angry or sad, but their partner's response was never anything like what the therapist was expecting people to do in the listener/speaker exercises.

Gottman's line of investigation demonstrates how learning to disagree with a partner is essential. His analysis of childhood conditioning illustrates the importance of negotiating conflict and disagreement. When an individual learns to keep his or her true feelings hidden from potential authority this may lead to lack of intimacy. The ability to engage in positive acts of communication includes allowing for variation and difference. These capacities contribute to whether the couple can allow for passionate gestures, try out innovative sexual positions, or reveal emotional vulnerability. Love maps can help partners see what is going on beneath the surface of the relationship since this permits different preferences and love styles.

As an alternative, the couple becomes aware of what they are actually feeling. Both parties can come clean about what they need and how to express emotional attachments. When the couple sees conflict as potentially positive, it revolutionizes the relationship. This prevents the couple from entrapment in obsessive dependency on the other partner, in similar ways that a child is on a parent. Interdependence places care giving, receiving encouragement, soothing, and security on inner resources. The contractual obligation and purpose of a relationship counselor or couple's therapist is to listen, respect, understand, and facilitate better overall functioning in the relationship, whether or not this means that the relationship has to end.

The basic services that couples counseling provides:

Couples counseling provide a confidential dialogue, which normalizes feelings and enables people to hear themselves while listening to the other. Counseling provides a mirroring therapist who provides understanding and supports the couple building skills that reflect the relationship's difficulties and potential paths for change. Many couples in crisis seek counsel to help them empower the relationship. Some request counseling to gain authority over their future direction and to establish common values. Others inquire about how to strengthen their essential decision making process or to repair the relationship if infidelity arise.

The counselor conveys relevant and appropriate information that identifies the repetitive, negative interaction cycles they are engaging in and to change this into a more functional and dynamic pattern. The counselor provides support so the couple can understand the source of the reactive emotions that drive the relationship toward ruin. The couple creates a blueprint of how they would each design a positive relationship. They use this as a tool to expand and re-organize key emotional responses in the relationship. Often when the couple facilitates a shift in their interactions, new patterns emerge spontaneously. Clear communication creates fresh and optimistic visions of what is possible and what is not. This fosters a secure attachment between partners and ultimately helps maintain a sense of intimacy.

Common core principles of relationship counseling and couple's therapy include the counselor encouraging the participants to give their best efforts to readdress their relationship with each other. One of the challenges here is for each person to modify their own responses to their partner's behavior. Other obstacles to the process include disclosing contentious, shocking, or disgraceful events. When revealing closely guarded secrets, not all couples put all of their cards on the table at first. This can take time. A couple's therapist helps keep the difficult lines of communication open.

There are a number of options available for working on intimacy issues.

Couples counseling: You might be considering couples counseling or marriage counseling. It is a big investment of time, energy, focus, and commitment. Working on problems and the desire to change must come from both parties. Each one is willing to communicate what he/she needs, and to face issues square on. When problems arise, counseling can support the couple making needed adjustments. It is important that both people feel at ease with the counselor for trust to emerge.

Spiritual advice: Some couples benefit from spiritual advice from a religious figure such as a priest, pastor, minister, or rabbi. This tends to work best if both persons have similar convictions about belief in God, and have a good relationship with their spiritual advisor, and faith tradition.

Emotional Intelligence: Another way of insuring that you can grow and sustain relationships is by developing emotional intelligence. Try using a holistic approach that encourages a balanced lifestyle, including mindful eating, sleeping, and sexual activity to develop a personal mind/body tool kit. This supports the couple's expressing intimate connection. This capacity is necessary for building emotional intelligence since a relationship that encourages emotional expression supports intelligent emotional processing. When we process emotions well this provides fertile ground that supports positive relationships in other areas of life.

Individual therapy: Psychotherapy is sometimes effective if one of the partners requires professional individual therapy and specialized help. For example, someone who is grieving the loss of a loved one may need counseling to help him or her process the grief. If your loved one needs help with an addiction, do not feel like you are a failure for not providing them with everything they need. No one can fulfill everyone's needs, and getting the right help can make a tremendous difference in your relationship.

Effective communication: Being able to commune with your partner is essential to maintaining open lines of communication. When we speak our truth with respect and encourage the other to do the same, we cultivate the secret garden of relationship by the water of appreciation and the sunlight of understanding. Then intimacy miraculously flowers. While communication may seem simple, there are skills you can learn to avoid misunderstandings and improve all your interactions. This is especially true in intimate situations where communication styles may conflict and sensitivities are more likely to arise.

Anger Management: Managing our anger is essential to clearing the air after dispute and conflict. If we cannot express deep animosity or resentment in our intimacy, it may display as an explosive rage toward the other. Couples benefit from effective anger management that includes conflict resolution and dealing with irritation. Anger management provides tools that assist you in expressing unpleasant and upsetting feelings in healthier ways and keeps your temper from undermining your relationships.

Humor: Good-humored, lighthearted, and playful communications in relationships are useful when they incorporate absurdity, wit, and the funny side of each other into the otherwise stuck and inflexible relationship dynamics. Bringing laughter into your daily interactions can strengthen your relationships in amazing ways since it encourages lightheartedness. Looking at the comedic aspect of life is a skill that can be effective when we need to apply a sense of humor and wit to a predicament. Positive conflict can provide an opportunity to strengthen the bond between two people.

Nonverbal communication skills: The majority of the messages you send are nonverbal. It is vital to understand and use body language effectively. How you carry yourself, your posture, and eye contact inform your partner of a vast storehouse of information. When your nonverbal skills are intact, you build better relationships both in the bed and in joint work.

CHAPTER THREE:
Attachment and Adult Relationships

⚜

The goal in an intimate relationship is to feel physically and emotionally connected and passionate about another.

We all attach to other people and build relationship in idiosyncratic ways based on our conditioning. We learn about how we first formed attachment bonds, ironically by looking at how attachment patterns continue to affect your adult relations. When we have successfully negotiated the art of positive attachments in childhood, we feel a supportive undergirding around the ongoing process of building healthy intimate relationships. The aspiration in any intimate relationship is to share the positive feeling of being together. Attachment patterns demonstrate the sensation of powerful physical attraction that arises when we are emotionally connected, and passionate about another. However to achieve this aim requires the art of forming attachments. At the heart of an intimate relationship, is a calm center of repose and relaxation. When we are deficient in the element of inner peace, it is often due to a feeling of powerlessness cause by the inability to create healthy boundaries. Strong boundaries allow a person to experience comfortable interdependence with other people. This results in well functioning relationships and positive self-esteem.

Take a self-inquiry to find out how you set boundaries and go about forming attachments.

I have discovered remarkable information about myself. This "to do list" provides insight into intimacy issues. Take the time to sit down and physically write an answer to these questions. See what you discover about yourself!

When you give up your boundaries in a relationship, what do you notice about your interactions?

When your boundaries are intact in a relationship, how do you feel?

Are you unclear about your preferences?

Do you have clear preferences and act upon them?

Do you notice when you are sad and must avoid confrontation?

Do you recognize when you are happy or unhappy?

Do you alter your behavior, plans, or opinions to fit the current moods or circumstances of another (live reactively)?

Do you acknowledge moods and circumstances around you while remaining centered (live actively)?

Do you do more and more for less and less?

Do you do more when that behavior gets results?

Do you take as truth the most recent opinion you have heard?

Do you trust your own intuition while being open to other's opinions?

Do you live hopefully while wishing and waiting?

Do you live optimistically while co-working on change?

Are you satisfied if you are just coping and surviving?

Are you only satisfied if you are thriving?

Do you let the other's minimal improvement maintain your stalemate?

Are you encouraged by sincere, ongoing change for the better?

Do you have few hobbies because you have no attention span for self-directed activity?

Do you have interest in self-enhancing hobbies and projects?

Do you make exceptions for a person for things you would not tolerate in anyone?

Do you have a personal standard, albeit flexible, that applies to everyone and asks for accountability?

Do you allow another person's flattery to cause you to lose objectivity?

Do you appreciate feedback and can you distinguish it from attempts to manipulate

Do you try to create intimacy with a narcissist?

Do you relate only to partners with whom mutual love is possible?

Are you so strongly affected by another that obsession results?

Are you so strongly affected by your partner's idea of reality and take it as fact?

Will you forsake every personal limit to get sex or the promise of it?

Can you integrate sex so that you can enjoy it but never at the cost of your integrity?

Do you see your partner as causing your excitement?

Do you see your partner as stimulating your excitement?

Do you feel hurt and victimized but not angry?

Do you let yourself feel anger, say "ouch" and embark upon a program of change?

Do you act out of compliance or compromise?

Do you act out of agreement and negotiation?

Do favors for your partner that you inwardly know is wrong for you to do but do not refuse because you cannot say no to him/her?

Do you disregard your intuitions or a hunch in favor of the others wishes or desires?

Do you only do favors you choose to do (you can say no?)

Do you honor intuitions and distinguish them from wishes?

Do you allow your partner to abuse your children or friends?

Do you insist others' boundaries be as safe as your own?

Do you mostly feel afraid and confused in relationships?

Do you mostly feel secure and clear?

Do you enmesh in personal dramas beyond your control?

Are you always aware of choices?

Are you living a life that is not yours, and that seems unalterable?

Are you living a life that mostly approximates what you always wanted for yourself?

Are you committed to yourself for as long as the other needs you to be committed (no bottom line?)

Do you decide how, to what extent, and how long you will be committed?

Do you believe you have no right to secrets?

Do you protect your private matters without having to lie or be surreptitious?

Now that you have taken this questionnaire, see what the professionals have to say about how adults form attachments and create intimacy.

Attachment Theory

> The desire for intimacy also has important ramifications on how we attach or form bonds emotionally and physically. The tool kit makes building psycho/spiritual relationships with others possible.

Proponents of attachment theory recognize the importance of intimacy in overall health and happiness. Bowlby (1988) identified basic attachment patterns in humans through out the life cycle. This process emerges as attachment theory. Bowlby suggests that the human propensity to make intimate emotional bonds to particular individuals is a fundamental component of relational life. Research demonstrates it is already present in germinal form in the neonate and continues through adult life into old age.

Simply put, the drive to connect with other humans determines the way we form attachments. This propensity is deep in our hardwiring. We desire intimacy throughout life, seek interpersonal connections and need others care during each phase of our development. Whatever age, gender, race, or creed one may be born into, each individual must forge bonds with others. It makes little difference in our circumstances since all humans share an innate desire and necessity to connect. The basic yearning for attachment is in our biology, but requires a caregiver to nurture that capacity. The primary instinct for all living creatures is to form attachments for basic survival. We are equipped to form attachments, even at birth. We are more likely to flourish throughout life when the need for appropriate attachments are met in effective ways by loving caregivers.

How we create bonds with others begins in the family and involves a strange mix of successful nature and nurture. Building relationships is at the center of attachment theory and demonstrates how this is a task each person must learn to negotiate. However, the catch is that we do not have control as an infant how we learn to connect since we learn how to relate from cues in our childhood environment used for adaptation and survival. How we learn to attach to others, (especially in terms of managing difficult emotions) like the need for love, care, physical contact, affection, warmth and tenderness are at the heart of the inquiry into how human form attachment.

Negotiating the often-chaotic realms of passion and desire is daunting at best. For some it is an area of mystery or confusion but is essential to how we go about meeting hidden domains that we split off into pornographic secrets while seeking to fulfill sexual urges and darker drives. The obsession we have for another is often a mask for unseen dangers that lead to negative attachments. Our emotional and physical well-being grows out of our psycho/spiritual relationships with others. Relationships that consistently fulfill the desire for intimacy lead to secure attachments. We first establish this between our parents and then apply it to the way we bond to future partners. In contrast, relationships that neglect to satisfy the desire for intimacy have less secure attachments overall.

Others in the field of relationship psychology have examined the connection between attachment and intimacy. Collins and Feeney define intimacy as a special set of interactions in which a person shares or reveals something important about him or her to the other. When you give time for your partner to respond to your disclosure, it is essential that the response is affirmative even if it is something that is difficult to hear. It is valuable to give the feedback in a way that makes the person who has shared something important feel validated, understood, and cared for.

These interactions commonly focus on verbal self-disclosure. Intimate interactions can also involve non-verbal forms of self-expression such as touching, hugging, kissing, and sexual behavior. From this point of view, intimacy involves the following: Both parties must be willing to expose authentic thoughts, speak true feelings, disclose irrational wishes, and share unspoken fears. The benefit comes from a mutual willingness to rely on a partner for care, emotional support, and intimacy. Then when engaging in physical intimacy, feeling secure to express what is really going on provides a foundation of love and mutuality to grow.

Self-revelation

A number of studies by Collins and Feeney (2004) demonstrate how each attachment style influences the other and affects how each person is oriented to self-revelation. The capacity to be intimate requires an incentive to engage in physical closeness. This requires good attachment dynamics. The more secure the attachment styles of each person, the more likely the two are to share personal details. These attributes allow the couple to be interdependent, disclose with confidence, and extend trust. Each one in the partnership is more excited about having physical intimacy in an attachment style that focuses on mutual sharing of work and play, hope and fear, win and loss.

Hiding is not intimate and does not foster familiarity, understanding, and warmth. However, the amount of intimacy in a relationship can vary due to differing personality types and circumstances, such as physical distance or illness. Accommodating various personality styles into intimacy is essential because each attachment style may enhance an individual freely expressing the unique way of living out the intimacy in which they share.

Attachment styles

For some couples, intimacy becomes suffocating. Mashek and Sherman (2004) report the need in intimate relationships for time apart, separate interests and the need for varying degrees of closeness with partners. Sometimes too much intimacy can be overpowering, may feel disgusting, or sickly sweet. People who are less "touchy feely" or emotionally inclined may want or need less intimacy with their partners. There is a direct correlation between attachment styles and proximity to closeness. People who tend to be afraid to feel vulnerable and open are more apprehensive of intimacy and display avoidant, fearful, and anxious styles.

This type easily becomes preoccupied with the other partner in unhealthy ways. This can lead to obsessive desire for more closeness for fear of the other becoming distant. People who are less caring and have a more dismissive style may tend toward avoidant attachment styles. They typically want less contact and desire some distance with their partners. Studies show that paradoxically, a large numbers of people admit to wanting less intimacy, over 50% less in some studies. However, for most people the desire for intimacy far outweighs the types that share less intimacy with their partners.

CHAPTER FOUR:
Self-Identity and Personal Boundaries

⚜

Who and what we are makes us unique and is essential to intimacy. It is virtually impossible to connect to another if have no relationship within.

To build thriving and positive relationships we need to have a strong relationship within. Two essential ways that we work on this ability include secure boundaries and a positive self-identity. Since all relationships consist of two or more people relating with each other, it behooves us to understand how we see our self. If we do not know who we are then our how can we know another? Each party must engage with a distinctly separate sense of his or her own identity. Without a clear perception of self, how can we relate with another with confidence or commitment? What happens to intensity and passion in a relationship if there is lack of self-identity? How can we enjoy time together? How can we build a life full of shared meaning?

A clear self-identity is essential to intimacy. It is virtually impossible to unite if we have no union within. Self-identity issues occlude the way we see problematic dynamics in intimate relationships. We need to know who we are, where we stand, and what we value if we are to extend understanding to another. To clarify communication or repair intimacy, both partners need a sense of self worth. This is the responsibility of both partners since self-identity supports clear statements of what is possible or not.

The reality is that you must communicate your desire to your partner. When you have a strong grasp of your own identity, you know yourself. Then you can easily recognize what makes your partner tick. You can better appreciate and love those qualities in your partner and honor what makes him or her unique. When two people come together, each with a clear definition of one's own individuality, the potential for intimacy and commitment is astounding. The similarities between two people may bring them together, but their differences contribute to their growth.

One feature of a healthy sense of self is the way we understand and work with boundaries. Personal boundaries are the limits we set in relationships for self-protection. Boundaries come from having a good sense of our own self-worth. They make it possible for us to have a separate self and to disconnect our body, thoughts, and feelings from those of others. Boundaries provide the core character structure that requires that we are accountable for what we think, feel, and do. Boundaries allow us to rejoice in our own uniqueness while maintaining intact boundaries that are flexible - they allow us to get close to others when it is appropriate and to maintain our distance when not. Boundaries are like an alarm system that alerts us to potential harm and cues us when not to get too close. Good boundaries protect us from abusive and manipulative people since our self-identity disallows such relationships. The act of managing personal boundaries paves the way to achieving true intimacy since it teach each person how to take care of his/her identity.

Unhealthy Boundaries

Many people are working longer hours, taking on more responsibilities, and are still falling behind. As one client, Janice put it, "It takes more and more to just to keep up. I am barely holding my head above water and my marriage is on the rocks." One income in the past could support a family, now it usually takes two working full-time. This has a major impact on the dynamics required to build intimacy.

In the coaching session, Janice expresses a need to explore how unhealthy boundaries cause her to feel ineffective, emotional unstable, and full of self-doubt. She broke down in tears, and bawling told me how she and her husband were financially drowning. "We neglect the important task of raising our children just to pay the bills." Often the needs or duties of parents or other adults in a family are so overwhelming that they feel like throwing in the towel. Janice began to take a step back from her obsessive drive to succeed and the fear of failure and financial ruin.

Janice used the life-coaching model to help her look at how poor boundaries around her work life leads to inconsistency in her ability to be a wife and mother. Janice uses the coaching to encourage herself in other directions, to stop relegating her responsibilities to the back burner. Janice discovers that when she sets aside time to be creative, work in her garden, cook healthy meals that mothering responsibility become more enjoyable. The take home message is that by altering her dysfunctional patterns, finding balance between work, family and self-care, Janice naturally finds a way to maintain intimacy, take pleasure in mothering, and work from a spirit of inner balance.

Robert came to counseling to work on anger management. He reports feeling that his family is a top priority, and yet he cannot control his inner rage. Robert confesses how his pattern of unleashing his anger on his family results in terrible upset for everyone, even the pet dog. Robert reports that he cannot stop yelling. He says it makes him feels like a super hero, authoritative, gigantic, and influential. He came for counsel to find ways to expresses this power, but not at his the expense of his family. He says, "It has become an enormous obstacle to peace. My anger slips out even when I try to be steady; it has become my habitual response."

Consider the role of a father like Robert who screams at his family in ways that have become intolerable for everyone. He reports becoming physically, emotionally, and verbally abusive with his family and dog, as a way of dealing with his own anger. Robert confesses that his needs come first, and the needs of his wife and children's safety, security, self-respect, and comfort come second. What Robert's children are likely to learn in this situation is that boundaries do not matter. As they grow up, they lack the anger management skills that include self-respect, delayed gratification and cannot support a healthy self-identity. In fact, they may learn that if they want to get their way with others, they need to intrude on the boundaries of other people, just as their father did with his lack of anger management.

Robert's children and many children raised in this manner will likely grow up with dysfunctional boundaries, especially around uncontrollable anger and inappropriate expression of intimacy. Life coaching helped Robert to explore proactive steps to work with anger and how to stop using anger to damage his relationships across the board. He explores how the need to express rage arises from his own lack of serenity. He named his anger as a response to the dysfunctional boundaries, (especially around anger and verbal abuse) witness in childhood. Robert's awareness of his problems with anger management supports new patterns of behavior. The coaching encourages Robert of transform the way he chooses to unleash anger onto his family rather than faced it with appropriate boundaries. Robert saw how his behavior had a negative affect on his children.

Growing awareness of how outer turmoil conceals inner truth helps Robert stretch his boundaries. In the coaching session, he reached a turning point. This led Robert to acknowledge how his father's dysfunctional patterns of expressing anger was negatively influencing his present situation. Problematic discipline patterns in his childhood muddled his current common sense approach to managing anger. Robert's wife learns that her rigid and inflexible boundaries may not be the way to handle her intimate relationship either. If one partner walls him or herself off in the relationship for safety or protection, consequently, both partners may find it difficult to form close interpersonal bonds.

Chronic boundary violations may lead to self-identity disorders. Unhealthy boundaries show-up in many relationships. Here are some remedies.

Self-Identity Disorder

When we lack a sense of our own identity and the boundaries that protect us, we tend to draw our self-image from our partner. We cannot imagine who we would be without our significant other. We become willing to do anything it takes to make the relationship work, even if it means giving up our emotional security, friends, job, and dignity. Independence comes with personal integrity since without self-respect; we may endure physical, emotional, or sexual abuse just to save the relationship.

The more balanced alternative is to find out who we are and what makes us unique. This is the only way we will ultimately feel comfortable in intimate engagement with another. Realize that your value and worth as a person are not necessarily dependent on having a significant other in your life. Recognize that you can function well as an independent person.

Life coaching helps Janice and Robert embark on a holistic approach to life. Janice is able to risk to knowing herself from the inside. She is willing to see herself as a powerful agent in her own right. She now engages in building skills that empower her to move into deeper self-love. After eight sessions, her intimacy with her husband began to take on a juicy feeling. Janice began to take a step back from her demanding career and embraced the responsibility of mothering. By accepting her role as a mother and wife, she gave herself the chance to grow in new areas. The capacity for intimacy began to flourish with her children and husband. The journey Janice took toward self-discovery is certainly a challenge but she found was highly rewarding.

Robert was initially reluctant to take on eight sessions of life coaching. Nevertheless, he knew he needed to work his anger. He used life coaching to discover how working with a trained coach was a way to challenge him to expose his old wounds that caused rage, renew appropriate boundary to stop verbal violations, and to design a workable family structure. Robert found a new lease on life by using the guidance of a coach. He now knows that he could not break through his negative pattern alone. He began to assume the leadership positions in the family, however in a much more effective manner, without the negative overlay of using anger as a weapon to avoid intimacy.

Settling for Second Best

Many cling to the irrational belief that it is dangerous to "rock the boat." You can easily deceive yourself and assume that things are good enough in the relationship. It is human to feel a measure of security in maintaining the status quo or thinking that this is as good as it is likely to get. In the process, however, we give up the chance to explore our sense of fulfillment in life. We relinquish our own life dreams in order to maintain the security of a relationship. There is a background fear of impending break-up if one of the partners grows and finds personal life fulfillment.

A healthy intimacy is one in which our boundaries are strong enough, yet flexible. You settle for second best when you feel that you cannot be yourself. If you do not thrive in your own individuality, there is a sense of disconnection that leads to grasping for another. When you can both be individuals, you allow each other to live as full a life as possible, and encourage each partner to explore personal potentials. We do not have to give up our sense of self for intimacy with another. Healthy boundaries allow interdependence and inner security to develop in the relationship.

Over-Responsibility and Guilt

One characteristic of growing up in a dysfunctional household is that we may feel guilty about our desire for affection. If we fail to achieve the same level of success and happiness of the other partner we feel accountable and guilty. Thus, in adulthood, we may come to feel responsible for our partner's failures and envious of their personal gains. The shame we feel when our partner fails may drive us to compromise our personal boundaries. We feel that we need to take on their burden or humiliation. We make ourselves available to the other person at all cost and on demand. When we feel overly responsible for another person's life experiences, we deprive them of one of the most important features of life, freedom. An independent, healthy, and mature relational life cannot come into existence if we are not empowered and empowering.

The ability to make our own life choices and accept the consequences of our decisions is at the core of intimacy. A healthy response is to show our partners respect by allowing them to succeed or fail on their own terms. You, of course, can be there to comfort your partner when times become difficult, and you can rejoice together when one or the other attains success and accomplishes an important goal. When boundaries are healthy, you are able to say, "I trust and respect you to make your own life choices." This statement conveys a kind of love that fuels your freedom of expression and encourages each other to reach full potential. We speak in the affirmative, as an equal partner, I will not try to control you. I will not take away your choices in life, but will offer freedom as the true source of intimacy.

The Difference between Love and Rescue

People who grow up in a dysfunctional family may fail to learn the difference between love and sympathy. Children growing up in these conditions may learn to have pity for the emotional crippling in their parents' lives and feel that the only time they get attention is when they show compassion for the parent. Children feel that when they forgive, they are showing love. Actually, they are rescuing the parent and enabling abusive behavior to continue. They learn to give up their own protective boundaries in order to take care of the dysfunctional parent.

In adulthood, we carry these learned behaviors into our intimate relationships. If one feels, "I can rescue my partner", they feel that they are showing love. They get a warm, caring, sharing feeling from helping their partner, and call this love. However, this may actually encourage their partner to become needy and helpless. An imbalance can then occur in the relationship in which one partner becomes the rescuer and the other plays the role of the helpless victim. In this case, healthy boundaries are lacking, which precludes both people living complete lives. Mature love requires the presence of healthy intimacy and includes flexible boundaries.

Sympathy and compassion are worthy qualities, but when distorted, they become obsessive and confused with love. Healthy boundaries lead to respect for the other, and an appreciation for the aliveness and strength of the other person. The feature of mature love is a mutual flow of feelings that course freely between the two partners. When one partner is in control and the other is in need, under the weather, or vulnerable, there is room for the normal give-and-take. For healthy intimacy to be available in the difficult times of the relationship, reciprocity between the care giving must occur.

Fantasy vs. Reality

Children from dysfunctional families often feel that things will get better someday, that a normal life may lie in the future. Indeed, some days things are normal, but then the bad times return. During these fallow periods, many couples are encouraged to hold the fantasy that all problems in the relationship are solvable, but just not in the current climate. When they grow up, these adults carry the same types of fantasy about intimate relationships, cannot distinguish what is real from what is flight of imagination or just plain fabrication. The personal dynamics established in childhood endure into their intimate adult relationships.

Lila came to counseling to explore an underlying disappointment in her relationship with her boyfriend of three years. She continued to bump up against her fantasy of what intimacy should entail and this caused her boyfriend to spin into a fight or flight pattern. Lila had an exaggerated view of her requirements for a happy, romantic relationship. She had problematic fantasies of what was required from an intimate partner.

In the session, we explore how she expresses these unrealistic fantasies to her boyfriend in a way that communicates her dissatisfaction with him and he feels disenchantment with her. We examine how Lila views her role in intimacy. She identifies intimacy means having a perfect situation and holds her partner to a faultless standard. Lila confuses the desire for perfection with having a perfect partner. She sees how her particular myth wreaks havoc in her relationship and causes problems with intimacy. She explores how her demands for an ideal relationship push love away.

Lila shares, "I pressure him to match up to my fantasy lover. My unrealistic expectations are hurtful to him, nevertheless when he falls short, I feel let down and angry. I experience our relationship as less than, it feels tarnished, and I need him to be flawless." Lila was able to work through this impasse to real intimacy. She recognizes that she and her boyfriend are actually anything but the perfect couple she had imagined in her fantasy. Lila challenges her need for flawlessness and then discovers that the relation she has is already perfect, in the sense, it is ideal for the two of them.

Lila explores various dimensions of her fantasy relationship versus the reality. She is surprised at how much her fantasy life obscures the real qualities that she appreciates in her boyfriend. This clears the doors of her perception. Lila discovers the reason she seeks perfection is to feel real and safe inside her skin. It is so overwhelming at times when "I insist that my boyfriend adopts the same fantasy of perfection I need." I ask, "Is this when the relationship spirals out of control?"

Lila says, "I feel uncertain, afraid of losing him, and not good enough. I revert to my old perfectionist stance, anorexic mentality, and insist that my real boyfriend meets up with my fantasy lover. When my boyfriend does not match up to my standards, I desperately seek my phantom lover. I go to mad extremes to force my fantasy onto my relationship, even when there are important issues we both need to discuss about the actual relationship."

Lila's view of an intimate relationship is one that must be perfect. However, this lends itself to contradiction and rebelliousness, in her boyfriend's behaviors. He feels that since there is no room for problems, he can continue to "pretend" to be flawless even when less than. He feels secure in the relationship illusion. In counseling, Lila notices a habitual pattern of ignoring abuse, manipulation, and imbalance, just to maintain control in a relationship. To compensate for a sense of internal emptiness, she must project an ideal image even when this does not match up. She is furious when this awareness dawns. She witnesses just how often she discounts negativity and problematic issues in life rather than accepting the good and bad, the perfect and imperfect, aspects of her relationship.

Lila uses ongoing coaching to confront the issues that may continue to arise as she works through underlying problems around her addiction to perfection. Lila looks at tangible difficulties, insecurities, and issues around financial worries. She realizes that the problems she tries to avoid through perfection put her at odds with her partner's desire to seek balance and equanimity. She grapples with her personal blocks and fears, begins to hear more from her inner voice than reasons why things will not be "perfect."

When Lila trusts that things will work out, even better than she imagined, she challenges her old fear based myth of intimacy that requires only an ideal partner for a sexual relationship. Lila's fantasy of a perfect future can be a reality since she now adjusts her expectations. Lila' take home message is dynamic balance as a way to transform the need for perfectionism and its destructive attitudes. Lila now takes on a healthy view of intimacy and seeks high standards while also establishing realistic boundaries. As she put it, "I do not have to collude with my fantasy of perfection."

Learning to have healthy boundaries is an exciting adventure.

As we see in Lila's story, establishing boundaries is an exercise in personal liberation. It means coming to know ourselves and increases our awareness of what we believe in and value. It also means self-acceptance and knowing that we are okay as we are, and worthy of the good things in life. When two people with healthy boundaries enter into a relationship, they encourage wholeness, independence, and a zest for life. They know that trust is possible and they can constructively work on the normal difficulties that arise in all relationships. They can find true intimacy as whole and equal partners. Ultimately, this is the ideal relationship!

The journey to a sense of healthy identity is not always easy - but it need not be impossible. It often means letting go of some of your old misconceptions about human nature, and the status of the world. It means treating yourselves with respect and appreciating yourself for who you really are. When you can do this for yourself, you can take the same approach toward your partner. Then true intimacy can become a reality.

Here is a list of healthy and unhealthy signs of intimacy

HEALTHY
Feeling like your own person
Feeling responsible for your own happiness

Balance between togetherness and separateness
Friendships exist outside of the relationship
Focuses on the best qualities of both people
Achieving intimacy without abusing substances
Open, honest and assertive communication
Commitment to the partner
Respecting the differences in the partner
Accepting changes in the relationship
Asking honestly for what one wants
Accepting endings

UNHEALTHY
Feeling incomplete without your partner
Relying on your partner for your happiness
Too much or too little togetherness
Inability to establish and maintain friendships outside the relationship
Focuses on the worst qualities of the partners
Using alcohol/drugs to reduce inhibitions and achieve a false sense of intimacy
Game-playing, unwillingness to listen, manipulation
Jealousy, relationship addiction or lack of commitment
Blaming the partner for his or her own unique qualities
Feeling that the relationship should always be the same
Feeling unable to express what you want
Unable to let go

CHAPTER FIVE:
Trust as Key to Intimacy

⚜

Trust is like a tiny seed; when nurtured it grows into a positive and healthy plant that is able to blossom into intimacy.

An intimate liaison is an interpersonal relationship that entails physical or emotional intimacy. We characterize intimacy by romantic or passionate sex that includes physical attachment and sexual activity. Intimate relationships play an essential part in the universal human experience. We all have a shared yearning to fit in and belong. Intimacy gives us a sense that we are special. When we feel intimacy, right with another, and in love, as a rule, we are more likely to be satisfied with our relationship.

Intimate relationships involve physical and sexual attraction between people. Intimacy often begins with an attraction such as "Exploring what I like about you" so liking and loving, involves romantic feelings. It can take on archetypal power as an intense craving that leads into mythic realms of hush-hush and surreptitious sexual liaisons. During the phase of courtship, we discover a shared understanding, engage in strong emotions, design alliance, and fulfill our communal need to love, and receive love. For many romance and early stages of sex is the most vital time in life. For many this is the most passionate of any life long experience, but when we are not confident in our own ability to trust, we cannot make such an intimate connection. We must all have a certain level of self-confidence to build intimacy.

It is easy to believe that an intimate relationship just happens, but we all know that without trust, sexual intimacy alone cannot sustain us. Trust is like a tiny seed; when nurtured it grows into a positive and healthy flower. Trust is cultivated in a seedbed of self-acceptance where mutual feelings and a deep sense of passion for life grow. Faith in the other is a requirement if you are to know they are trustworthy. Therefore, to develop an intimate relationship, you must first honor the qualities of truthfulness, faithfulness, and dependability.

Intimacy normally refers to the sense of being in a close personal association and trusting that you two belong together. It is a celebrated sensation of having an emotional connection with another. Intimacy in this sense is a result of an attachment that is formed through familiarity and understanding. Authentic human relationships call for intimacy based on conversation, directness, openness, and give-and-take. The meaning of the verb "intimate" is "to state or make known." Intimacy is an action word requiring knowledge about the other and necessitates both parties creating intimacy together. To discover intimacy we must be "intimate" and allow our self to know another. The activity of "making known" undergirds the meanings of "intimate" and refers to a person with whom one has deep knowledge.

The significance and intensity of intimacy fluctuate within and between relationships over space and time. In anthropological research, mating ritual that involves intimacy includes conquering the other thorough elaborate courting ceremony and captivating styles of seduction and seduce. The socialization process buildings special knowledge of and unique understanding about another; enabling both parties to feel safe sharing what was formerly hidden away in undisclosed thoughts and feelings. Intimate conversations become the starting point for "assurance" (clandestine information shared) that connects people together and builds trust.

Self-differentiation

To sustain intimacy for any length of time requires highly sensitive emotional and interpersonal responsiveness. Intimacy requires an ability to simultaneously be separate people and a unified whole. Murray Bowen called this "self-differentiation" and noticed how the capacity results in building a relationship with expressive range that links both partners and encourages full-bodied differences, and passionate devotion to the other. Inability to distinguish oneself from the other is a form of enmeshment. Intimacy cannot thrive under such symbiosis. Real intimacy is actually a state of entwined contact, even if feelings of closeness are similar to the state of enmeshment.

From a center of self-knowledge and self-differentiation, closeness bonds those in intimate love, as well as creates intimacy among family members and friends. Intimacy evolves through reciprocity, where self-disclosure is mutual, reciprocated, and sincere. Too much exposé of self can lead to trying to become too close too hastily. When we have adequate skills in the task of self-differentiation, we allow the other to have authority over their own life choices without trying to control their decisions.

Intimacy requires openness so we allow our intimate partner to develop friendships apart from us. Adults, who have trouble forming and maintaining intimate relationships, may still need to deal with negative attachment patterns from childhood. This helps avoid serious psychological problems down the road, since if not address in a straightforward manner can lead to enmeshment. Individuals may experience the personal limitations of their partners with an increasing sense of dread, especially when there has been infidelity and duplicity. The intimate relationship has to confront difficulties as they arise if they expect to repair trust. Studies show that fear of intimacy may lead to acting out, unfaithfulness, and disloyalty since many believe that comfort and emotional closeness is potentially dangerous.

Types of Intimacy

Other common forms of intimacy are the bonding between a mother and child. Four types of intimacy include physical, emotional, cognitive, and experiential. Physical intimacy is tactile and involves some form of touching, such as being inside someone's personal space, holding hands, hugging, and kissing that lead into caressing, petting, and other sexual expression. Emotional intimacy often means having sexual relationships. It naturally develops after bodily bonds (including carnal knowledge) recognize and identify the expressive bond of "falling in love." This feeling is powerful since it accompanies a biochemical factor. We feel it through reactions in the way our body senses stimulation by the sex drive and innate sexual magnetism.

The social facet motivates intimacy by "conversing" together in ways that result from habitual corporeal familiarity. Sex is a symbol for bonding together, becoming one body. Balanced intimacy takes place when two people discuss thoughts, ideas, and feelings that include taking pleasure in sharing areas of likeness and difference that involve discussing beliefs and judgments about sex. When we are encouraged to do this in a close and relaxed manner, intimacy grows in all areas of the relationship.

No-nonsense intimacy is when two people get together to actively involve themselves with each other, predominately for physical congress, and most likely need to say very little to each other. Deep levels of intimacy do not require that we share much of anything, including our thoughts or feelings. This kind of intimacy involves the two engaging in joint activities, sharing time, and activity with one another. Imagine observing two dancers who are playing out a duet on the stage. They may be surprised to think that they were occupied in an intimate activity, however from the point of view of the audience they would be seen as very intimately occupied with each other.

Physical and emotional intimacy requires love. Love is an essential dynamic in physical and emotional relationships. Love is qualitatively and quantitatively different to liking, and the distinction is not merely in the presence or absence of sexual attraction. There are two forms of love in a relationship, one is passionate or infatuated love and the other is supporter or association love. Supporter love involves building upon the influential feelings of affection like security and dependability. This creates a long-term attachment and provides a sense of mutual loyalty.

The deep emotion of reciprocal loving-kindness and sensitivity cause both partners to be proud of the other's achievements. They both take in mutual pleasure that comes from sharing a common outlook on life. In distinction, love that arises only in sexual craving and on again, off again passion, is infatuation. It feels intense and enthralling but is actually an obsessive fixation on the other. In the fit of elation, the excitement feels like love, but is not intimacy. What drives sexual closeness is a compulsive feeling of the potential feeling of orgasm and the desire for ecstasy. However, this enchantment can take over the capacity for reality testing.

Shakespeare eloquently expresses this sentiment in the words of Titania who proclaims the power of love.

Sleep thou, and I will wind thee in my arms....
So doth the woodbine the sweet honeysuckle gently entwist;
The female ivy so enrings the barky fingers of the elm.
O, how I love thee! How I dote on thee!
– Titania, A Midsummer Night's Dream, Act 4, Scene 1

A couple is two people who are in an intimate relationship, especially if that couple places some permanency in their relationship. These couples often provide the emotional security that is necessary for the two to accomplish other tasks, particularly forms of labor or work. Although at times it may seem intimidating, intimacy is rewarding and when put into practice challenges us to grow in intimacy. We bring to light what makes us happy and share in what makes each partner truly whole.

We become capable of a profound or peak experience with another that encompasses physical bliss, orgasmic potential and tangible achievements on many levels. Intimacy results in both reaching a shared zenith of sexual health and accelerates closeness. The experience of a deep sense of belonging takes over that includes nostalgia and happy memories. When we begin to experience the positive side of intimacy, we know a deep sense of beauty. Fulfillment is possible while also tolerating times of vulnerability and openness. We know the relationship is worth it since it provides love, supports our highest aims, and knows the ideals of both.

The foundation of trust building is a living, breathing, and activating rapport between two engaging parties. Trust refers to a dynamic and continuing evaluation of our own and the other's aptitude for being trustworthy. Ultimately, trust is the capacity and potential for being upright and faithful since it requires some sense that the other is able to be present and relate in a manner that also meets our expectations. Integrity is the degree to which each person honors the principles that both deem acceptable in the relationship.

Trust is based on:
- Consistency of past actions that includes reliability and stability
- Credibility of communication involving dependability and truthfulness
- Commitment to standards of fairness that honors evenhandedness and fair dealing
- Congruence of the other's words and deeds resulting in reliance and assurance
- Consideration of the other and treat him/her with compassion and kindness

Trust building requires that the trusted individual be concerned enough about their partner's wellbeing to advance his or her interests or in the least, not to hold them back. Honest and open communication, delegating decisions, and sharing control are evidence of one's goodwill. Although, these dimensions each contribute separately to influence the level of trust within a relationship. However, sharing affection, empathy, and integrity are likely to be most influential demonstration of intimacy early in a relationship, as information of one's goodwill needs to emerge for trust to build. The effect of compassion will increase, as the relationship grows between the partners.

The next section describes in more detail how trust develops in relationships.

Levels of trust development

Early theories of trust describe it as a one-dimensional occurrence that enlarges or decreases in magnitude and strength within a relationship. However, recent studies of the effect of reliance on trust suggest that trust builds along a continuum of hierarchical and sequential stages. As trust grows to higher levels, it becomes stronger and more resilient and may change in character or quality. In the early stages of a relationship, the act of trust is calculated. In other words, an individual will carefully determine how the other is likely to behave in a given situation. This is determined depending upon the rewards for being trustworthy and the penalties suffered for untrustworthy behavior. In this way, rewards and punishments guarantee that a trustor ensures the trustee's consistent behavior.

Individuals deciding whether to trust the other mentally may contemplate the benefits of staying in the relationship with the trustee versus the benefits of "cheating" on the relationship. They may consider the costs of staying in the relationship versus the costs of breaking off the relationship. Trust extends to the other to the degree that this cost-benefit calculation indicates that the continued trust will yield a net positive benefit. Over time, trust builds as individuals manage their reputation and assure the stability of their behavior by behaving consistently, meeting agreed-to deadlines, and fulfilling promises.

From this perspective, assurance that the other is trustworthy is largely a matter of cognitively driven evaluation of the other. When grounded on the judgment that the other is consistent, trust arises from a shared history of predictability and reliability. However, as the two come to a deeper understanding of each other, through repeated interactions, they may become aware of shared values and goals. This allows trust to grow to a higher and qualitatively different level.

When trust evolves to the highest level, it functions as identification-based trust. At this stage, trust builds to the point that the parties have internalized each other's desires and intentions. They understand what the other party really cares about so that each party is able to act as an agent for the other. Enhanced trust is available at this advanced stage when the couple designs a strong emotional bond between each other, based on a sense of shared goals, values, and ideals. It arises from the experience of perceptions of interpersonal care, ongoing concern, and mutual need satisfaction.

Practical Implications for Building Trust

In psychology, trust means that the person who is trusted will do what they say and say what they do. They will and can be dependable, sincere, and trustworthy. It starts within the family and extends to others. According to the psychoanalyst Erik Erikson (1959) during the first two years of life, we develop a sense of basic trust that is the first condition of psychosocial development. Achievement of trust results in feelings of safety, confidence, and hopefulness, while failure directs a person's psycho/social development towards an orientation of fear, insecurity, and mistrust.

A person's temperament influences the propensity to trust others. We regard it as a character trait, and as such is an accurate forecaster of happiness and the quality of the good life. Psychologists note that as trust increases, so does personal contentment since it boosts the value of one's interpersonal relationships. Happy people are capable of nurturing belief in self and have faith in others, and so naturally have more high-quality intimate relationships.

Trust is fundamental to the idea of how we build a society of dependence. We rely on social influences to maintain confidence in each other, simply because it is easier to persuade someone who is trusting to go along with us. Conversely, once again, discernment of truthfulness, genuineness, and meaning correspondence (somewhat analogous to compassion and good will) are indispensable. On the other hand, there is a wide range of approaches to discerning whether to engage in the act of trust or not. Trust requires being open to the words and actions of a significant person, we listen to them and trust their remarks. Steadfastness and reliability reflect the characteristics that support others being willing to trust you.

The positive expectations we hold toward another person, believing in their trustworthiness, feeling secure and close with them enhances our inclination to rely on people in general. On the contrary, once trust has gone, even if understandable infringements of trust or a fundamental confidence breached, it is difficult, if not impossible, to regain trust. Thus, there is obvious disproportion in the formation of trust since there can be irreparable damage to our ability trust some people. Therefore, being and acting honorably should be the priority. When our relationship is well thought-out, we consider the impact of negligence and double-dealing. Trust becomes the prerequisite and single most important way to maintain a level of optimism and positive expectation.

Trust building is a bilateral process

Trust building is a bilateral process that requires mutual commitment and effort, especially when attempting to de-escalate conflict. Nonetheless, there are several ways individuals can act on their own to initiate or encourage the trust building process. This is accomplished either by taking steps to minimize the risk that the other party will act in dishonest ways, or by keeping watch over one's own actions to guarantee they are trustworthy. You profess trust to another by your confirmation of actual being honest and vice versa.

Individuals can take several steps to strengthen another's trust in them, particularly when these steps are performed frequently, within numerous, and diverse contexts of the relationship. To build trust both parties need to know, execute specific duties and responsibilities proficiently. When we continue to make every effort to show the other that we care, this may initially require renewing our interpersonal skills. These abilities demonstrate that we can establish trust on a firm foundation that fosters a safe space for emotional growth. By establishing consistency, we build certainty. We can advance the level to which others will regard us as trustworthy. However, when we do not behave in consistent and predictable ways every effort we make ensures that our words are not congruent with our ensuing actions. When we honor another, we communicate from a firm and balanced position. We vow to keep our commitments, we secure our integrity, and we reinforce the aim of intimacy, trust building. Therefore, it is vital to keep our word.

When communication is accurate, open, and transparent, it is natural that you tend to act candidly. That is, you must be unambiguous about your intentions and clear about the motives for your actions. This helps the other person determine your sincerity. Therefore, they can accurately determine your level of trustworthiness. Most people are more willing to act clearly and keep an eye on the other's trust when the relationship is for the fulfillment of both. You need to be trustworthy to receive trust in return. There is symbolic value in requesting participation and sharing decision management with others. Likewise, when person hordes such power, others feel that they are not trusted. This happens with monitoring and shadowing behavior where you are not transparent. You may be more likely to act out against the trust with behaviors that strengthen a suspicious exterior position.

One of the most effective ways to show concern for others is to be trustworthy. The trust others have in you will grow when you show sensitivity to their needs, desires, and interests. Performing in a way that respects and protects the other builds trust. It supports the process of us abstaining from engaging in selfish pursuits that harm or disadvantage the other. It will also contribute to ensuring that the trust others place in you is solid. When you violate someone's trust, the other may deem that you are acting in your own self-interest. Accordingly, they may divert their attention to their own self-interest and self-protection rather than on conflict resolution.

Prescriptions for trust building entail a number of additional steps: Strengthening trust establishes a common identity; we nurture a familiarity that creates a sense of unity between two people. Discussions and actions that pull together a sense of a "we identity" rather than a divisive "me or you identity" encourages individuals to work together.

One of my favorite ways to build trust is to create mutual projects and goals with another person. Working toward a shared success creates a marvelous atmosphere that fosters a feeling of unification. This sense of togetherness can bring the two into concert in new ways that strengthen an important aspect of trust, a shared identity. When I create projects and engage in creative activities with another, we activate our commonality, this enlivens our intimacy, and makes us both feel unique and special in the eyes of the other.

When we promote common values, we also discover there is innate attraction and magnetism in the power of mutuality. When we model a concern for other people by getting to know them, we engage in active listening, focus on their interests, recognize the contributions they bring to the table, and demonstrate confidence in their abilities. This ensures more trust across the board.

CHAPTER SIX:
Patience in a Relationship

ॐ

Be mindful in situations that challenge your patience.

Patience is the ability to persevere and maintain composure in situations that necessitate understanding, mandate tolerance for delay, and incite emotional intensity. Patience refers to a virtue or a habit, and practicing patience is an action. Therefore, patience is something that we must develop. Relationships present many circumstances that call for patience. Tolerance is necessary to have a healthy and functional relationship.

Patience Exercise:
You can learn patience by following these instructions.

Step 1:
Focus on your mindset. You may have thoughts, beliefs, and ways of thinking that are not conducive to practicing patience. In order to learn how to be more patient, it is necessary that you prime your thinking in a way that promotes serenity, lack of complaint, and staying power.

Be mindful in situations that challenge your patience. Take note of the emotional, physical, and mental responses you are having so that you can learn to recognize the ways in which you react to such triggers. Understanding how you react to things that challenge your patience is tantamount to coping with relationship challenges. If you learn to practice patience when under stress or conflict, you are well ahead of the game.

Eliminate thoughts that center around what you feel "must" or "should" happen. Impatience is often the result of unfulfilled expectations. Remember that life is unpredictable. Many circumstances are outside of your control. For example, replace thoughts like, "men must put the toilet seat down at work" with thoughts like, "it would be nice if my male co-workers put the toilet seat down" in order to take the immediacy off the issue and downgrade it to something more manageable and less testing of patience.

Practice self-talk: When relationship issues that test your patience arise, mentally recite affirmations that you can and will be patient. For example, if you feel that you are getting impatient during a discussion with your spouse, you may say to yourself, "I am capable of practicing patience. I will calm down, and listen."

Step 2:

Check your ego. Determine how much of your impatience is due to your desire to be right or to have things go according to your plan. To develop patience, you must acknowledge that a relationship involves two people, and that your perspective is only part of the equation

Step 3:

Encourage open communication. Commit to practicing patience even in the face of things you may not agree with or may not want to hear. Relationships require open and honest communication, and the more comfortable both of you are with sharing thoughts and feelings, the less likely it is that you will display passive-aggressive behaviors that challenge patience.

Step 4:

Take note of your relationship dynamic. You will notice that each of you have certain strengths and weaknesses, and that you must work together in order to make the relationship work. It is possible to learn patience by focusing on your cooperative efforts. Be mindful of how you each contribute to the success or failure of the relationship.

Step 5:

Spend time in personal reflection. You cannot have a relationship alone, but you can only develop patience through your own effort. Designate some private time for thinking about how you may practice patience in your relationship.

Enthusiasm is necessary if you ever want to accomplish anything of value.

You need larger-than-life excitement in whatever it is that you are doing for it to be successful. You can amass incredible enthusiasm within your relational life, you simply have to follow through with the 10 methods I am about to discuss just below:

Be passionate

You have to have a passion for what you are doing if you want to build enthusiasm for it. You need to be excited about it as you wake up in the morning and as you go to bed at night. This passion is what will keep your enthusiasm high, even during rough patches, which we all go through. Simply put, love what you do and enthusiasm will follow. You might want to read or discuss ways that other people demonstrate passion in relationships. Gaining from other's experiences can help you get the ball rolling as to figuring out what your ultimate passion really is!

Be grateful

One of the ways that I build my enthusiasm with my work is that I always remind myself everything that enthusiasm has given me. I express gratitude for all that I have and this helps me become even more excited about what I'm doing. As we go through the daily grind, it is very easy to forget about all the little things that make our life easier and comfortable. Remember all the good things that you have going on in your life and be grateful for being who you are today. This is a wonderful method to create powerful enthusiasm in your life.

Be positive

Enthusiasm cannot survive in a negative environment. If you always have negative thoughts and are always looking at the glass as half empty, you will find your enthusiasm dissipate very quickly. You need to be positive for your enthusiasm to thrive. Look at the unseen benefit and positive aspect. Look on the bright side of things. Take away positive lessons out of seemingly bad situations, and you will find yourself submerged by a wave of amazing enthusiasm that will help carry you along the way towards your goals.

Be proud

Whatever it is that you want to build enthusiasm for, make sure that you are proud of it. Talk about it with your peers, discuss it with your friends, and mention it to your family. Pride is very important to create lasting enthusiasm, as anything that is worth being proud of, is worth having enthusiasm for. Talking about anything that you are proud of builds a terrific excitement that only helps in the continuation of it in a positive direction.

Be creative

You can never have enough creativity. Enthusiasm generates resourcefulness and vision triggers enthusiasm. Be innovative and creative in whatever you are doing and watch your enthusiasm skyrocket. Always look for better and newer ways to go about it, always look for an easier path, and always think outside the box. Being creative is one of the fastest and most effective ways to create enthusiasm.

Be proactive

When you are the initiator, the one that makes things happen, you transform your dedication to enthusiasm seamlessly. Being proactive creates massive enthusiasm in that you promote something that you have a stake in, perhaps something that you are passionate. I have discussed above how passion helps with enthusiasm. This follows along the same line. Be the captain of the ship. Be the leader, be the inspiration, and you will notice your enthusiasm is contagious.

Be reasonable

The quickest way to destroy your excitement along the way is to be completely unreasonable. Be realistic and understanding...this will ensure that your enthusiasm sticks for the long haul. Being unreasonable leads to guaranteed disappointment and thus creates an aura of negative energy. Building enthusiasm in such an environment is impossible. So be sure to stay logical and reasonable for your enthusiasm to survive.

Be patient

Following from my previous point about being unreasonable, the same applies to patience. Being impatient and expecting everything right away will only crush your enthusiasm when reality slaps you in the face. If you want to have long lasting enthusiasm, it is required of you to be very patient. The more patience you have, the more solid your enthusiasm will be. After all, what we want is enthusiasm that lasts a lifetime, so learn to have patience in your endeavors.

Be enlightened

You can build incredible enthusiasm with stillness. You can have amazing enthusiasm with full peace within your entire being, and living in the never-ending present moment. You do not need to be agitated to feel excitement. You can be completely still, calm, and still enjoy unparalleled enthusiasm.

Be evolving

Understand that life is all about improving yourself and that you are in a constant state of evolution. Knowing that you are getting better and better everyday is a wonderful way to create enthusiasm. Being aware that each step, each moment has a meaning and a purpose is incredibly rewarding and builds a solid foundation on which you can build up your enthusiasm. Always evolve, and never look back.

As you can see, each of the methods above compliments each other. Add each one of these to your tool kit. You will witness your gusto for life growing stronger. You are unstoppable because nothing can prevent you from being all that you ever wanted to be and so you encourage others to do the same.

CHAPTER SEVEN:
Curiosity in Relationships

❧

To keep the vitality in a relationship, it is critical to stay curious.

Curiosity may kill the cat, but it definitely deepens a relationship. After all, relationships are not only an opportunity to love another person but they are also occasions to become curious about another person. Interest in another brings the energy of inquisitiveness, attention, and joie de vivre. Why do relationships stagnate and fall apart? One reason is that partners are not curious about each other. After the honeymoon phase, they stop asking what the other cares about and stops being curious about what the other wants out of life.

You can engage in deeper acts of curiosity when you offer a quality of active listening. You need to pay attention to the subtleties of another, as this evokes trust when they know you are being sensitivity to their insecurities and fears. Curiosity reflects back that you really are interested. To know another requires curiosity since you convey that you know their hopes and dreams. Then you truly delight in knowing the other and the many facets of their life.

To keep vitality in a relationship, it is critical to stay curious. If we maintain a real interest in fully knowing a person, the energy stays alive. Sometimes, we have to listen. Sometimes, we have to probe. Much of the time, we have to practice the fine art of asking follow-up questions. "What about that fascinates you?" "I didn't realize you were frightened."

"Do you know why I like to walk to work?" "Why do you think you love cooking so much?"

Sometimes, we may not be curious about some aspect of our partner's life. That is fine! Nevertheless, that is no justification for not asking open-ended questions and showing curiosity. This is another person, and we need to get below the surface. This requires that we not only care about the big picture, but also are paying attention to every particular detail. We desire to know more by engaging deeper and being aware. The finest opportunity we will ever have to know another genuinely is to want to know what drives the other and how they tick. We start being curious about the simple quirks our partner displays since they become delightful and precious, even if they are annoying at times. We need to be curious about the true nature of the other. To love another is a kind of fascination. We really know someone by curiosity. Only when we actively pay attention do they know we really care.

A child asks, "What killed the cat?" adults respond with the adage "curiosity killed the cat!" This wise saying is supposed to keep them from doing unsafe and risky things. When I heard this, all I could think back then, and now, is that cats must have an abundance of curiosity to get though all nine lives. In bringing this to relationships, what I never heard, and wish I had, was, "Lack of curiosity killed the relationship." Like a cat, a relationship can have many lives, but when we stop bringing curiosity to our partner, those potentials within the relationship diminish. The relationship quickly suffers; it is like a cat pouncing on a mouse. Moreover, the consequence will be similar for the relationship as it is for the mouse.

Relationships suffer when one person considers the other person's life story boring, unremarkable, or embarrassing. They are not interested what motivates his/her feelings and thoughts. Often one party minimizes the others issues and think they are better off or consider the other's life more trouble-free. Everyone is full of mystery and magic if we are curious enough to explore the complexity of his or her personality with interest. We discover that the other is not only an intricate individual but also one who encompasses surprising, mysterious, and fascinating attributes.

You can and must show real curiosity. Creating healthy relationships with stronger bonds shows you are interested in the other. This requires open-minded curiosity and not nosiness and prying. You need to be inquisitive about that other person. We all need to stop jumping to conclusions, and start using curiosity to gather information about others that are accurate rather that jumping to negative conclusions. We will deepen the interconnection rather than set up division.

Even more important may be curiosity about oneself. When I assume, judge, and "know" things about me that are depressing and off-putting, this may sabotage my intimate relationship. An example of negative self-talk is "I'm a loser," "I'm a lousy lover," "I am not good enough," or "I am a crazy fool." Negative self-dialoging makes it impossible to have healthy, flexible bonds with other people.

Psychotherapy can help you rediscover curiosity about your own life, both its glories and struggles. You begin to find meaning and purpose where before there was confusion, heartbreak, and disappointment. You empower curiosity in others by first being curious about yourself. Many schools of therapy help challenge your assumptions about your life, as do spiritual counseling, self-help groups, and 12 step programs.

Curiosity is the key ingredient to creating a healthy relationship with yourself and others. That is why I encourage curiosity with my clients. Such inquisitiveness embraces all aspects of the relationship so that "curiosity does not kill the cat" but provides for revival in having "nine lives." Rather pouncing on others, like a cat on a mouse, we become curious about what motivate their actions and inspire their dreams.

We all desire to be in relationship with parents, children, spouses, siblings, lovers, and friends in ways that fosters curiosity and real interest. The benefit of giving our presence to another is that we empower them to share their concerns without fear of rejection or being shamed. We do not judge or condemn others without asking for their view since staying curious moves us toward deeper understanding. We want to know significant people in our lives, as they really are, rather than as the person who we want them to be. In addition, to know them in this way opens a portal into the other's soul. We allow ourselves to know ourselves for who we are–in all our magnificence, and in all our imperfection.

Did curiosity kill the cat? I do not think so. Curiosity makes each cat's life richer and more exciting. Here is an example. Not too long ago, I was standing with a friend who recently divorced from her husband. As she was telling me about her current struggles, my body started to get tense, and unsolicited advice followed. I was suddenly aware that I had some firm assumptions about her situation that mirrored my own divorce. I noticed something did not feel right in the interaction, but I felt stuck between not saying anything, and giving advice. I started offering suggestions rather than being curious about her view of divorce. At one point she responded, "You know, it would have been better if you were a little more curious about my experience, instead of giving me your opinion."

In that moment, a light bulb went off. Now I try to bring curiosity more often to my relationships. I became more curious with my friend around her painful divorce. It has been enormously helpful for both of us. It is a wonderful thing to bring curiosity to our intimate relationships, but is equally valuable in all interactions. Most of us want to feel appreciated, valued, and welcomed. Curiosity enables this because it says, "I'm interested in you, I'm paying attention, and I care about you." This facilitates trust, people's guards to come down, which creates valuable opportunities for real connection.

If we practice curiosity, we will be less likely to fall into the mind trap of fortune telling and mind reading games. This happens when we make assumptions what another person is thinking or feeling. If I always assume, when my partner walks by without smiling it is because I did something wrong, then I am assuming the worst. I may be incorrect about his motive and way off the mark. When someone in my family is short-tempered, I assume it is probably because they had a bad day at work. If I assume they are mad at me, I may become angry, anxious, or unhappy. We all know where presumptuous thinking gets us, nowhere! When I assume, I make an "ass out of u and me."

So today, practice being a bit more curious in your relationships. Intentionally check your automatic judgments at the door, read between the lines, and dig a little deeper. Instead of jumping to conclusions you might ask, "What do you mean by that?" or "How was that for you?" or "I'm not sure I understand, could you say more?" We can all try to be a bit more curious with our husbands, wives, children, partners, friends, colleagues, clients, employees, bosses, or whoever.

Try it out. You may just like it. When you are curious about another, rather than apathetic, your interactions share knowledge, thus creating a living wisdom that benefits all.

CHAPTER EIGHT:
The Way to Solve Any Relationship Problem

☙

You must both agree to respect each other's opinions.

Here are several things that must happen for a relationship conflict to be resolved:

Phase 1: In solving a relationship conflict, begin by committing to respect. The commitment to stop yelling and shouting at each other in the course of talking about the problem is essential. You must both agree to respect each other's opinions.

Phase 2: Begin by actually identifying the issue and then enlighten your partner to your specific complaint and how you feel. These two steps are a prerequisite, or the process of negotiating some kind of compromise will be pointless and insincere.

Phase 3: You need to adhere to several fundamental principles that can apply to any relationship.

Principle #1: Do not keep score

You and the other, whether, your spouse, parent, child, co-worker, boss, friend, or partner should never keep a running tally of "wins" and "losses" in your interactions. Score keeping damages the effectiveness around how you negotiate differences and conflict.

Sadly, this is one of the biggest mistakes that I see people make who are intimately involved on a daily basis. Most people will not come clean about this or speak of it aloud. However, trust me, most people are silently keeping track. People are keeping score on the inside, just waiting for the day they finally get to "triumph." When you hear anyone, especially your partner (or yourself) complaining, "You always get your way. It's my turn now!" it may be time to recognize that score is being kept.

You should not keep track of victories and losses since usually over time things balance. It would only make sense to win an argument sometimes, and I will grant you that your relationship should be a mutual and reciprocal partnership. The problem with keeping score is that the win-loss record usually becomes the most important factor in resolving a dispute, rather than the need to figure out each issue on its own merit.

Judy, a co-worker of mine, once smugly told me that she had gotten her way four times that week. I was curious about her comment. I wondered about what she meant. Judy answered, "I got my way twice as much as my boyfriend. He only got his way once." Judy did not care if she was right or wrong, just as long as she got in the last word, won the argument, and was the victor in their fight. Giving in for her meant that she was somehow "weak" and losing control. Although, Judy had made significant strides in overcoming her fear that men were with her to manipulate and use her for sex, I thought she was completely off track to keep a tally. I encouraged Judy to understand how this behavior would only serve to drive a wedge between her and a potentially positive relationship.

Finding the middle ground is not a sign of failing nor is it exposing a weak point. It is all right to let your partner come out on top sometimes. Compromise can be an extremely hard thing to do when the relationship has fallen into a pattern of win or lose. However, dare yourself to wash the slate clean before you tackle a new relationship issue. If you are only interested in keeping a score, you will most likely not see the impasse clearly. Very dire conclusions that might irretrievably damage your relationship are likely to happen.

Principle #2: Use your words carefully.

Sticks and stones may break my bones but words hurt even more at times. The language you use toward the other, whom ever, your parent, partner, or even a pedestrian is critically important in determining the outcome of any predicament. Even though you may be right, you may not get your way if your method of communicating is not effective. It will do you no good to put the other person on the defensive right away with accusatory language or a harsh tongue. When someone feels attacked, it is a natural defense mechanism for him or her to fight back, retreat into a shell, or bury his or her head in the sand. Some hope that by denying the resentment, the difficulty will just go away. In either case, you will unlikely find any good solution.

Here are a few examples of language choices that will get you nowhere fast:

Stop using the words always and never. Saying something like, "You never help out around here!" will stop any reasonable discussion dead in its tracks. It sounds like you are exaggerating, and your partner will invariably be challenged to fight back in their defense. They will probably respond with something like, "That's not true! Remember that time two weeks ago that I helped with yard work and took your laundry to the cleaner?" It turns into a "he said, she said" debate, and the real issue gets lost in translation.

So catch yourself when you use words that imply unqualified or ambiguous conclusions. It would be better to start by saying, "I'd like to talk to you about your share of the workload," and "It would be great if sometimes you put me first. I feel like I am playing second fiddle to your friends, relatives, and co-workers."

Stop using insults and name-calling. Some of us grew up believing that the more belligerent and loud we were, the more we would command attention. Nothing could be further from the truth. Sure, this technique may intimidate and belittle your partner into compliance, but you will also make them angry and resentful. They might not have the guts to tell you to your face, but they will secretly feel that you are an insensitive jerk.

Every time you or your partner call each other "stupid" or an "idiot" or an even nastier insult, a little bit of your relationship gets destroyed in the process. On top of that, you obscure the original difficulty in a bombardment of obscenities, so nothing is ever resolved. Therefore, if you are being insulted, the right move is to say, as calmly as you can, "I can't continue to talk to you right now if you're going to use that language," and then offer to pick up the conversation later when your partner has calmed down. If they continue to escalate and violently attack you verbally, then you need to question whether you will be able to stay in a relationship with someone who is acting emotionally and verbally abusive.

Saying "or else!" Many people resort to this threat and tack this little warning at the end of a command; for example, "You better do things my way, or else!" Apparently, many people feel they will get their needs met more quickly if there is an insinuation of some consequence. Even so, the real question should be "Or else what?" What will you really do if your partner ignores your request? How will you retaliate? The problem with this choice of words is that very few people respond favorably to a threat. For most, the response to a threat will actually do the opposite just to show that they will not allow the other to bully them into a demand to a specific action.

Your bluff may be called, and then what will you be prepared to do? If you back down, then your intimidation is empty. Instead, think through your response very carefully and tell your partner, "Here's what I'm going to do if you don't respond to me." It is certainly okay to provide a consequence if your partner fails to correct a problem in the relationship, but that consequence needs to be well defined. You need to actually be able to carry out the consequences. Never make a threat and then back down because this sends a very harmful message.

So how can you guarantee respect? Do you know when the other is listening? Ask yourself, are they hearing me? If this is significant then inquire deeper. How can the other pledge that they will listen? There are better ways to communicate what you need or will tolerate. However, how you convey your preferences to another is vital and requires a level of self-development.

Apply the following examples to any relationship problem:
"I'd like it if we could take some time today to talk about something that's really important to me."
"I feel that this is a problem we can work on together."
"This is really difficult for me to bring up, but I just want to tell you how I feel about..."
"I just need you to listen and try to reserve judgment until I'm finished."
"I'm just asking you to hear what I'm saying -- we don't have to fix the problem right this second."

Principle #3: One thing at a time

You will have more success by focusing on one issue at a time. One of the biggest challenges during conflict is to keep the two people from swerving off into too many directions at once. It is nearly impossible to analyze more than one major issue at a time, which is why problem solving often fails miserably. Recently a friend asked me support around time-management issues in terms of intimacy with her husband. She told me how she saw the problem. "We start with affectionate touching and small talk but before we knew it, we ended the conversation by deliberating the amount of money we spend. Suddenly, we both saw how we put our budgeting concerns before making time for intimacy. We caught our mistake and got back to the topic of spending quality time, but it did take some energy to stay on topic.

My suggestion to my friend was to make a commitment to focus on one issue at a time. I know it sounds difficult, but the payoff will be well worth the extra effort. Be aware, though, that your partner may try to derail the discussion by veering off onto another topic. Often when things start to heat up, one may use a sneaky little tactic to shift the conversation, especially when things are not going well. Therefore, every time you catch your self-avoiding the issue, bring the topic back in focus. When your partner or whomever it is important to communicate with avoids the topic at hand, try to bring the issue back on the table.

Get back on the pathway by saying, "Let's slow down and refocus. Let's attempt to deal with ___ now and get to ___ [the other issue] afterward."

Principle #4: Negotiate the problem

Setting the right stage for discussion is essential. There is a correct time and place to work on your problems. Let us deal with place first. I cannot tell you the exact place or perfect time to deal with an important issue. Think carefully about what will work for you and the other involved. A good rule of thumb is to find a location that is quiet and comfortable, where both parties feel safe, and respected. It just should not be in public, or at a communal gathering space such as work or in a social setting. Major discussions deserve a sacred space so that exploring the problem happens in a consistent, appropriate location. Forgetting to set the scene is a central error made by many people who are engaged in conflict, esp. when couples fight in front of children, friends, or a co-worker.

The right time for the negotiation is just as important as the setting. I believe that there are three important considerations in this area:

First, you must (and I cannot stress the word must enough) point out a problem the very first time it arises. You will have a better advantage if you do not allow something to snowball into a habitual pattern of behavior. Many people finally put their foot down when their partner has made a major mistake for about the hundredth time, but by then it is simply too late. The reality is this: The longer you allow your partner to get away with intolerable behavior, the harder it will be to have any power to get them to stop. If you hold your tongue and just hope that your partner will change, do not complain that you never get what you need.

Second, make sure that you have enough time available to discuss the problem completely. People seek holistic life coaching for issues with intimacy and often bring up an extremely sensitive issue right before our time is up. When I say that we have to end the session, they become upset. They act annoyed and report that the session is over and they received as much as they could. The same principle applies to your intimate relationship. Notice when you are most likely to start a fight. If you and your partner begin to argue just as you are leaving for work or getting ready to go out for dinner, then the discussion will be upsetting and unhelpful. Alternately, if you do not want the problem solved then continue to put off the issue. However, the danger is that if you wait too long, you run the risk that the problem remains up in the air. So set aside an appropriate length of time for a face-to-face meeting. When dealing with intimacy issues, notice that an email, text, or a cell phone conversation is generally not personal enough.

Third, when you and your partner have been haggling for hours, all the hammering away produces more confusion, and less clarity, maybe it is time to stop. Suspend the discussion for the time being. Often the problem arises again and you have a fresh start to address it then. When you both get tired and start feeling dizzy, know that you are on a merry go ride. It may be time to take a break. It is acceptable to say, "I have had enough for one session" "How about we agree to disagree for now." "What about picking up our discussion later when we are both feeling more up to the challenge?"

Principle #5: Apologize and Make Amends

Admit that you are regretful that there has been a breach in the relationship. Express your truth by saying, "I'm sorry." If you act in a disrespectful or hurtful way toward your partner things will only spiral downward. Acknowledge that you are not perfect. Occasionally, unintentionally (or intentionally) you may hurt someone's feelings. This can happened at times without you noticing your partner's feelings. You may say mean-spirited things in the heat of the moment that you instantaneously lament. So swallow your pride, apologize, and ask for forgiveness. For the same reason, you should also expect an "I'm sorry" from your partner if your feelings were hurt by disrespectful behavior.

I know there is a possibility that you grew up in a family where people had arguments or where there was abuse. Many people had parents that were abusive towards the other parent. The negative energy expressed as maltreating each other became the norm. Your parents have set the cast and model for you a certain kind of relational patterning.

You may have become afraid of relationships or wary of that intimacy gives another potential power over you. These kinds of situations weigh you down and contribute to significant troubles that become a drain on the relationship. I will bet that when someone mistreated you, there was no apology for the actions.

So be different -- become truly free in your relationship by admitting that you were wrong. Really, value your partner, and do not let your relationship have an unhappy ending. As the old cliché goes, it is never too late to have a happy childhood. Now you are ready and have access to some very important negotiating and compromising skills. Use these practices in any disagreement and see what happens. You can make the most of these techniques and will have much greater success in solving difficult relationship problems.

CHAPTER NINE:
Positive Reinforcement

⚜

The most common types of positive reinforcement are praise and reward, and most of us have experienced this as both the giver and receiver.

The power of positive reinforcement:

Have you ever wanted another person to behave or respond in a specific way, often according to your expectations? Have you ever allowed another to be truly who they are? Then you know what I mean by positive reinforcement and you "get" how this is fundamental to building healthy relationships. For most of us, positive reinforcement enhances motivation.

Here is a familiar example of positive reinforcement. I work in a residential rehabilitation program for sex offenders with mental illness reentering society. The weekly group, I run, provides education and coaching to support clients building positive relationships after incarceration. The group offers psychosocial education around the risks of criminal behavior, sexual acting out, and the prevention of recidivism.

Our program director tires of seeing the clients sitting around in their rooms doing nothing. He offers three non-mandatory groups per week on the residence. The only requirement is that the clients show up, but he also wants the clients to contribute and benefit from the support group. He knows that the clients love pizza, and so he begins to provide pizza at these groups, but only if the clients participate. Subconsciously, the clients begin to associate going to the group with something good, the pizza.

The pizza is the positive reinforcement the program director provides to help with increasing the attendance. The group is a supportive setting for offering education, tutoring, and redirection, while also getting to eat a favorite food. Program director considers that by rewarding clients with positive reinforcement, (the pizza), this will help solidify the desired behavior, (coming to the group to learn how to maintain safe behavior) coupled with something that they consider a reward, (pizza).

However, for positive reinforcement to succeed, the behavior has to have a consequence. The behavior (coming to the group) then leads to (pizza for lunch). As a product of that outcome (eating pizza), the behavior (coming to the group) is more likely to take place. The program director knows clients like pizza, so by using positive reinforcement they come to the group more often.

Let us take the same issue of positive reinforcement when working with personality conflicts in relationships. What kinds of positive reinforcement influence you? This will differ for each individual and vary from person to person.

Reinforcement

The term reinforce means to strengthen, and is used in psychology to refer to any stimulus which strengthens or increases the probability of a specific response. For example, if you want your dog to sit on command, you may give him a treat every time he sits for you. The dog will eventually come to understand that sitting when told to will result in a treat. This treat is reinforcing because he likes it and will result in him sitting when instructed to do so.

This is a simple description of a "reinforcer" (Skinner, 1948), the treat, which increases the response, sitting. We all apply reinforcers everyday, most of the time without even realizing we are doing it. You may tell your child "good job" after he or she cleans their room; perhaps you tell your partner how good he or she look when they dress up; or maybe you got a raise at work after doing a great job on a project. All of these things increase the probability of repeating the same response.

There are four types of reinforcement: positive, negative, punishment, and extinction. We will discuss each of these and give examples.

Positive Reinforcement

The example above describes positive reinforcement. Think of it as adding something in order to increase a response. For example, adding a treat will increase the response of sitting; adding praise will increase the chances of your child cleaning his or her room. The most common types of positive reinforcement are praise and reward, and most of us have experienced this as both the giver and receiver.

Negative Reinforcement

Think of negative reinforcement as taking something negative away in order to increase a response. Imagine a teenager whose mother nags him to take out the garbage week after week. After complaining to his friends about the nagging, he finally one day performs the task and to his amazement, the nagging stops. The elimination of this negative stimulus is reinforcing because it will likely increase the chances that he will take out the garbage next week.

Punishment

Punishment refers to adding something aversive in order to decrease a behavior. The most common example of this is disciplining (e.g. spanking) a child for misbehaving. The reason we do this is that the child begins to associate punishment with the negative behavior. The child does not like the punishment and therefore avoids it; he or she will stop behaving in that manner.

Extinction

Extinction is a behavior modification based on removing or taking something away in order to decrease a behavior. You decrease the negative response by taking something away; such as the object that one desires or enjoys.

Research demonstrates how positive reinforcement is the most powerful of any of these. Adding a positive to increase a response not only works better, but also allows both parties to focus on the positive aspects of the situation. Punishment, when applied immediately following the negative behavior can be effective, but when not applied consistently or at the wrong time can have negative results. Punishment can also invoke other harmful responses such as anger and resentment.

CHAPTER TEN:
Intimacy from the Neck Up

✤

Brain to brain intimacy is when two people, without to much difficulty, are able to characterize their relationship's vitality from the head up

There are many different ways to look at what makes an intimate relationship to work.

The practice of intimacy from the neck up and through the eyes is a profound discovery for couples. Many people start relationships from below the neck. Consider using a rating scale of 1-10, with 1 being low and 10 being high. Rate you and your partner's relationship from the neck up. See how well you do together.

Eye to eye, contact reveals how radiant you and your partner look to each other. Conscious eye-to-eye contact exposes you completely as our eyes are the window to the soul. When the two of you engage, whether it is a sober dialogue or casual babble, do you look at each other and hold eye contact? To perceive with the eyes is a particular perspective. It is a visual portal into how the other's beauty reveals a hidden Source. Intimate eye-to-eye witnessing is important in setting the aperture to widen the scope of union.

When you look at your partner, what do you witness through the visual portal of your eyes? Do you discover in the gaze a sense of attraction and affirmation? Are you loving and affectionate when looking at your partner? Do you share a sense of the importance of this experience with eyes wide open? Is it difficult to bring open face-to-face contact when discussing a thorny matter? Can you keep eye-to-eye contact even in the heat of an argument or in the throes of ecstasy?

Ear to ear contact is critical to building intimacy because active listening is the gateway to understanding. Do you hear what your partner has to say and enjoy listening to them? Do you find the description of their day interesting to hear about? Do you seek out and want to listen to their thoughts, opinions, and ideas? Do you like the sound of their voice? Do you understand what they say? In good hearing like good harmony, you can hear your partner at different levels of meaning. When your partner speaks to you, can you often hear what they say with understanding at more than one level?

Mouth to mouth contact encompasses two intimate acts of a relationship, talking with and kissing your partner. Do you share in witty conversations that allow playful talking and kissing? Do you taste your partner and sense the delight of a fresh a mountain spring or does it taste like toxic waste? Do your lips meet like good dance partners or are you tongue-tied and uncomfortable? Does it feel natural? Do you feel better after having mouth-to-mouth contact with your partner? Is this something you look forward to doing in your relationship? If mouth to mouth contact has not happened for a while, do you invite the practice or bring it to your partner's attention? How often does your day begin or end with a kind word or meaningful kiss?

Partners who are in balance share by talking, kissing, and taking turns starting the practice. While there are many styles of kissing and talking, each couple finds their own poise. These go from light lip brushes to a full and fervent "French" kiss. When your mouth is more than the words, but envelops the tone and nuance of how it sounds to the beloved's ear there is intimacy from the neck up. From this tender receptive place, both partners connect from the heart, pillow talk soften into a tender soul-searching conversation.

In healthy relationships, couples keep the process going at all ages and stages of their relationship. It makes no difference what age; a mouth-to-mouth renaissance is a vital part of intimacy throughout the lifespan. Moreover, words like "I" as in "I love you" confirm and words like "you" as in "you make my life worthwhile" celebrate value and worth of the partnership. The word "we" as in "we have a great rapport" shows up for the most part as it conveys appreciation, support, and affinity. The actual measure of mouth-to-mouth renewal is how often you find time to linger in the intimate experience. Can intimacy happen by merely kissing? I would divinely say, yes!

Head-to-head contact is vital to longevity in intimate relationships. While sharing of minds is more than just a brain connection. We must have brain intimacy because the brain is where desire originates. In relating from the head up, we engage through the energy of perception, intelligence (both intellectual intelligence IQ and Emotional Intelligence EQ), and brainpower. Notice how you think about your partner. What are your thoughts and feelings? Are they clear, affirmative, and effortless to describe?

Brain-to-brain contact challenges you to trust yourself and your partner's intelligence by understanding thoughts and feelings. Can your partner describe them to you? Brain to brain intimacy is when two people, without to much difficulty, are able to characterize their relationship's vitality from the head up. When your do this simple practice, intimacy naturally moves to the center of your shared life since you are interested in what the other person thinks. With a communal vision of the path, your relationship will naturally take a positive trajectory into the future and you will keep active with brainstorming and problem solving.

Nose-to-Nose, while it may seem insignificant, our smell is perhaps the most important of the five senses for above the neck connecting. The sense of smell reveals a significant aspect of the other's body, and evokes a desire of physical closeness. If a potential partner smells bad to us and has a foul scent, their body odor can be an immediate turn off. We participate in all the senses for survival since we need adeptness with each one to maneuver through initial stages of intimacy. Each person has a particular preference when it comes to the sense of smell. The nasal aroma links us to deep memories and creates unconscious longings. Why do certain scents of perfume take use immediately back to the scent of a lover, child, or even a place lost in time? People seem drawn to certain smells more than others are. While good hygiene is important, remember that the nose knows of subtle regions linking us to a perfumed passion from the past.

Take a few moments and see how your relationship above the neck measures up. Congratulations, if your score was high. That means that you and your partner are already connecting from the neck up. Continue with whatever you are doing. If your score was lower than you would like on any of the senses, it is time to get back to intimacy by face-to-face, from the neck up contact. Make time to be with your partner and make some decisions about what it is you have to do to get more of a heads up reactivating intimacy in your relationship.

CHAPTER ELEVEN:
Seven Strategies for Healthy Sexuality

⚜

Now you have a practice to work on intimacy from the neck up. Here are seven strategies that support healthy sexuality from the neck down. You will be surprised just how easy it is to dissolve common issues around sexuality. The benefits of this practice are healthier displays of affection, more mutually enhancing sex, and improved attitudes toward intimacy in the relationship.

1. Mutual Respect:

Without respect, all is lost in the realm of sex. If we do not have this, well, reciprocal sex that is both pleasurable and passionate is not possible. Sex is going to be a bumpy ride. This does not mean you concur with everything your partner says or consent to anything. It means that you have high regard for each other, and a secure base to express amorous feelings and affection.

Respect is the ability to "see again" and includes holding the other in high regard and being willing to see through problems to underlying desire for sex. This act preserves the intimacy, but without the negative cost disregard. For positive sexuality to remain strong throughout your relationship, ground the love in intimacy that arises from mutual respect. You also hold the other in awe, appreciate the magic of union, and show the relationship reverence.

Marriage therapists often can tell in the first few minutes of a session whether a couple will make it together for the long haul or merely crash and burn. If there is no mutual respect, they are not going to make it. How can the therapists tell with such amazing accuracy? Many discover that if there are any signs of disrespect in their attitude toward the other, the relationship suffers. Disrespecting the intimacy contaminates sex in the bedroom and affection in the home. The relationship usually does not endure. Mistreatment whether it is physical, verbal, or emotional abuse, forecloses mutual respect.

2. Disagree without Fighting

I have never seen a healthy couple that does not quarrel. However, they never exchange blows and battle in hurtful ways that display disrespect. They may differ and disagree on various issues but can use problem-solving skills. They are more successful at resolving conflict and agree to disagree. If a couple comes for holistic relationship coaching and tells me, they are always in harmony, I wonder! Sometime avoiding conflict creates more conflict.

You can argue without fighting. Arguing is non-combative if you and your partner state your points of view without calling names or raising your voice. Sometimes you consent to diverge and that is all right. Figure out what is "non-negotiable" and what is not. Discuss things that you will not shift your position. Now change that list. I like the saying "You can either be right, or happy." When our values and those of our partner's match up well, it is amazing how that makes things so much easier in terms of intimate communication and sex!

3. Synchronization around Sex

You are both okay with how often you have sex, how you engage in sex, where you have sex, and that there is mutual participation. Do not withhold sex as punishment. Sex is not for penalizing the other. If you or your partner is not comfortable with a facet of your sex life, you can talk about it openly, without censure. You also find time to have sex if you have passion for each other, no matter how busy or tired the two of you are. There is always time for sex.

4. Agreement on Parenting

There are essentially three major styles of parenting:
1.) Authoritarian: The rules are the rules are the rules and no exceptions.
2.) Authoritative: This is what I refer to as a "single party rule". There are rules, and kids can give their contribution, but the parents have the last word.
3.) Lenient or "Lassiez-faire": There are nominal rules.

If the two partners disagree on a parenting style, you need to talk. You may have each grown up with different parenting styles - and we each tend to act toward our children in ways that are similar to how our parents treated us. If you do not have children but are planning to, this is an important conversation to have with your partner.

People can change parenting styles but often personalities are in the hardwiring.

5. Equality with Money

Even if one of you contributes more to the finances, you both have an equal say about where your money goes. There are no "hidden accounts", and you decide together before you make large purchases. If you are the one in charge of the bill paying, you pay the bills on time. If you cannot pay the bills on time, turn over that job to your partner or hire someone to do it for you. You decide on separate accounts if sharing a joint account is getting too complicated or frustrating. Does that hurt the intimacy of a relationship? No, it actually helps your intimacy. You are no longer fighting about money.

6. Common Goals and Values

Couples with very different interests can have healthy relationships. The key is that they share common goals and values. Couples of different religions (or non-religion) and cultural backgrounds can have healthy relationships - what makes a healthy relationship is sharing core beliefs. You may both share the belief that giving back to your community is important. You may both share the belief that extended family members are welcome to live with you at any time. Values and beliefs differ for everyone.

Common goals include intangibles like raising happy and healthy children, and tangibles like saving up for a house. You can work together on setting one-year, five-year, even ten- and twenty-year goals. Working towards something together strengthens your bond.

7. Fun

"Sexiness wears thin after a while and beauty fades, but to be married to a man who makes you laugh every day, ah, now that's a real treat." - Joanne Woodward

Enough said. Make time to have fun. Life gets too serious without receiving regular doses of humor. If there is one thing that psychological research and personal experience will reveal to every one of us, it is the positive impact relationships have on our happiness, level of success, and overall well-being. Having healthy relationships means so much for every area of our life. Relationships offer us joy, love, and support in times of need. They also help us expand our aspirations and level of achievement through support, knowledge, and interpersonal connections. In general, relationships can help us to grow and become better people. Therefore, whether your focus is on intimate and loving relationships, or more professional business relationships, there are certain qualities of pleasure and delight that will make any relationship more fun, meaningful, and long lasting.

Here are five additional attributes:

1. Commitment - Relationship success and commitment go hand in hand. When we are committed to a relationship, we are willing to put in the effort to make it work. It is more likely there will be a plan to stick together, and a growing sense of loyalty, and trust can develop. When we are committed to a partner of any kind, dedication and allegiance provide stable plans and goals for the future.

2. Compassion - Being able to connect with others emotionally is so crucial to building a strong relationship. If you want to have more than just superficial interactions, you need kindness. When we want for others what we want for ourselves and truly care about their well-being, it provides an amazing foundation for making real connections. Connecting with others comes from having empathy and caring about how they feel, just as we do about ourselves. Developing compassion and empathy will offer great security for a long-lasting relationship.

3. Generosity - In a healthy relationship, the more we give the more we get. Wanting to make others happy and offering our support to help one another is a staple of loving and caring relationships. Being generous is about being willing to give of yourself when you may not immediately get something directly in return. This can require having a "win/win" attitude or a "what's mine is yours" mentality. By practicing this habit alone, you will find amazing benefits that help deal with internal conflict and outer strife around intimacy.

4. Tolerance - Everyone makes mistakes. A tolerant and open-minded perspective goes a long way in building relationships. Taking a non-judgmental attitude and learning that there will be differences in opinion serves the purpose of making relationships a safe place to iron out differences and be tolerant. If we feel understood, we are confident that we will receive honest praise when deserved or positive guidance, not criticism for making mistakes. It is not about being perfect. When we can be our real self, we experience much greater fulfillment and growth.

5. Kindness - This one area, (being kind) says empirical research demonstrates the most benefits on peoples' happiness and life-satisfaction. When we engage in random acts of kindness, it benefits everyone. Kindness can come from a nice gesture, doing favors for others, or by simply treating others with respect. We can to show we care about them as a human being by showing consideration. Kindness stems from a general loving heart where we feel affection and warmth for others. What act of thoughtfulness can you commit today?

Incorporate these five traits into your current relationships. Especially try this on whenever you are entering a new relationship. You will cultivate more positivity so you will both benefit. Relationships are about coming together for enjoyment, mutual purpose, and helping each other to be better people. Simply practice these behaviors and intimacy will thrive.

Jealousy is that green-eyed monster

You may have lived with this "monster" of a habit for many years or perhaps it is a recent development. Whatever the case, when you jump into jealousy, you and your relationship are both bound to suffer. We are here to help you practice building trust so that your love relationship can be passionate and connected.

Take off the mask of the green-eyed monster and you will likely find fear, feelings of insecurity, low self-esteem, and belief that you are not good enough to deserve faithfulness. On the surface, jealousy may seem angry and even hostile, but a deep sense of anxiety and vulnerability tend to drive this destructive habit. In order to turn jealousy around and open up space for building trust, it is important to work with these feelings.

If you tend to be a jealous person, perhaps you grew up feeling like there just was not enough love to go around. You may have felt unwanted due to lack of attention. It may not go as far back as childhood, but maybe you experienced a trauma that left you traumatized and feeling alone. You were left feeling not good enough or somehow flawed. Perhaps you have just never gotten over it. You may have experienced a broken heart and never really recovered. You may have never gone through a particular loss such as a lover having an affair on you for these feelings to develop. It might come down to feeling inferior and unworthy of love and then expecting the ones you care about to treat you accordingly.

As difficult as it is for the person prone to jealous feelings, it is also tricky for that person's partner. Jealousy in a relationship does nothing but build walls of mistrust between you and your partner. Try to stand on one side of a literal brick wall with your partner on the other side and then attempt to embrace one another. As we know this is virtually impossible. In fact, it is also hard to communicate clearly with that literal wall between you. Relationship walls may not be as easy to see, but they can feel just as solid and impassable as a concrete barricade.

Adam and Eve's Story

Adam and Eve had just started dating. They love to spend time walking hand in hand in the park, and going out to dinner and the movies. They both feel excited about this new relationship. Eve, however, has an ongoing problem with jealousy. Distrust has become a habit that she has adopted to deal with her insecurity. She recognizes that in most of her relationships, she ends up feeling jealous. This attitude causes her to act distrustful and guarded resulting in the ending of the relationship.

There is always a fear that her partner will become tired of her and move on. When Adam and Eve are out in the park, she is always aware of the other women walking by or sitting on a bench—particularly the ones she thinks are attractive. She is hyperactive with suspicion; ultra attentive to the direction of his gaze. Eve looks to see if he also notices the other women. When Eve is away from Adam, she asks many questions. Adam comes how to a barrage of questions: Where have you been? What have you been doing? Who are you spending time?

Adam has begun to notice a certain change in Eve. She has become suspicious and dubious about Adam's faithfulness. Adam notes that he feels like this relationship could be something special but Eve's mistrust makes him feel uncomfortable and irritable. He decides to talk about his feelings with Eve before her pattern of jealousy snuffs out the fire between them.

As bleak as this all might seem, there is reprieve in view! Being aware that you or your mate has a jealousy pattern is a first important step. Here are two suggestions to get you started building trust.

1.) Look Deep Within

Whether or not you are the one with the jealousy pattern, you can both benefit from looking deeply within yourselves. Set aside some time when you can be alone, on your own, and undisturbed. Now do a reality check and really confirm how you are feeling. When in the heat of feeling overwhelmed by jealousy, if you can manage to look within you have some advantage. It is important that you stay focused on how you are feeling. Allow the stories of who, what, and where go for now. You can never be sure how accurate the stories you tell yourself. Work with the feelings as they arise. Do not either grasp or push away. Be at the center of the storm and witness what is happening in your body, what are you physically experiencing. This act alone will help.

When a feeling comes up for you-- like fear for example-- no matter how much you want to resist, allow it. Look at what you are feeling and notice where it comes from. It might be that you fear abandonment and you can trace that back to feeling abandoned as a child. Childhood traumas are not the sole cause of later habits, but they can significantly contribute to them. Again, let go of the stories that go along with your emotional turmoil. Remind yourself that you are now safe and that you care for yourself very well. The abandonment fears may not totally disappear with this reminder, but you may find relief.

2.) Uplift

As Adam and Eve sit down to talk about how they are both feeling, it is important that they speak with honesty. However, they must not continue to bring the other person down. The jealousy habit is already doing that! In order to build trust, be sure to speak from where you are and not from a place of blame or judgment. This may not be easy as many of us automatically judge and criticize internally.

Perhaps Adam starts by sharing with Eve that he would like to see their relationship continue and grow but that he feels a wall building between them. Instead, he would like to work with her on building trust. For her part, Eve may be able to be honest about her fears. She may even choose to share some of the history behind them. Only then can Eve "own" the feelings of jealousy and let Adam know she also wants to build trust and work on letting go of the past.

Nothing has really changed for Adam and Eve except that they both took a huge step towards each other by honestly sharing feelings. They may have not even mentioned the word jealousy, but they did put out there what they want—a more trust-filled relationship. Just as Adam cannot make Eve's fears of abandonment go away, you cannot allay the feelings that underlie your partner's jealousy habit. What you can do is be honest about where you are and be uplifting to your partner. Keep the focus on what you want and on the good stuff that is going well between you.

As Eve begins the healing process, she trusts more and takes the mask off her green-eyed monster. Eve also appreciates the way that Adam is supporting her with and showing fidelity and reliability. She can share with him in a new way and starts to uplift them both out of the pit of suspicion. Eve can consciously choose to uplift herself when difficult feelings arise. She might come up with an effective routine to use when that familiar jealousy makes an appearance as when the green-eyed monster rears its ugly head.

One example she tries is to use self-loving quotes that she carries in her purse or she sings a soothing song to herself. Whatever brings relief to those feelings, will help stop the jealousy in its tracks. No matter how much jealousy forms between you and your partner, you can make a change. With an honest sharing of feelings from the heart and the intention to uplift one another, you can start to build trust.

Dispositional Authenticity

Humans have evolved to build committed social bonds. We do this primarily for self-protection, maintenance of the species so to raise offspring to maturity. When it comes to romance, the advice to "be your self" might be right on, according to new research. Studies suggest that peoples' ability to stay true to their values and act consistently with their beliefs, affects their relationships. The results show that those who reported being true to themselves also reported positive dating relationships. Common sense tells us that if you are true to yourself, it is easier to act in ways that build intimacy in relationships.

One study involved 62 heterosexual couples, all college students. The participants completed questionnaires in three separate sessions that took place about two weeks apart.

The first part of the study, participants rated items meant to measure their "dispositional authenticity," or how true they were to themselves, such as: "For better or for worse, I am aware of whom I truly am."

The second phase, participants answered questions examining various aspects of their relationship functioning, including their willingness to discuss emotions with their partner, and issues of dealing with honesty and secrecy.

The third phase involved measures of relationship satisfaction and personal well-being. Overall, men and women who reported being truer to self, built deeper intimate relationships with their partner, and felt their relationship was more upbeat, positive, and secure. In addition, those who were more authentic also reported greater personal well-being.

Relationship and Gender roles

Such research reveals an interesting gender difference in how authenticity in men and women affected their partners. Men who were more true to themselves had partners who showed more healthy relationship behaviors. However, the reverse was not true: there was no significant connection between women being true to themselves and men's relationship behaviors. That finding might be the result of relationship gender roles in our society, since typically in dating and marital relationships, the women tend to be 'in charge' of intimacy in the relationship. Therefore, when men have this dispositional authenticity, and want to have an open, honest relationship, it makes women's job easier since they can more easily regulate intimacy. While men have less of a role in developing relationship intimacy, authenticity in their partners and being true to them or not, did not figure significantly.

Staying true to yourself does not mean you should accept all of your flaws and not try to make positive changes in your life. However, you should be aware of both your limitations and areas where you can improve. One payoff could be better romantic relationships. When it comes to romance, the advice to "be you" might be right on, according to new research that looked at how peoples' ability to stay true to themselves, including seeing themselves clearly and objectively, acting in ways consistent with their beliefs, and interacting honestly and truthfully with others affected their relationships.

The results show that those who reported being more true to themselves also reported positive dating relationships. If you are true to yourself, it is easier to act in ways that build intimacy in relationships. Truthfulness is going to make your relationship more fulfilling. It seems that when men have a disposition to be authentic, and wants to have an open, honest relationship; it makes the female partner's not have to take on the role of monitoring intimacy. Studies suggest strengthening our capacity for truth telling also improves the quality of our authenticity intimate relationship.

Polly and Justine's Story

Polly had been married to Justine for ten years when she first consulted me for help. When asked what she wanted coaching around, she blurted out, "Intimacy." Polly said her relationship with Justine was lacking in closeness mainly because she was uncomfortable with intimacy. "I can't stand being in this marriage anymore." She continued to explore the upset. "We have two wonderful children and I do not want to break up this family, but I m miserable." I asked Polly what aspect made her so anxious so much of the time. She said, "I feel like I'm always walking on eggshells and I can't be myself." I asked, "What are you afraid will happen if you are yourself?"

Polly ponders a moment, "I know it sounds crazy because a part of me wants out of this marriage, but I am more afraid that James will leave if I express my needs and desires." In our exploration, Polly reveals her feelings. "I fear I will be alone the rest of my life." Her fear of being independent and looking in-depth at her own choices, gave her new insight into her role in the anxiety around intimacy. She said, "I think that if I take care of myself and do what makes me happy, instead of taking care of Justine's feelings and needs, he will leave."

We analyze this fear. I ask Polly, "What is lurking behind the dread of abandonment and rejection?" Polly expresses her view. "I'm afraid to find out that Justine really doesn't love me. What if the only reason he is with me is only because how devoted I am, I take care of him." I ask, "Do you fear that if you stop letting him dump on you, it would end?" Well, Polly continues, "If I stop having sex when I don't feel turned on to him, he will leave me for someone who will give him continual sex. He gets furious at me when I say no to sex." Polly opens to a deeper possibility of healing and intimacy. "I'm afraid to find out that he really doesn't care about my happiness at all."

Polly addresses her fears and agrees to works on intimacy by working on her relationship within. This step requires that she is pro-active and willing to take the first step. By courageously challenging his lack of intimacy, she can also explore the underlying reason she is so needy. Thorough inner work, Polly began to accept some of the concealed reasons her husband may demand that she conform to his wishes rather than attune to her own desires.

Polly, I share, "it sounds like you are telling yourself two things that are making you feel miserable and anxious. One voice is telling you it if you do not take care of Justine's feelings, he will leave you. The other is saying that you will not be okay if he leaves you." This comment stirs Polly. She says, "I understand that my misery and anxiety are signals from my deeper inner guidance system." Yes, I echo, "It allows you to hear what you are telling yourself unconsciously, that you are not worthy of Justine's love. You recognize a new voice coming from within. This voice helps you distinguish between what is good for you and what is not."

Polly acknowledges this strength inside. She can now allow her feelings to be in alignment with her highest good, and, to identify the warning sign when she is not.

Here is a transcript from a session.

I begin, "Let us start with the belief that you will not be okay if Justine leaves. Are you sure this is true?"
Polly responds, "Actually, I know it isn't true. I love being alone, and financially there is enough money that I would be okay. Moreover, I know that Justine loves our children and me. He would never abandon us."
I respond, "So if you tell yourself that you will be fine if Justine leaves, then how do you feel?"
Polly says, "That feels good! I know that is the truth!"

I reply, "Okay, then if that is the truth, what do you have to lose by being yourself?"

Polly says, "I m scared to death to find out that Justine doesn't really love me. I guess it's not about being alone after all, but about not feeling loved."

I coach, "Polly, please go inside and ask your Inner Child if she feels loved by you when you give yourself up just to sexually please Justine?"

Polly says, "When I am a door mat for him I am living a lie."

Therefore, I add, "Your inner child feels that you have to be inauthentic to be loved?"

Polly exclaims, "No, she (my inner child) doesn't feel loved at all! She hates it when I don't take care of her and take care of him instead."

I say, "So, do you think it is possible that even if you found out that Justine doesn't love you that loving yourself would make things okay for you?"

Polly responds, "Yes, the first step is to be true to me, and I need to love myself!"

After this coaching session, Polly began use this simple form of inquiry to process her inner feelings. She starts to take care of herself. She stops being a push over for Justine. Polly does not allow Justine to dump his anxiety about his manhood onto the marriage bed. She gets back on track by connecting with her inner child. Polly finds more intimacy than she knew was possible and displays it in passionate lovemaking, but has sex only when she feels like being intimate. At first, Justine is angry, but when he discovers that his anger does not get him anywhere, he starts to take better care of himself. Instead of discovering that she has to give herself up to receive Justine's love, Polly discovers that loving herself works wonders in their marriage. Being her true self enhances her life and fosters deeper intimacy than she ever thought possible.

CHAPTER TWELVE:
Maintaining Intimacy

⚜

No two people are alike or have the same interests, and while you will naturally seek commonalities to share, accommodating both differences and compatibilities is essential for long–lasting connection.

Any type of relationship whether it is between a lover, family members, people we work with, friends, or clients we serve, takes a lot of work but is worth it. In addition, much of the work that improves our relationships involves developing trust, compassion, and acceptance of both self and the other. As well, we learn to consider there will be differences in preferences and styles. No two people are alike or have the same interests, and while you will naturally seek commonalities to share, accommodating both differences and compatibilities is essential for long-lasting connection.

Step 1: Know Thy Self

Long stated by many people, this simple adage is essential for good relationship building. If you do not know your own needs, wants, preferences, and limits, you risk using relationships as a source of your own validation, which can easily lead to co-dependency, clingy behavior, aggressive possessiveness, manipulation, or other unhealthy reasons for wanting to be with others. Self-knowledge enables you to be a creative, resourceful, and whole. Self-awareness is an uplifting force rather than a destructive, Debbie Downer one. You will find yourself able to celebrate in other's successes, achievements, and strengths rather than resenting them.

We are always attracted to people who make us feel good about ourselves and ultimately, this is the number one skill in improving our relationships with others.

Step 2: Know the Other

Learning all you can about a wide range of people is not always easy, but it makes such a difference. We can even apply this to people we meet only once. This act alone of feeling the other is interested in knowing us, can touch us deeply. For example, think of the salesperson who engages you in a conversation about your life, rather than acting like the one they couldn't care less whether you were there or not and only going on about the product or sale. A successful sale happens simply because the salesperson acknowledges that they are in a relationship with the customer as a human being, not as a consumer. Take time to build rapport, no matter how brief a connection with another person, and you will be greatly impressed by how much easier your interactions with others become.

Ask simple questions about big things. Get to know other people's values and beliefs by asking them. For those people you intimately connect with, what do you know about their views on the world, other people, laws, ethics, marriage, faith, spiritual fulfillment, etc.? Share your views and values too. However, be prepared to challenge what others think and believe without being negative, confrontational, or opposition in response. You do not have to give up what you believe in to be accepted. You may just learn something by truly being open to understanding the other person's perspective.

Feel comfortable in asking questions about other people's values; many people love the opportunity to open up some more. However, do not probe or twist their responses and be particularly caring about those people who are still working out their values, who seem confused, or who simply find this sort of conversation overwhelming. Not everyone feels comfortable opening up about values but most people do appreciate compassionate guidance.

Step 3: True Self-Worth

At times, we do not feel good enough unless we are in a relationship with a significant other. Many of us come across as needy precisely because we feel we are not whole unless we are part of a couple. Being single is not always a choice but it is important to make the most of it when we are in the situation of going solo. If single, we can continue to reach out to others as a friend and as a fellow human being, rather than constantly seeming needy, and lost without an intimate partner. Learn to spend time with yourself in positive ways. It is about being alone as healthy rather than lonely, and as simply another spectrum of your complete self.

For those who come from dysfunctional family situations, there can be a deep yearning to recreate a family that "works". There is nothing wrong with this desire provided you do not let it compromise your values. You need not abandon enjoying the life you have until you find the perfect partner. Do not put your life's fulfillment on hold because of a contingency you have not yet met (and remember that the idea of what "works" is very abstract). It is important to put your needs first, but not to the extent that you go on the defense, or put life on autopilot.

In addition, continue to be part of the lives of those family members whom you still relate to and care about from your family. They are still your family, and they can be a source of strength and grounding. For those whose former family situation was so bad that they cannot return to any family members for support or love, find other people you can rely upon for love and support, such as good friends, extended family members, or people who have meant a great deal to you through life. We are all one human family after all.

Step 4: Living, Loving, and Sharing:

Living: To live and let live means allowing others to live as they choose insofar as that does not infringe the dignity of others around them. Do not try to change people or direct their life's choices - while there is room for guidance, do not force your preferences onto others. It also means actively enjoying being with other people by being present for them and truly listening to them. Many times, we are not present to the moment of being with another. We give our presence to someone or something else such as to answer an insignificant cell phone call or text. We let our minds wander over other matters rather than concentrating on the person before us. Cultivate living, loving and sharing by being present. This is the best gift you can ever give to another human being.

Loving: Love means giving love to others unconditionally. One of the hardest things to do for most relationships is caring for another person's well-being, in the sense feeling responsible or worrying for another person. When we place conditions on our love as a way of shaping the outcome, the outcome unfortunately is less than loving.

Sharing: Try very hard to get beyond the temptation to withhold and simply love people for who they are. If you see warts, keep scraping until you find the gem underneath. Sharing both your strengths and weakness creates harmony in a relationship. Harmony and balance are a part of any relationship structure since the relationship is not only about you but also about the shared intimacy. Intimacy is actually about being real, and making a true connection.

Step 5: Grasp the other's perspective

Perspective change is another important relationship improvement skill. Use this technique to walk a mile in the other person's shoes. It is impossible to know another person's motivations, reasons, and actions until we look with care and listen with an open heart. It is easy to dismiss a person because they have done or said things we are not in agreement with. When we feel hurt on a superficial level, we prefer to lick our own wounds instead of looking at the real motivations of the other's underlying intent. Is it possible that your own reactions are causing another person to react to you in a way that makes things harder between you?

For example, if you keep pushing someone who is a reluctant talker to expose their feelings about you, and they end up saying even less, consider that by you having been so pushy, it may cause the other person to clam up. Alternatively, if this person did finally open up but you jumped down their throat with your annoyance, you have not grasped the other's perspective. You may show anger at the things they have said, which confirms for them that keeping quiet is the best option around you.

Instead, try the following whenever you are in a relationship situation where you feel confrontation, unease, or misunderstandings arising between the two of you:

Stop talking your self and simply listen.
Take a moment to digest what the other person has said.
Repeat your understanding of what the other person has said back to them (the gist, not verbatim). Keep summarizing what the other person has said until they agree you have nailed it. Start seeking a compromise. Rather than bombarding the other with what you think they "don't get" about your side of the story.

Step 6: Face difficulties as they Arise

Do not let problems in a relationship fester. This is a recipe for disaster as it fuels misunderstanding and anger, which can ultimately lead to a rupture in your relationship. Talk to one another openly about feelings, issues you have, and concerns about things you have heard. Avoid prejudging and resist gossip. Try to clear the air when someone you interact with seems to have said or done something that reverberates negatively on you. When discussing things openly, there is no need to confess all your sins and give them your whole life story. Be circumspect about what you say and get to the point. Making up sob stories so others feel sorry for you wears thin very quickly.

Step7: Take full responsibility for your own words and actions

After childhood, the expectation is to be responsible for what you say and do; unfortunately, there are many adults unable to grasp this simple notion. Many feel safer, for one reason or another, in placing blame for their own inadequacies and actions onto others. After a time, this causes relationships to falter because nobody wants to receive blame for things all the time. It is both boring and exhausting to be around someone who constantly blames others but never takes personal responsibility. One very fast way to improve relationships is to remove blame from the equation. Accept responsibility where it's due, and find solutions instead of complaining.

Step 8: Grow together.

Expecting someone to remain the same person they were 5, 10, or 20 years ago is both unrealistic and unfair. You really do not want people to remember you as the same person you were 20 years ago. You have grown and changed in that time. Good relationships make space for growth and both parties accept this growth in each other. In fact, not only allow this space but also nurture it; help the person to become more and more the person they feel best as, and help them to grow their strengths. Bring out the best in others. This is one of the greatest experiences of being part of relationships affords, whether it's family, lovers, students, staff, coworkers, friends, clients, guests or whoever.

Remember, that as each of you grows, the changes do not necessarily mean the end of a relationship; instead, it is just a different type of relationship. If you can accept the fact that your relationship status has changed, it may be the beginning of something completely special in a new way. Naturally, though, some growth means that you grow apart and things are not compatible anymore. That is normal too but just be sure you really are unable to reach acceptance before finally cutting ties.

Step 9: Nurture your relationships.

Every person and all relationship need nurturing to flourish. Left untended, or uncared for, the survival rate is slim to none. This means setting aside time, however brief, to spend with this person. In intimate relationships, the time needed together will be far greater than the time we set aside for other daily contacts. In every single case, the time spent must be dedicated, focused, and of quality, in order to nurture the relationship. Give your full attention; show that you care and that you are interested. Be authentic. This shows you are mentally and emotionally present when you spend time together.

If someone lives far away from you, send him or her email now and then, or call him or her up. Arrange to meet up occasionally, or if that is impossible, try a video link chat. All our amazing technology makes it possible to seem like you are in the room with another person halfway across the world, so make the most of it!

Step 10: Believe

Believing in people and trusting them is not always easy. Certainly, there are people who will abuse your trust and will not live up to your belief in them. However, it is always far better to assume that others will do the right thing and that they will seek to live up to your belief in them than to view the world through fearful or angry lenses. Use your wits and common sense about what feels right when interacting with other people. You do not want to end up physically harmed or emotionally abused but try to be a source of encouragement.

Enlighten other people in your life by giving them an indication that you really do believe and trust in them above all. It is far harder for people to break trust and to let another person down when they are fully aware of that trust, and that to break it they must make active choices that bring about harm. In many situations where coercion is absent, assuming good faith about a fellow human being will bring you the reward of a much improved relationship. When we assume the best about another, the result is often a lifelong commitment to this person as friends or trusted partner.

Stand behind those you trust. Show others that you support them and believe in them too. People are more complex than we often give them credit. In many cases, this is because it is easier to make erroneous assumptions about people. When we only see things in black and white, we can be stuck in negative patterns. When we are able to bring a holistic approach to our relationship, we get on with our lives. This often does a service to another human being because we stop assuming things that are often inaccurate or mistaken.

In doing so, you appreciate the value of what you already have. You start to seek understanding and peace more than being right and in control. You stop feeling as if you are the victim of life and stop needing to find someone to blame. In addition, it is more likely you will learn more about yourself in the process of knowing another in this open and compassionate way. The ultimate aim is for you to create deeper realms of intimacy throughout your life.

Conclusion

❧

Anything of value in life involves human connection. A priest once shared with me, "God works through others." All our basic needs, deepest desires, hopes, and fears involve other people. Just think of how many people contribute to bringing clean water to our glass. Our relationships must spring from a pure source within but this requires a willingness to step outside our comfort zone. Traveling with a companion or journeying solo, this book speaks to creating a relationship within. We take another's hand, fully embrace for a moment, or a lifetime, and touch each other's world, but ultimately we live and die alone.

When two join in unconditional love they relate to the Higher Self within each other. Namaste, "I bow to the divine within you" is the term many use as a spiritual greeting. It announces that I speak from my higher self and welcome the beloved within you to speak your truth. I have invited you to embark on a personal journey to the experience of "falling in love from the inside out" via union with your Higher Self.

Union with your Higher Self gives you a secret advantage in life since this connection signals to others that you have self-love. "I treat you as I treat myself." If partners grasp at each other out of fear or blind desire, the oneness becomes entrapment. Thus, I emphasize the deeper purpose of building a relationship is always life enrichment for the greater good. By extending freedom to the other, we develop integrity, and grow in spirit. As the poet Rilke says, "Two solitudes protect and border and greet each other." We all need internal space to help us build, repair, and maintain our many relationships throughout life. Nevertheless, at the center remains the definitive goal; connecting with your Higher Self.

Every great teacher speaks to the power of a hidden realm beyond the physical. On the ordinary level, we try to live with compassion, but often find we exist from routine patterns of selfishness, and personal inclination. In rare moments, we can all transcend the ego and experience compassion for everyone. We surprise our self with gestures of kindness and operate from a place of higher intelligence. This kind of wisdom resides in a clandestine region of psyche where each person must establish his or her own inner authority. However, much of the psychological work we do on relationship building is not always patently obvious. The process of individuation is real, and takes real moral work to break free of our illusions. Turning to the Source is not a fantasy, but requires an awareness of an enduring presence that like the divine child, invites us to follow something mysterious, odd, and even weird. This ephemeral psychological activity is much like trying to take hold of a dream upon awakening. We suddenly wake up, on the inside, and acknowledge the fundamental nature of any relationship. Relationship Within is the real meaning of union and heart of relational life.

Relationship Within draws you into divine intimacy, that is both elusive and yet closer than your skin. I trust this material will nourish the transformative potency inside so you can apply personal energy to this undertaking. No one can show you the way, since there is no set course. Do not seek a linear pathway or set itinerary. The formal structures for union are deep within you already. Persistence, practice, and patience determine your passageway.

One example of this conduit is Jesus' profound understanding of divine love. Jesus faced his demons and encountered the dark devilish principle within human nature. He chose the inner path, the course away from self-aggrandizement and violence. He turned the other cheek and looked to his Source. Jesus' initiation provides us guidance on how to build a relationship within. His profound knowledge of the inner realm is the outpouring of love. This act of self-emptying shines through in the lives of mystics throughout history.

Jesus' story illustrates a new human potential, the opportunity of giving and receiving unconditional love. His love demonstrates a truly evolved human being, one who embodies a new life perspective, a radical state of presence. Jesus' far-reaching act of love is also our life work; self-emptying brings the collective consciousness of each generation to a new perspective since it encourages loving human interactions regardless of outer form or circumstance. This capacity arises from building character, a moral fiber to face the ongoing challenge of living in a diverse community. We address the harmful patterns in our own life. We face up to selfishness, ego aggrandizement, and personal greed in all their many forms.

As we consciously chose to reach deeper levels within, we desire wide-awake interactions with others. We share this new consciousness of love since this act alone brings joy. A sacred life force fuels our relationships since we demonstrate that we hold common values and stand behind a culture of compassion rather than violence. Love and acceptance for all people, regardless of who they are, symbolizes the ideals of a higher love. Jesus' life exemplifies a person who is willing to give his life for others. Our God given endowment is consciousness that all people have the right to pursue life, liberty, and happiness. Here we discover eternal life, in the here and now, and witness the power in our daily interactions.

However, you may say, Get real! Relationships are often upsetting, frustrating, and problematic. Think about any relationship, has it always been smooth and easy? Remember that your desire for positive human relationships mirrors your longing for divine union. When human relationships do not match up with our ideal image, what are we to do? The good news is awareness of our deeper Source gives us self-assurance since we know that no one else can fulfill our deepest longing. We stop looking for love in all the wrong places.

You have read this book because you are on a personal path to a relationship within, whether you know it or not. I hope this book will continue to inspire you to return to your Source. Regardless of where you may be now, a relationship within enriches your relationships across the board. With this in mind, you do not sabotage your relationships since you now know how much work it takes for any relationship to thrive. If we do not attend to our own grief, we cannot sit with someone else's suffering. We notice how relationship entanglements arise when we erect secret walls out of anxiety or guilt. We can learn to deal with personal responsibilities and ask for help if we need it, but we do not ignore our own tasks.

I am hopeful you will to take the challenge and boost your relationship muscles. If you practice the exercises provided, your relationships will thrive. The ones that were once superficial, become more significant, and those that were useless are easily set aside for something more appropriate. You become precious to yourself and take care of how valuable you truly are. A well-crafted relationship is the Jewel in your Crown. It is a prized crystal created from an enduring love light shining within you. This light draws you out of your own selfishness and allows you to share love with others.

The inner dance of relationship is a partnership with your Source and is the energy behind All Things. As you ponder the material presented here, I hope you continue to engage your intuitive vision, start seeing through the literal appearances of relationship difficulties, and understand the symbolic realm of unity consciousness. Love opens you to a universal intelligence. This astuteness helps you distinguish what is possible between two human beings and what is not. Your truth moves to the center of your life.

I trust this book will continue to shed new light on your process of creating a relationship from the inside out. I leave you with a few inquiries.

What can I do individually to create a culture of respect?

What can culture do to create communities of people who value one another?

What tools do we need to build and maintain meaningful relationships through out our life?

How can we ensure that from infancy to old age, that the power of building relationships will remain at the core of our every day experiences?

How can we interact with others to help preserve world peace?

How can we teach tolerance so open communication encourages the expression of diverse feelings?

What principles inform how we confront conflict within the world?

What basic human rights do we extend to others and to ourselves?

I hope this material will continue to offer you up-to-the-minute resources for returning to your Source. Now you have the language to speak about the symbolic dimension of your relationships. The unfathomable vastness within you provides the ultimate resource for the journey ahead. Wherever you go, your divine self is your primary companion. I cheer you on to discover the archetypal meaning of human connection for yourself. This is the goal of each new generation, to have a direct experience of the enduring mystery. So do not forget, "God is inside of everyone."

The take home message is that you can experience conscious awareness of your divine essence. This is profound spiritual work when you integrate both the good and bad sides of your personality, and try to correct your individual shortcomings. You bring new light to your relationships, release narrow-mindedness, and start observing spiritual, emotional, physical, and mental developments as a single synchronism. You finally end your obsessive searching for something outside yourself since, "You are your own discovery." This is the language spoken by enchanted and enlightened people throughout history. It is a basic human right to learn this native tongue.

As I have emphasized throughout *Relationship Within*, we can use anything humans do, no matter how outrageous, brutal, or ridiculous as a doorway into a deeper capacity to love. I encourage you to pick up the book from time to time and continue practicing concrete solutions to problems as they arise. Notice how you apply this information in your relationships. Discover the areas where you need more practice. Find your own workable solutions. Now that you have read this book, you should have self- assurance, since you know what to do. You turn to your Source!

References

Anonymous Co-Dependents Anonymous, Phoenix: Co-Dependents Anonymous, 1st ed. 1999, ISBN 0-9647105-0-1, 3-6.

Aronson, E. (2003). The Social Animal, Ninth Edition, New York: Worth Publishers.

Beekman, Daniel. (1977). The Mechanical Baby. Westport, CT: Laurence Hill.

Blavatsky, H.P. (1889), The Key to Theosophy, p175. ISBN 0-8356-0427-6

Bowen, M. (1988), "Family Evaluation: An Approach Based on Bowen Theory, co-written with Kerr, M.E. at The Family Center at Georgetown University Hospital," New York: Norton & Co.

Bowlby, J. (1988). A secure base. New York: Basic Books. Brunell, A. B., Pilkington, C. J., & Webster, G. D. (2007). Perceptions of Risk in Intimacy in Dating Couples: Conversation and Partner Perceptions. Journal of Social and Clinical Psychology, 26, 92-119. Bowen, M.(1978), Family Therapy in Clinical Practice, Northvale, NJ: Jason Aronson Inc.

Bowlby J (1999) [1982]. Attachment and Loss Vol. I (2nd ed.). New York: Basic Books. ISBN 0465005438 (pbk). OCLC 11442968. LCCN 00-266879; NLM 8412414.

Bowlby J (1988). A Secure Base: Clinical Applications of Attachment Theory. London: Routledge. ISBN 0415006406

Bowlby J (1979). The Making and Breaking of Affectional Bonds. London: Tavistock Publications. ISBN 978-0-422-76860-3.

Bowlby J (1988). A Secure Base: Clinical Applications of Attachment Theory. London: Routledge. ISBN 0415006406.

Bretherton I, Munholland KA (1999). "Internal Working Models in Attachment Relationships: A Construct Revisited". In Cassidy J, Shaver PR. Handbook of Attachment: Theory, Research and Clinical Applications. New York: Guilford Press. pp. 89–114. ISBN 1572300876.

Broderick, C.B. & Schrader, S.S. (1991). The History of Professional Marriage and Family Therapy. In A. S. Gurman & D. P. Kniskern (Eds.), Handbook of Family Cassidy J (1999). "The Nature of a Child's Ties". In Cassidy J, Shaver PR. Handbook of Attachment: Theory, Research and Clinical Applications. New York: Guilford Press. pp. 3–20. ISBN 1572300876.

Campbell, W. Keith Rose, Paul. (2004). "Greatness Feels Good: A Telic Model of Narcissism and Subjective Well-Being". In Shohov, Serge P. Advances in Psychology Research 31: 3–27. ISBN 978-1-59033-958-9.

Carnegie, D. (1964). How To Win Friends And Influence People.

Casement, Patrick (1996). Further Learning from the Patient. London. p. 131.

Cassidy J (1999). "The Nature of a Child's Ties". In Cassidy J, Shaver PR. Handbook of Attachment: Theory, Research and Clinical Applications. New York: Guilford Press. pp. 3–20. ISBN 1572300876.

Cervone, D., & Pervin, L. (2008) Personality Theory and Research. Hoboken: John Wiley & Sons, Inc

Chopra, D. (2001). The Higher Self. New York, NY: Simon & Schuster, Inc.

Collet, L (1990). "After the anger, what then? ACOA: Self-help or self-pity?". Family Therapy Networker 14 (1): 22–31.

Collins, N.L. & Freeney, B.C. (2004). An Attachment Theory Perspective on Closeness and Intimacy.

Compton, William C (2005). "1". An Introduction to Positive Psychology. Wadsworth Publishing. pp. 1–22. ISBN 0-534-64453-8.

Dalton, M. (1959) Men Who Manage, New York: Wiley. Erikson, Erik H. (1959).Identity and the Life Cycle. New York: International Universities Press.

Diagnostical and Statistical Manual of Mental Disorders, (1994). "Cluster C Personality Disorders," in DSM-IV, Washington: American Psychiatric Association, 4th ed. 1994, ISBN 0-89042-062-9, 662-673.

Erikson, Erik H. (1968). Identity, Youth and Crisis. New York: Norton.

Farrell, Warren. (1999). Women Can't Hear What Men Don't Say, N.Y.:Penguin

Ferrini P., (1996), Love without Conditions, Heartways Press, (p.146.)

Anthony Flew, ed. (1979). "Golden Rule". A Dictionary of Philosophy. (1979). London: Pan Books in association with The MacMillan Press. p. 134. ISBN 0-330-48730-2.

Friedberg, JP, Suchday, S, and Srinivas, VS (2009). Relationship between forgiveness and psychological and physiological indices in cardiac patients. International J of Behavior Med. 16 (3): 205-211

Furnham, A., & Crump, J. (2005). Personality Traits, Types, and Disorders: An Examination of the Relationship between Three Self-Report Measures. European Journal of Personality, 19, 167-184.

Giddens, Anthony (1992). The Transformation of Intimacy: Sexuality, Love and Eroticism in Modern Societies. Cambridge:Polity

Gottman, J. (1999). The Marriage Clinic: A Scientifically Based Marital Therapy, Norton.

Gray, J. (19920. Men are from Mars, Women are from Venus, A practical guide for improving communication, and getting what you want in your relationships. Harper Collins. ISBN 978-0-06-016848-3.

Haley, J (1984). Ordeal Therapy: Unusual Ways to Change Behavior (Jossey-Bass).

Haley, J (1996). Learning and Teaching Therapy (Guilford Press) (1999).

Hanegraaff, J. (1999)."New Age Spiritualities as Secular Religion: A Historian's Perspective." Social Compass 46.2.

Hayes, Louise (1984). You Can Heal Your Life. Hay House Inc., ISBN 0-937611-01-8

Jung, C.G. Psychological Types. Collected Works Vol.6., par. 757

Holcombe, Alfred D., and Suzanne M. Holcombe. (2005): "Biblically-Derived Concept of Mankind's Higher-Self-Lower Self Nature." Journal of Religion & Psychical Research 28.1, p.20-25.

Jacobi, J. Complex, Archetype, Jung quoted in Symbol (London 1959) p. 113-4

Jung, C. G. (Shamdasani, S). (2009). The Red Book. Pg 208 (par. 3) Verona, Italy: Mondadori Printing.

Jung, C. G. (1962). Symbols of Transformation: An analysis of the prelude to a case of schizophrenia (Vol. 2, R. F. C. Hull, Trans.). New York: Harper & Brothers.

Jung, C. G. (1976). Campbell, Joseph. ed. The Portable Jung. New York, NY: Penguin Books. pp. 178.

Jung, C.G. ([1921] 1971). Psychological Types, Collected Works, Volume 6, Princeton, N.J.: Princeton University Press. ISBN 0-691-01813-8.

Jung, C.G. ([1961] 1989). Memories, Dreams, Reflections, New York, N.Y.: Vantage Books. ISBN 0-679-72395-1.

Jung, C.G. (1966). Two Essays on Analytical Psychology, Collected Works, Volume 7, Princeton, N.J.: Princeton University Press. ISBN 0-691-01782-4.

Kagan, J. (1994). Galen's Prophecy: Temperament in Human Nature. New York: Basic Books

Keating, T. (2009). "Intimacy with God: an Introduction to Centering Prayer," 15-28.

Khaleque, A. (2004). Intimate Adult Relationships, Quality of Life and Psychological Adjustment. Social Indicators Research, 69, 351-360. Mashek D.J & A. Aron A., (Eds.), Handbook of Closeness and Intimacy, pp. 163–188. Mahwah, NJ: Lawrence Erlbaum Associates.

Lee, JA (1973). Colors of love: an exploration of the ways of loving. Toronto: New Press. ISBN 0-88770-187-6.

Lee, JA (1988). "Love styles". In Barnes MH, Sternberg RJ. The Psychology of love. New Haven, Conn: Yale University Press. pp. 38–67. ISBN 0-300-03950-6.

Mashek D.J & A. Aron A., (Eds.), Handbook of Closeness and Intimacy, pp. 163–188. Mahwah, NJ: Lawrence Erlbaum Associates.

Mashek, D.J., & Sherman, M.D. (2004). Desiring less closeness with intimate others. In A. Aaron and Mashek, D.J. (Eds.), Handbook of Closeness and Intimacy (pp. 343–356). Mahwah, NJ: Lawrence Erlbaum Associates.

deMause, Lloyd. (1974). The History of Childhood. New York: The Psychohistory Press.

Mellody, P. Facing Codependence, (1989). "A Brief History of Codependence and a Look at the Psychological Literature," in: New York etc.: Harper San Francisco, ISBN 0-06-250589-0, 207-217.

Miller, Rowland & Perlman, Daniel (2008). Intimate Relationships (5th ed.). McGraw-Hill. ISBN 978-0-07-337018-7

Minuchin, S. (1974). Families and Family Therapy. Harvard University Press

Minuchin, S. & Fishman, H. C. (2004). Family Therapy Techniques. Harvard University Press.

Mitchell, S. (1988). Tao Te Ching. Harper Collins Publishers.

Moore, M. (1985). "Nonverbal Courtship Patterns in Women: Contact and Consequences", Ethnology and Sociobiology, 6: 237–247.

Mumford, Lewis. (1951). The Conduct of Life. New York: Harcourt, Brace.

Myers, Isabel Briggs with Peter B. Myers (1980, 1995). Gifts Differing: Understanding Personality Type. Mountain View, CA: Davies-Black Publishing. pp. xi–xii. ISBN 0-89106-074-X.

Nanda, Serena. (1987).Cultural Anthropology, Third Edition. Belmont, CA: Wadswoth Publishing.

(NAS) New American Standard

(NIV) New International Version

(NKJV) New King James Version

(NRS) New Revised Standard Version

Pennington, M. Basil (1980). Centering Prayer: Renewing an Ancient Christian Prayer Form. Garden City, NY: Doubleday. ISBN 0-385-14562-4.

Pennington, M. Basil (1986), "Centering Prayer: Refining the Rules," "Review for Religious," 45:3, 386-393.

Perlman, D. (2007). The best of times, the worst of times: The place of close relationships in psychology and our daily lives. Canadian Psychology, 48, 7–18.

Phillips, Adam (1994). On Flirtation. London: Harvard University Press. p. 54. ISBN 0-674-63440-3.

Phillips, A. *Winnicott* (1988), Harvard Press.

Rappaport, Alan, PhD. (2005). Co-Narcissism: How We Adapt to Narcissistic Parents. In The Therapist.

Rappaport, Richard L. (1997). Motivating Clients in Therapy (Routledge,) p. 66.

Ridley-Duff, R.J. (2010) Emotion, Seduction and Intimacy: Alternative Perspectives on Human Behaviour (Third Edition), Seattle: Libertary Editions, ISBN 978-1-935961-00-0

Riso, Don Ricard & Hudson, Ross (1996). Personality Types Using the Enneagram for Self-discovery, Mariner Books.

Rogers, Carl. (1951). Client-centered Therapy: Its Current Practice, Implications and Theory. London: Constable. ISBN 1-84119-840-4.

Rogers, Carl. (1961). On Becoming a Person: A Therapist's View of Psychotherapy. London: Constable. ISBN 1-84529-057-7.

Rogers, Carl. (1977). On Personal Power: Inner Strength and Its Revolutionary Impact.

Rogers, Carl. (1980). A Way of Being. Boston: Houghton Mifflin. Rowan, J., Subpersonalities (London 1990) p. 144

Rowan, J., Subpersonalities (London 1990) p. 144

Sadock, B.J. & Sadock, V.A (eds), "Codependence," in: Benjamin J. Kaplan & Sadock's Comprehensive Textbook of Psychiatry on CD, Philadelphia: Lippincott Williams & Wilkins, 7th ed. 2000, ISBN 0-7817-2141-5, ISBN 2-07-032070-7.

Satir V (2001). Self Esteem. Berkeley, Calif: Celestial Arts. ISBN 1-58761-094-9.

Satir V (1976). Making Contact. Berkeley, Calif: Celestial Arts. ISBN 0-89087-119-1.

Satir V (1978). Your Many Faces. Berkeley, Calif: Celestial Arts. ISBN 0-89087-120-5

Satir V; Bandler R; Grinder J (1976). Changing with families. Palo Alto, CA: Science and Behavior Books. ISBN 0-8314-0051-X.

Satir V., Stachowiak J. &Taschman, H.A. (1994). Helping Families to Change. Northvale, N.J: Jason Aronson. ISBN 1-56821-227-5.

Satir V; Baldwin M (1983). Satir Step by Step: a guide to creating change in families. Palo Alto, CA: Science and Behavior Books. ISBN 0-8314-0068-4.

Satir V (1988). The New People Making. Palo Alto, CA: Science and Behavior Books. ISBN 0-8314-0070-6.

Schultz, JM, Tallman, BA, Altmaier, EM (2010). Pathways to posttraumatic growth: The contributions of forgiveness and importance of religion and spirituality. Psychology of Religion and Spirituality, 2(2): 104-114.)

Seligman, Martin E.P.; Csikszentmihalyi, Mihaly (2000). "Positive Psychology: An Introduction". American Psychologist 55, pp. 5–14,:10.1037/0003-066X.55.1.5. PMID 11392865.

Seigel, DJ (2007). The Mindful Brain: Reflection and Attunement in the Cultivation of Well-Being, WW Norton.

Seigel, DJ, (1999). The Developing Mind: Toward a Neurobiology of Interpersonal Experience published by the Guilford Press.

Sheehy, Gail (1976). Passages: Predictable Crises of Adult Life. New York: E. P. Dutton.

Skinner, B. F. (1948). Walden Two. ISBN 0-87220-779-X(revised 1976 edition).

Sholevar, G.P. (2003). Family Theory and Therapy. In Sholevar, G.P. & Schwoeri, L.D. Textbook of Family and Couples Therapy: Clinical Applications. Washington, DC: American Psychiatric Publishing Inc.

Smith, L. D.; Woodward, W. R. (1996). B. F. Skinner and behaviorism in American culture. Bethlehem, PA: Lehigh University Press. ISBN 0-934223-40-8.

Stace, Walter T. (1937,) The Concept of Morals Reprinted 1975 by permission of MacMillan Publishing Co. Inc., Also reprinted January 1990 by Peter Smith Publisher Inc). The Concept of Morals. New York: The MacMillan Company; and also reprinted by Peter Smith Publisher Inc, January 1990. p. 136. ISBN 0-8446-2990-1.

Steer, R. "Basic Christian: The Inside Story of John Stott" (2010). Leicester, Inter-Varsity Press. ISBN 0-8308-3846-5, ISBN 978-0-8308-3846-2

Sternberg, R. J. (1990): Metaphors of mind: Conceptions of the nature of intelligence. New York: Cambridge University Press.

Sternberg, R. J. (1997): Successful intelligence. New York: Plume.

Sternberg, R.J.: (2007) Wisdom, Intelligence, and Creativity Synthesized. New York: Cambridge University Press

Stevens, Richard (1983) Erik Erikson: An Introduction. New York: St. Martin's.

Stoia-Caraballo, R; Rye, MS, Pan, W, Kirschman, KJ, Lutz-Zois, C, Lyons, AM (2008). Negative affect and anger rumination as mediators between forgiveness and sleep quality. Journal of Behavioral Medicine, 31(6): 478-488.)

The Cloud of Unknowing and other works. Penguin Classics. (2001). ISBN 978-0-14-044762-0. Translated by A. C. Spearing

Totton and Jacobs (2001). Character and Personality Types. Philadelphia, PA: Open University Press.

Toussaint, LL, Williams, DR, Musick, MA, and Everson-Rose, SA (2008).

Why forgiveness may protect against depression: Hopelessness as an explanatory mechanism. Personality and Mental Health, 2: 89-103.

Winnicott, D.W. (1966).The Family and Individual Development. New York: Basic Books.

Winnicott, D. W. (1971).*Playing and Reality* (London: Tavistock).

Winnicott, D. W. 1971). Therapeutic Consultation in Child Psychiatry (London: Hogarth Press, 1971).

Winnicott, D. W. (1971) The Piggle: An Account of the Psychoanalytic Treatment of a Little Girl (London: Hogarth Press).

Winnicott, D. W. 1984). Deprivation and Delinquency (London: Tavistock, 1984).

Zeisset, Carolyn (2006). The Art of Dialogue: Exploring Personality Differences for More Effective Communication. Gainesville, FL: Center for Applications of Psychological Type, Inc. p. 13. ISBN 0-935652-77-9.

Acknowledgements

✣

I dedicate this book to my children, Kristin Smyer Dubrow and Daniel Asher Dubrow, the two great gifts of my life, with whom I love with all my heart. You grace my journey and make it all worthwhile.

With special thanks to my wonderful parents, Ingrid Smyer Kelly and Sidney William Smyer, Jr. who gave me life. You are my first companions on the long journey, and have been steadfast each step of the way.

My appreciation goes out to Richard Higgins, my brilliant editor. His advice, guidance, and camaraderie made the process, not only possible, but also pleasurable. I wish all writers could have such a wonderful editing experience.

I pay tribute to the many people who have worked with me over the years on the art of building relationship. I send out a special cheer to the people who have supported my ongoing journey to a Relationship Within; Rusty Brown, Susan Braus, Stephen Calloway, Connie Crittenden, David Dubrow, Eric Godin, Lisa Northcutt Guyton, Jean Marie Pitmann, Hal and Mary Smyer, Harry Stafford, Paul Sullivan, and Victor Wallgren.

In addition, I want to thank my family and friends near and far, some of you go first, and others of you may come long after. I thank the staff and clients at The Staniford House who encouraged me to write this book from the material of our Building Relationships Group. Finally, I am grateful to everyone who courageously shared your personal experiences on the path to a relationship within and who supported my writing process. You know who you are!

About the Author

INGRID FRANCES SMYER PH.D.

❦

Ingrid has been in the helping profession for thirty years, after completing a Master's degree from Yale Divinity School, she began her clinical training at Yale/New Haven Hospital, New Haven, Connecticut as a chaplain and member of the clinical pastoral education treatment team at Connecticut Mental Health Center.

Ingrid holds a doctorate degree in clinical psychology from Pacific Graduate Institute and is currently working as a mental health counselor in residential treatment program for sex offender rehabilitation. She also maintains a private practice as a certified Holistic Life Coach, Cyberdream therapist, and MBTI practitioner in Boston, MA.

Ingrid lectured before the House of Lords London, England, April 19, 2007 on a panel for the International Federation of Women United against Fundamentalism and for Equality, (WAFE) titled "Beyond Fundamentalism: Healing the Trauma of Fundamentalist Extremes. Her publications include, *Animism* for The International Encyclopedia for the Social Sciences, Vol. II, and (November 2007).

Professional Business Entrepreneur: Sole Proprietor, The Apple of Boston Guest House, Boston, Massachusetts.

Printed in Great Britain
by Amazon